OF THOMAS EARLE OF STRAFFORD, LORD
12th of May, 1641.

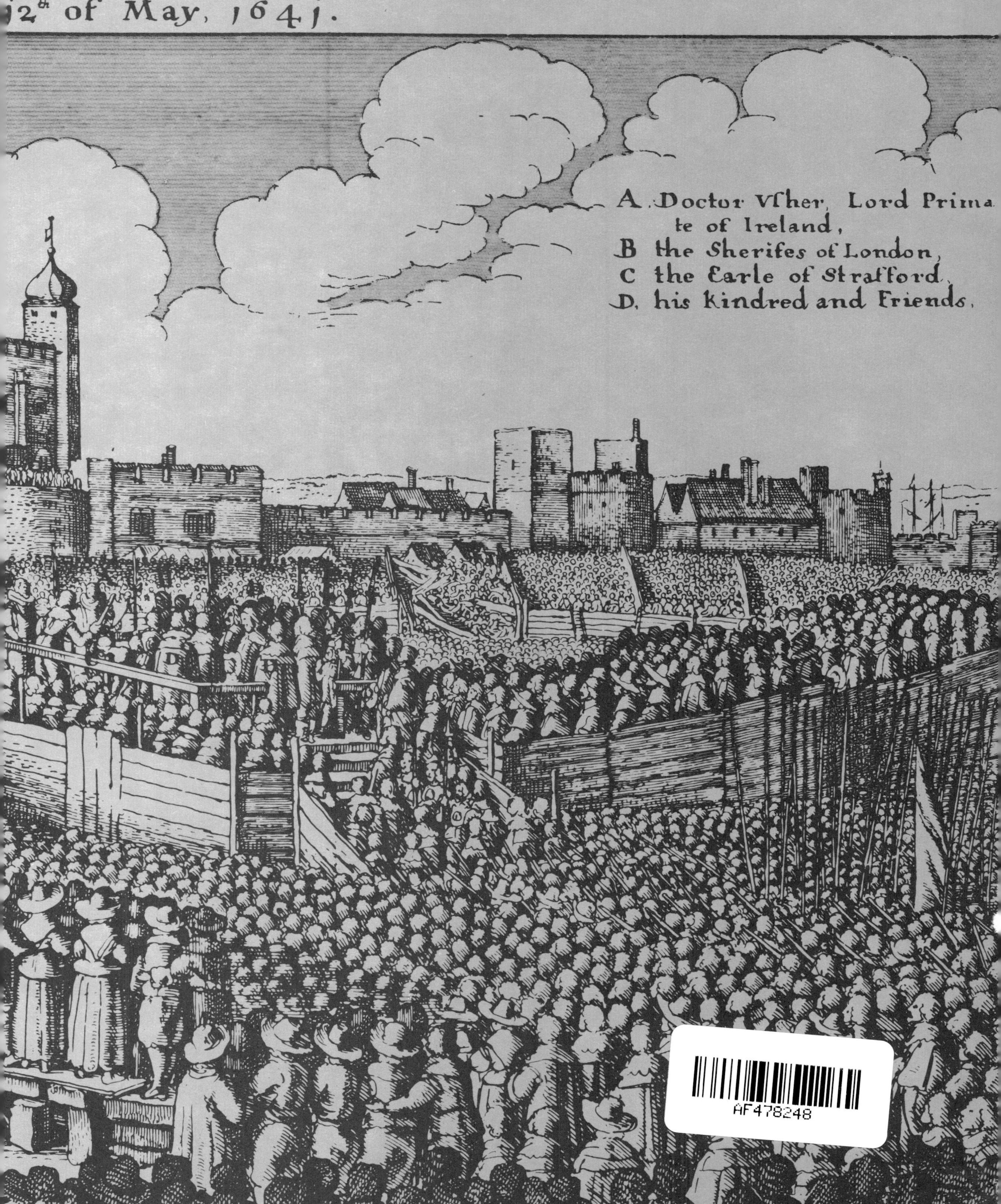

HOLLAR

DRAWINGS

HOLLAR
DRAWINGS

VLADIMÍR DENKSTEIN

Foreword by Professor Michael Kitson
Professor of Art History at the Courtauld Institute, London

ORBIS PUBLISHING · LONDON

LIST OF ABBREVIATIONS

S followed by an Arabic numeral refers to the catalogue number in Franz Sprinzels's *Hollar – Handzeichnungen*, Prague–Vienna 1938.

P followed by an Arabic numeral refers to the catalogue number in Gustav Parthey's *Wenzel Hollar, Beschreibendes Verzeichniseiner Kupferstiche*, Berlin 1853.

G followed by an Arabic numeral refers to the number in F. G. Grossmann's exhibition catalogue, *Wenceslaus Hollar 1607–1677: Drawings, Paintings and Etchings*. City of Manchester Art Gallery 1963.

S followed by a Roman numeral refers to the catalogue number in Francis C. Springell's *Connoisseur and Diplomat*, London 1963, dealing with the Earl of Arundel's diplomatic mission to Germany in 1636 and listing the drawings executed by Hollar on this journey.

Translated by D. Orpington

ISBN 0 85613 231 4

The monochrome collotype plates printed in Czechoslovakia by Polygrafia 4, Sadská. Introduction and colour plates printed by Polygrafia 1, Prague.

Endpapers: *The Execution of the Earl of Strafford*
Etching P552, in or after 1641. (The Fotomas Index/British Museum, London)

CONTENTS

FOREWORD

The Bohemian-born artist Wenceslaus Hollar is best known in Britain and America today for his etched views of seventeenth-century London and its buildings and for his illustrations of women's costumes and fur muffs. As a draughtsman he is less well known. This book, by the former Director of the Prague National Museum, is about Hollar's drawings, especially those which he made on the Continent before and during his tour of the Rhine and the Danube in the company of the Earl of Arundel in 1636. Dr Denkstein discusses these early drawings of Hollar's, of which more survive than from any other period of the artist's life, with a thoroughness and sensitivity that has not been shown before; he demonstrates that Hollar was a draughtsman of considerable seriousness as well as charm.

The object of this foreword is not to go over ground which the author has covered so admirably but to try to place Hollar in his historical context. When he was born in Prague in 1607, the city was still the seat of one of the most astonishing courts in Europe, that of the Emperor Rudolf II (1576–1612). A recluse, a pervert and a passionate devotee at once of old superstition and new knowledge, Rudolf formed an amazing collection of rarities of all kinds, in which natural objects were arranged side by side with artistic and technical artefacts, in an assembly designed as a kind of real-life encyclopedia of the whole world. The pictures which contributed to this assembly consisted partly of Italian and German Renaissance works and partly of works by living Northern Mannerist artists, such as Bartholomeus Spranger, Hans von Aachen and Roelandt Savery, whom Rudolf attracted to Prague. After his forced abdication in 1612, his successors began removing the collection to Vienna, but a good deal remained in Prague, and Hollar, as the son of a government official with pretensions to minor nobility, probably had access to it. He almost certainly saw it when he visited Prague with the Earl of Arundel in 1636. The influence of this collection is reflected in Hollar's work, not only in the Mannerist style of his earliest figure drawings (illustration nos. 6, 7, and 11), but also, in a broader sense, in the all-round curiosity with which he viewed the world – its landscapes, its buildings, its fashions and its living things (illustration nos. 42–4).

It is true that topographical landscape as such was probably not practised in Prague, but there was a strong interest both in maps, including bird's-eye views, and imaginary landscapes, the painters of which no doubt produced occasional realistic sketches from nature. It is not at all incredible that, as Dr Denkstein suggests, Hollar made a few black-chalk or pen-and-ink sketches of his native city (illustration no. 8) before leaving Prague at the age of twenty in 1627.

By that date the situation in Bohemia was much less favourable to art than it had been at the beginning of the century. Not only had the court removed to Vienna, but the rebellion of the Czech nobles in 1618 and their ultimate defeat by the imperial forces two years later at the Battle of the White Mountain had radically undermined society; and when, in 1627, the nobility were ordered to join the Catholic Church or forfeit their estates, it must have seemed like the final blow. Whether or not Hollar was a religious refugee (which seems to be in some doubt), his primary reason for leaving Prague was surely to go in search of wider artistic opportunities. Perhaps because the majority of Rudolf's artists had been Northerners and because one of his favourite earlier painters was Dürer, Hollar went to Germany rather than, as might have been expected, to Italy. In western and southern Germany, following the German tradition of the *Wanderjahre*, he spent a number of years moving from city to city. In Stuttgart he found art-lovers for whose autograph albums he made drawings (illustration nos. 6, 11 and 12); in Frankfurt he found an engraver, Matthaeus Merian the Elder, who taught him the rudiments of topography (illustration nos. 14 and 15); and in Strasbourg and Cologne he found publishers for his prints (illustration no. 9). Above all, in the years between 1627 and 1636, when Hollar formed his style as a landscapist, he encountered for the first time the new Dutch approach to landscape, which had been developed only a decade before; as early as 1628–9 he made a series of landscape etchings representing the *Months of the Year* after the Dutch engraver, Jan van de Velde, and in 1634 he himself visited the Netherlands, including Amsterdam (illustration nos. 2 and 21).

This approach involved the use of an eye-level viewpoint, a nearly empty foreground, and the placing of the principal motif – usually buildings of some kind, including a church spire, surrounded by trees, or shipping off the coast – in the far middle-distance. The horizon is low (because of the low viewpoint) but, in order to avoid at this stage the inclusion of a high sky, the format of the picture is itself long and low (illustration nos. 13, 21 and 26). The composition is often built on a receding diagonal formed by the far bank of a river, with the river itself filling the foreground. There are sometimes figures in the foreground standing on a narrow strip of land (illustration no. 15). It was an approach to landscape clearly suited to a flat country intersected by wide waterways, and Hollar was well able to adapt it for views on the Rhine.

In 1636, Hollar met the Earl of Arundel in Cologne. The Earl was then on a diplomatic mission from England to the Emperor Ferdinand II, the object of which was to obtain the latter's agreement to the restoration of the son of Frederick, the Protestant Elector Palatine, to his hereditary lands in western Germany. However, partly because England had no military means of bringing pressure to bear on the Emperor and partly because of Arundel's own obstinacy, the mission failed. While the fact that Hollar was a Bohemian may have helped to recommend him to the Earl, the chief reason why he was taken on was undoubtedly his skill as an artist, coupled with the fact that he would have known where works of art were to be found in western Germany and Prague. To add to his art collection was Arundel's object at least as much as, if not more than, the fulfilment of his diplomatic task.

A young Englishman, William Crowne, who also accompanied the mission, has left a detailed account of the journey (though he nowhere mentions Hollar).* The party, which filled at least one medium-sized boat on the Rhine and three or four smaller boats on the Danube (illustration no. 27 and plates, *passim*), travelled as far as possible by river. They were towed or rowed up the Rhine and the Main as far as Frankfurt, then went overland by way of Würzburg and Nuremberg to Regensburg, where they embarked once more on the Danube. After meeting the Emperor at Linz in Upper Austria, the party continued on a sightseeing trip to Vienna and Prague, where they inspected the collections of Rudolf II. On the way back, Arundel had a second meeting with the Emperor at Regensburg, and thence they returned to England by the same route as they had come out. The tour lasted from 7 April to 27 December 1636.

The predominant impressions left by Crowne's journal are of the exchanges of diplomatic courtesies, which took place at most towns on the route, and the constant signs, in a country which had suffered almost twenty years of intermittent warfare, of casual violence. The mission met no large armies and saw no battles but here and there a church, whole villages or parts of a town would be burnt down and pillaged, and the Earl and his suite would have to move on to the next town to stay the night. Marauding bands and undisciplined local troops were also a frequent danger, and outside Regensburg the Earl's Gentleman of the Horse and his trumpeter, who had gone on an errand, were brutally murdered. Yet Hollar's drawings, apart from a set-piece illustration of the execution of some rebel leaders in Linz, show nothing of all this. In contrast to his great

*Published in London for the Earl of Arundel, 1637; reprinted in F.C. Springell, *Connoisseur and Diplomat*, London, 1963.

contemporary Callot, who made a memorable series of etchings of the horrors of war in Lorraine, Hollar was an artist of peace, whose sole concern was to show the handsomeness of the cities, towns and castles which Arundel and his entourage passed on their journey. His panoramic views, carefully labelled with the place-names – in German in the drawings made on the spot (see the plates in this book), in Latin in the finished versions – are like illustrations to a book of 'wonders of the modern world'. They are, so to speak, realistic, eye-level variations of the fantastic bird's-eye views which formed the staple of topographical engraving at the beginning of the century.

Hollar's method is to stand well back from the motif and view it from a point far out in the river or from the opposite bank. The buildings thus 'sit comfortably' in the middle distance; in the case of large cities like Mainz or Prague (plates 4 and 54), Hollar simply stretches the composition lengthways to accommodate the view. In composing his subjects like this, he was indebted to the Dutch. But unlike Dutch artists, who were comparatively indifferent to topography for its own sake, Hollar made the identity and specific character of the place he was representing the principal aim of his art. The precise details of buildings, down to ordinary houses, are faithfully rendered, an end which he was able to achieve through the linear clarity of his style. This is not to say that he was insensitive to light and atmosphere or to pictorial qualities but he had no aesthetic prejudices or preoccupations to obscure his objective. He was as ready to record the details of Gothic as of more recent buildings, he had little interest in picture-making or the picturesque, and he had no interest in people other than as bystanders or spectators of a scene (in consequence of this, his towns and cities tend to appear uninhabited). All this makes Hollar probably the greatest and certainly the most lucid topographical artist of the mid-seventeenth century, that is, of the period between the decline of topography as an offshoot of map-making at the beginning of the century and its rise as a popular art form in oils as well as drawing and engraving a hundred years later. Perhaps the nearest contemporary equivalent to Hollar is the Frenchman, Israel Silvestre (1621–91), who worked in Florence, Rome and Paris. But Silvestre's style is more classical. Hollar's, though of Dutch origins, is quite his own.

When Hollar returned to England with the Earl of Arundel at the end of 1636, he must have been intended to produce a series of etchings after his drawings executed on the tour, perhaps as an accompaniment to Crowne's written account. But this did not happen and, instead, he was put to work making reproductive etchings of the pictures and other works of art in Arundel's collection. He also made his first etched views of London (illustration nos. 28, 29 and 34) and produced his marvellous etchings of women's costumes and muffs (illustration nos. 32, 33 and 41), which show a wittier, more seductive side of his art than his topographical and architectural views. He was probably busier and more successful in these years (1637–44) than at any other time in his life. He was living at Arundel House in London with his English wife and he extended the range of his art to embrace a wider variety of subjects than before. His friend, the diarist John Evelyn, after listing the painters in the Arundel Collection whose works Hollar engraved, described his repertoire thus: 'landskips, townes, solemnities, histories, heads, beasts, fowles, insects, vessels & other signal pieces:' in short, an abundance reminiscent of Rudolf II's collection but with a more functional and antiquarian bias. No previous etcher or engraver in England, where portraiture was the consuming interest, had offered anything like such a range.

Nevertheless, Hollar was now making far fewer drawings than he had on the Continent, to judge by what survives, and there are signs that he was being compelled to spend too much of his time on hack-work, as has so often been the fate of gifted foreign artists in England; the making of endless reproductive etchings after paintings by other artists was beneath his talents and was also not his forte, since his style was not sufficiently robust. In the early 1640s, the political situation was also becoming unfavourable. In 1641, Charles I had to consent to the execution of the Earl of Strafford, his greatest minister; Hollar etched the scene on the scaffold (see endpapers), which was watched by a crowd estimated at 100,000. In the following year the Civil War broke out and Hollar's patron, the Earl of Arundel, left England. Soon other artists and art-lovers went too, and in 1644 Hollar himself, after serving briefly as an attendant to the ten-year old Duke of York (later James II), moved to Antwerp. He remained in Flanders for eight years, supporting himself chiefly by continuing to work on the Arundel Collection and by producing further etched views of London. Other than publishers, few patrons seem to have come his way, and he took the opportunity of peace in England under Cromwell to return in 1652. In London once more, he found work making illustrations for books by scholars and antiquarians like Elias Ashmole and William Dugdale, whose *History of St Paul's Cathedral* he illustrated in 1658 (illustration nos. 4 and 39). The thirty-odd plates Hollar etched for this publication, all executed with his usual meticulous clarity, are a precious visual record not only of the medieval cathedral but also of the alterations made to it during the 1630s by Inigo Jones. The whole building was, of course, destroyed during or as a consequence of the Great Fire of London in 1666, and Hollar subsequently produced what is still perhaps his most popular print, the *Parallel Views of London Before and After the Fire*, in which his gift for composing very wide panoramas without losing visual unity came fully into play.

Later in 1666 Hollar was given the honorary appointment of 'His Majesty's scenographer, or designer of prospects', and in 1668 he undertook his last commission: to accompany the English fleet as official draughtsman on its expedition to secure the fortress of Tangier, the dowry of Charles II's Queen, Catherine of Braganza. Like the Earl of Arundel's mission this expedition also failed, but Hollar was able to make at least thirty drawings of the fortress from various viewpoints, and later translated fifteen of them into prints. Here a new role for the topographical artist emerged, which was to be important in the future: that of military surveyor.

Hollar died in London in poverty in 1677. During his career he had executed over 2500 prints; no wonder the adjective most frequently applied to him at the time and later was 'indefatigable'. But Evelyn wrote of his work that 'there is not a more Usefull or instructive Collection to be made', and described him as 'this very honest, simple, well-meaning man'. Just as he was the first, so he was also one of the last etchers and engravers able to turn his hand to a wide range of subjects in England. After Hollar, the reign of the specialist began to reassert itself.

But, if Hollar is chiefly of interest to the historian today for his prints, it remains true that his topographical drawings have a quality of rare distinction in a European context, as this book shows. As the Earl of Arundel put it a few days after meeting him in Cologne: 'I have one Hollarse with me, whoe drawes and eches printes in strong water quickely, and with a pretty spiritte.' Hollar also counts as a forerunner of the English school of landscape watercolours. One of the artists who knew him in his old age and was influenced by him was Francis Place (1647–1728), who usually stands at the beginning of modern histories of English watercolour painting. The next group of drawings of views of the Rhine after Hollar's to be made for an English patron was by J. M. W. Turner, no less, who travelled by boat up the river in 1817, making pencil sketches as he went and producing on his return fifty-one finished watercolours of Rhine scenery for Walter Fawkes.

MICHAEL KITSON

PREFACE

The seventeenth-century Czech draughtsman and etcher Wenceslaus Hollar left behind him an *oeuvre* of vast range, remarkable for its artistic value and technical accomplishment. His work, the fruit of tireless creative effort during a career full of misfortune, can be seen today as one of the foundation-stones of European graphic art. It was respected and loved by contemporaries, admired in successive generations and finally secured Hollar a place of honour in modern art history. Now, three hundred years after his death, Wenceslaus Hollar's name can be added to the roll of men honoured throughout the world.

Hollar's drawings account for only a fraction of his output and are less familiar than his more numerous and famous prints sought by collectors. Artistically, however, they are no whit inferior. His sketches have the spontaneity of form, and the personal and intimate approach to their subject that characterizes Hollar's work. They are the first expression of the artist's feelings and imagination, the authentic evidence of the individual hand at work.

Private collections of Hollar's drawings were already being amassed in England during the seventeenth and eighteenth centuries, while in the nineteenth they started appearing in Europe as well. The majority of the drawings passed later into public collections, and today around four hundred of them are in private or public hands. The largest and best integrated sets are in the Staatsmuseum in Berlin-Dahlem and in Prague's National Gallery. Valuable groups also survive in the Royal Collection at Windsor (including those of London scenes), the British Museum and the Duke of Devonshire's collection at Chatsworth. Francis Springell's notable collection at Portinscale, Keswick, with the beautiful series of drawings produced during the artist's trips along the Rhine and Danube in 1636, formed the basis of the 1963 Hollar Exhibition at the Manchester Art Gallery.

The drawings and prints in the Prague National Gallery's Print Collection constitute what was known in older Czech and international references as the Hollareum. This was created in 1863 when the Czech nations purchased a large number of Hollar's etchings (2817 prints) from the estate of Hermann Weber, a dealer in engravings from Bonn and a fervent admirer of the artist. The Hollareum, first owned by the Society of Patriotic Art-lovers in Bohemia, passed into the hands of the National Museum in Prague after the First World War and twenty years later became the core of the Prague National Gallery's Print Collection. The Hollareum was originally comprised only of engravings, but from the end of the nineteenth century drawings by Hollar were also included; thirty-six of these were acquired between 1893 and 1918 while the Hollar specialist F.A. Borovský was Keeper of the Collection. Many more were bought in subsequent years, though Hollar's drawings were then keenly sought after by collectors throughout the world. At present the Prague National Gallery's collection includes fifty-two of them, though several are of doubtful attribution. They include examples from Hollar's early period as well as from his later years, most notably the exquisite series recording his journey with Lord Arundel's mission in 1636.

The plates in this book are taken from the original drawings in Prague's National Gallery collection, which are reproduced here in their entirety for the first time, with the exception of the doubtfully authentic ones. Two drawings from Stuttgart are reproduced in the text by permission of the State Gallery and the Württemberg Landesbibliothek in that city. Most of the illustrations in the text are of etchings, reproduced from the original prints in the Prague National Gallery collection. Apart from two, these are all prints executed by Hollar from his own drawings. They thus supplement our picture of Hollar's draughtsmanship and evoke thematically, and in some other respects as well, those periods and genres that are not represented by original drawings in the Prague National Gallery. They also give a vivid impression of places and people significant in Hollar's career and furnish some idea of his masterly and versatile achievement as an engraver. A few illustrations have been taken from reproductions in books and periodicals.

The prime source of information on Wenceslaus Hollar's drawings is the catalogue in Franz Sprinzels's book *Hollar – Handzeichnungen*, published in 1938 in Vienna. The numbering in this list is internationally accepted for Hollar's drawings, as those in Parthey's are for his etchings, and are accordingly quoted throughout the text. A list of all Hollar's authenticated drawings in the Prague National Gallery's Print Collection was published by Jan Dvořák in the catalogue to the 1959 exhibition of these works in the same Gallery. Precise details concerning the selection of Hollar's drawings and prints appeared in the compendious catalogue of the Gallery's 1969 exhibition covering both drawings and etchings, for which we are indebted to Jiřina Volková. We have drawn on both catalogues in the present work.

Where it has been necessary in describing the drawings to refer also to some of the prints, we have for simplicity called these 'etchings'. However, the word is not fully adequate since Hollar used a combination of techniques and achieved delicate effects by finishing his work off with a burin or light touches of the needle.

The author wishes to thank the directorate and staff of the Prague National Gallery's Print Collection for facilitating his study of Hollar's drawings.

Wenceslaus Hollar was born at the beginning of one of the stormiest centuries in European history. The Bohemian insurrection and its defeat at the White Mountain by the Catholic League in 1620 marked the onset of destructive wars that gradually involved the countries of Europe, great and small, in the religious and political conflict known as the Thirty Years' War.For three decades a large part of Europe was an open battlefield across which mercenary armies passed in successive waves, leaving behind them ravished towns and burnt-out hamlets.

Hollar left Bohemia after the Battle of the White Mountain and for the next ten years was variously employed in Germany. Circumstances finally led him to England, where, apart from an eight-year period in Holland, he remained until his death. The convulsive years of the English Civil War were hardly conducive to tranquil artistic work, yet Hollar's skill developed and ripened here in a way that has led him to be ranked among the greatest masters of European draughtsmanship.

The seventeenth century was characterized by the confrontation of two great ideologies – the Catholic Counter-Reformation transformed by the Spanish temperament into an aggressive fanaticism, and the sober and severe Reformation of northern Europe. In the fine arts both systems of thought adopted and adapted the heritage of the Renaissance, exemplified in the Mannerist and baroque styles of the late sixteenth century and after. These fostered both the distortion and exaggeration of reality and the development of an unidealized naturalism.

Faced with this choice, Hollar opted unambiguously for realism. Unaffected by the hysteria and dramatic exaggeration of Baroque art, and taking Renaissance rationalism as his starting point, he strove from the start to express reality as he objectively saw it. With maturity he developed elegance of form, individuality of style and a sensitive and precise observation. In the sharply-observed landscape sketches of his finest years Hollar could express the emotional overtones of what his senses saw. His work went along with the realistic stream of seventeenth-century European art, while in style and attitude, particularly in still life and landscape work, it approached the highest achievements of the Dutch masters.

Hollar's view of the world around him was conditioned from the start by his austere temperament and by the moral principles he adopted in early youth. His English friends refer unanimously to his modesty and good nature, his tireless energy and conscientious routine, and his temperance and strict self-discipline.[1]

The unsentimental and rigorously moral elements in his character were clearly reinforced in his youth by the strict evangelical training he was given both by his family and in the schools of pre-1620 Prague. As the son of an official of the *Land* Records Office the adolescent Hollar may well have found employment in the Imperial court where similar principles – Puritan and stoic ideals of hard work and self-denial as the path to wisdom – were encouraged. The ideas of the northern humanists, Erasmus of Rotterdam and Justus Lipsius,[2] were imported to Prague by German and Dutch artists who had been brought up on them. Neo-stoic views

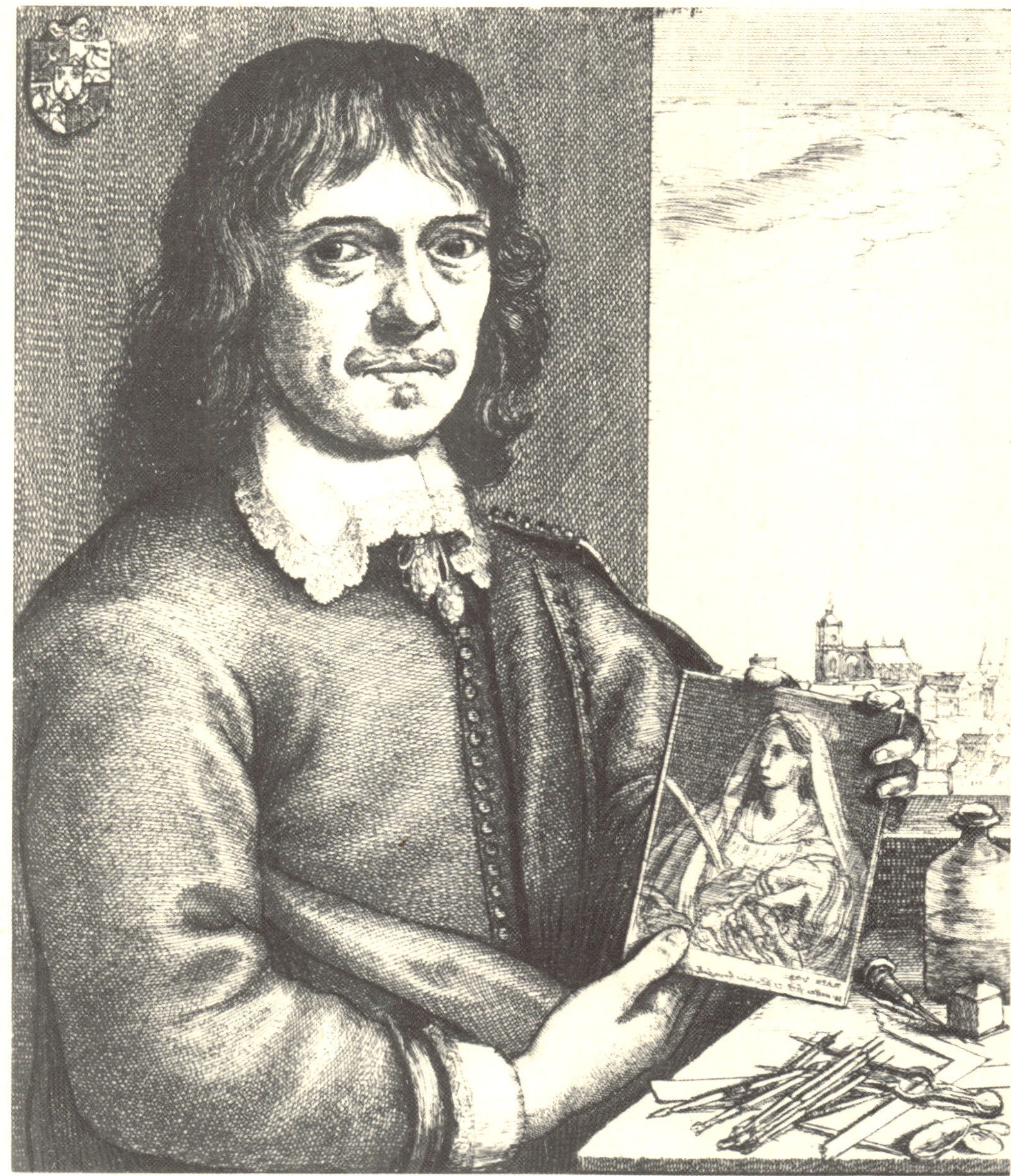

1 *Portrait of Wenceslaus Hollar after Jan Meyssens* Etching P 1419/I, published 1649. The portrait of Hollar by Meyssens from which this etching by Hollar is taken was made during Hollar's stay in Antwerp (1644–52). He is shown holding a copper plate after a picture of *St Catherine* in the Arundel collection then attributed to Raphael – the plate is a sample of his skills. On the table beside him are the tools of his profession: etching needles, a burin, a scraper, dividers, a set square and what look like shells for holding watercolour washes. The bottle probably contains acid for biting the plate, and the small box may contain ink. Through the window in the background can be seen a view of Hollar's home city, Prague. Beneath the plate is an inscription in French (not reproduced) outlining his career down to his arrival in Antwerp. (British Museum, London)

had become common at court in the time of Rudolf II and were expressed in a language close to Hollar's own vision of a transitory but beautiful world, which is so well reflected in the early drawings in his journals. The tags from Ovid and Vergil in his dedications show the level of his culture and his appreciation of philosophical thoughts. The choice of allegorical subjects extolling the certainties of virtue, art and science amid the turmoil of life shows that the wide-ranging themes and ideas in the works of Protestant artists at the Prague court furnished a favourable climate indeed for Hollar's budding affection for the Dutch masters. In such an atmosphere a young artist, after his initial intoxication with humanistic allegories, might well grasp the true meaning of the Dutch feeling for natural reality.

All this may provide a clue to the contentious question of what faith Wenceslaus Hollar was actually reared in. Though his art is decidedly secular (only a few works, mostly illustrations, have biblical subjects) its affinity to the northern manner and especially its realism, which is so different from the emotional exaltation of baroque Catholicism, corresponds to the Protestant outlook. Hollar's religious affiliation as a young man is very important in clearing up obscure events in his life; if we were certain about this, we could narrow down the possible date of his departure from Prague and guess his initial destination in Germany, and this would in turn throw light on the development of his art during his first years abroad.

Older sources, relying on the memoirs of Hollar's English friends, took his family's Protestantism for granted and regarded him accordingly as one of the refugees from Bohemia after the Battle of the White Mountain. Early in this century a different view was put forward.[3] This was based on the argument that Hollar's father could not, as a non-Catholic, have remained an official of the *Land* Record Office until his death in 1630, nor could the son, when visiting Prague in 1636 with the Earl of Arundel, have obtained the consent of the Emperor Ferdinand to the formal addition of his mother's surname to the family title. But these are not conclusive arguments. The population of Bohemia was ninety per cent non-Catholic around 1600 and only a small fraction left after 1627 when the entire Czech nobility was threatened with expulsion unless they embraced the Catholic faith by a given date. Most Czechs stayed for material reasons and changed their church under duress. Hollar's father may likewise have turned Catholic only after 1627. As for the title acquired in 1636, Katherine S. van Eerde recently pointed out that Hollar was in Prague as a member of the English lord's entourage and under his patronage.[4] The Earl of Arundel must have carried some weight, considering that the Prague Jesuits organized theatrical performances in honour of the Anglican diplomat, in which England was allegorically eulogized as the Defender of Peace.

There are several strong reasons for believing that the Hollar family was evangelical, however. Jan Hollar and his younger brother Jakub, both elevated in 1600 to the minor nobility with the title 'of Prácheň', came from Horažd'ovice, where practically the entire population was non-Catholic. According to the town archives,[5] after Jakub's death in 1624, his son Jan Jiří was summoned to the town hall with the rest of the citizenry, where they were asked why they did not 'conform in religion' with the authorities' instructions. All those present decided to appeal that they be allowed 'to remain in faith under the two kinds', that is as Protestants entitled to sacramental dispensation of both bread and wine. Jan Jiří was thus demonstrably Protestant and the same can safely be concluded of his father Jakub and his uncle Jan. Jakub's denomination is also indicated by the wording of his will, and particularly by the fact that it was witnessed not only by his brother Jan but by his brother-in-law Pavel Aretin, the publisher of an important map of the kingdom of Bohemia. Aretin was a zealous evangelist, follower of and secretary of Václav Budovec z Budova, who was among those executed after the White Mountain battle in 1621. (Aretin himself was persecuted for his faith, fined in 1624 for his part in the rebellion and finally forced into exile.) As for Hollar's father, there is a convincing piece of evidence: in 1600 he wrote a brief entry in Czech in the journal of the evangelical humanist Master Matouš Günther of Jihlava, alongside various quotations from the classics in foreign languages. This motto – *Samému Bohu čest a sláva* (Honour and glory to the only

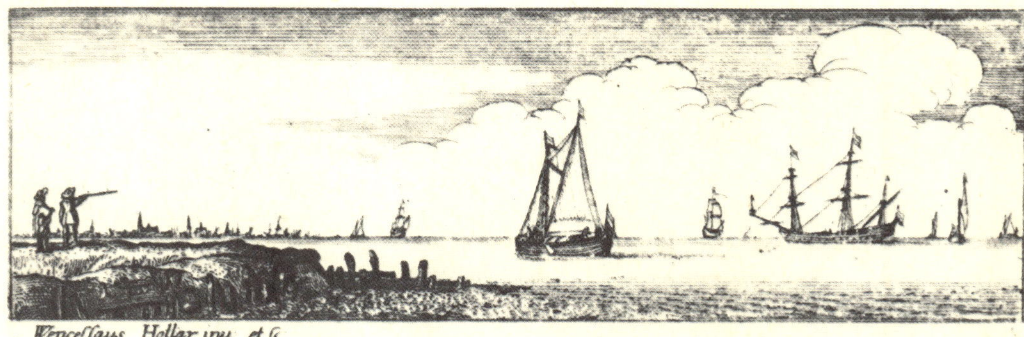

2 *Shipping off the Dutch Coast* Etching P 1255, *c.*1634. Hollar first visited the Netherlands in 1634, and it is likely to have been on or shortly after this trip that he made this etching. As might be expected, the style reflects contemporary Dutch treatments of shipping. (British Museum, London)

God)[6] – quoted in the language of the Melantrich and Kralice Czech Bibles, is itself a reflection of Calvinist influence on the church of the Czech Brethren at the end of the sixteenth century. And Calvinism was most probably the faith of Hollar's mother Markéta von Löwengrün, who came from a knightly family in the Upper Palatinate, which was Calvinist in the late sixteenth century.[7]

The body of indirect evidence for Wenceslaus Hollar's Protestant upbringing is supplemented to the point of near-certainty by the entry in the Horažd'ovice archives. There is therefore no need to question the two following statements in old English sources. John Aubrey recalls Hollar saying that his father was subjected to a property fine after he was found taking part in a secret assembly – an evident reference to the meetings of the Bohemian Brethren, who never fully accepted the official Czech Confession and had accordingly been persecuted by the Emperor Rudolf II. (We also know from Aubrey's diary that Hollar was buried as a Catholic.) Hollar's friend John Evelyn noted that Hollar was persuaded to convert to Catholicism under pressure from the Antwerp Jesuits. There is therefore ample reason to suppose that religious persecution was one motive for Hollar's departure from his homeland. On 31 July 1627 Ferdinand II issued an edict requiring all members of the Czech nobility to switch to the Catholic faith within six months or emigrate. This would bring the probable date of Hollar's move to the late summer or autumn of 1627, since the first mention of his presence in Germany refers to November of that year.

It is certain, however, that religion was not the only reason for his departure. Hollar was encountering serious obstacles to his artistic ambitions at home through quarrels with his father, who had planned a career for him as a public servant, and through the decline of Prague as an artistic centre after the Battle of the White Mountain in 1620. Although these facts must have weighed on the young man's mind, it was the Imperial edict that no doubt tipped the balance. The part of Germany to which Hollar made his way was one that had been markedly Protestant for a century. (It was also the destination chosen by another young Czech artist, Karel Škréta, whose whole family had suffered for its adherence to the Church of the Czech Brethren.)

It was during his stay in Germany that Hollar's realistic feeling for the world around him took firm root. Here he acquired the experience in landscape sketching that completely dominated his work in those years. In German art he found a reflection of late sixteenth-century Dutch realism, while the engravings of

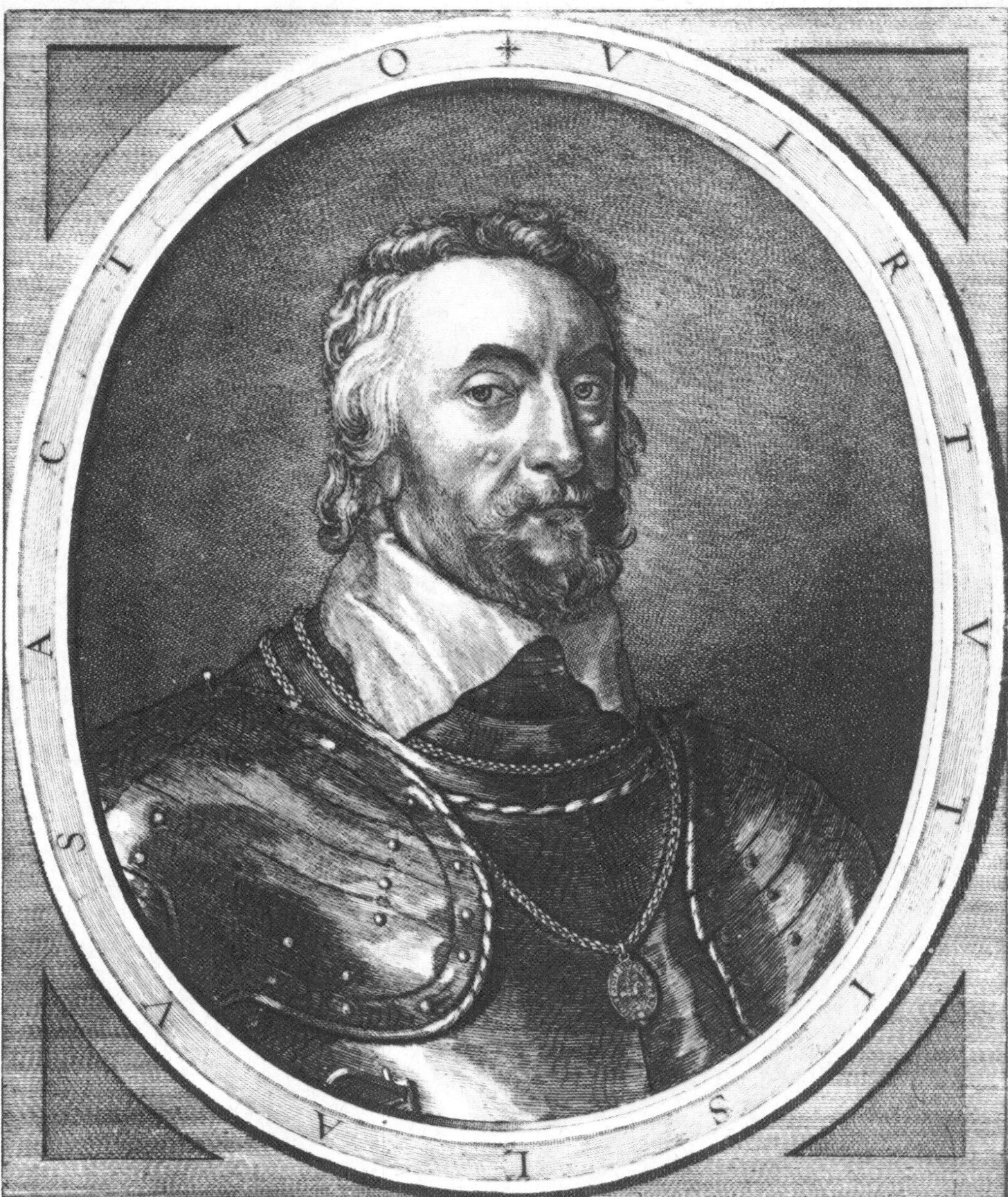

3 *Portrait of Thomas Howard, 2nd Earl of Arundel* Etching P 1351, dated 1639; this is based on a portrait by Van Dyck of the earl with his young grandson, Thomas, painted *c.*1635 and still at Arundel Castle. The earl was Hollar's principal patron, and Hollar describes himself as *Coelator* (engraver) to his lordship on the print. The Earl of Arundel (1585–1646), called by Horace Walpole in the eighteenth century 'the father of *virtù* in England', was the most significant, and probably the most serious and influential, of the English patrons and connoisseurs whose tastes were developed in the reign of James I. He was particularly celebrated in his own time for his collection of classical sculpture but he also formed a superb library and owned pictures, drawings, prints and curios of all kinds. He was the first patron of the architect, Inigo Jones. A proud and obstinate man, he was a courtier (Earl Marshal) and diplomatist and spent much of his time abroad, where he died. (British Museum, London)

the Antwerp school showed him the principles of contemporary Flemish landscape painting. His first journey to the north in 1634 brought him into contact with the Dutch countryside and with Dutch art, which in the 1630s held pride of place in realistic landscape work and was close to Hollar's own convictions.

In 1636 Hollar met Thomas Howard Arundel in Cologne, then making his way on a diplomatic mission to the Emperor Ferdinand II. This sophisticated art lover was enthralled by Hollar's drawings – he described him in a letter as 'executing drawings at breakneck speed and engravings of his own inspired works' – and asked him to join his mission as a draughtsman. Hollar's finest drawings were produced during their journey along the Rhine and Danube to Vienna and Prague, and it was this achievement that paved his way to England and determined his subsequent career.

On his arrival in London Hollar entered a world of philosophical ideas akin to the Protestant view of the real world that was familiar to him from his upbringing and from which his own artistic principles had sprung. Many reasons have been suggested recently for supposing that Lord Arundel's circle may have acquainted Hollar with the empiricist ideas of Bacon and Hobbes and the rationalism of Descartes. Similarities have also been pointed out between Hollar's view of nature and that of another Czech emigré, Comenius.[8] It was in London that Hollar formed a life-long friendship with John Evelyn, one of the founders of the Royal Society, which was established as an official body in 1662 to foster scientific research.

All this left its mark on Hollar's work during the third quarter of the seventeenth century, when he began illustrating books on history and natural science. Moreover he learnt about applying scientific method to the investigation of nature and human history and devoted his skill and creativity to their furtherance. He was working at this period on subjects taken from the world of nature as illustrations for books typical of the contemporary taste for fauna and exotic travelogues, and could draw on the experience he had gained at the start of his English sojourn when he was drawing butterflies and other insects for the catalogue to Lord Arundel's collection. The precision of Hollar's illustrations was highly thought of and in his book on prints John Evelyn wrote: 'We can justly say of Hollar's works that no series could be more useful or instructive.' To justify this opinion Evelyn mentioned the remarkable range of Hollar's drawings, their outstanding artistry and in particular their natural and discriminating quality, which in comparison with those of other draughtsmen were 'copied from life and hence more deserving of appreciation than those which rather depict chimerical curiosities and things non-existent in Nature'.[9]

Hollar's objectivity was even more valuable when applied to human artefacts. A large part of his output after his return from the eight-year stay in Antwerp consisted of illustrations for works of historical and antiquarian scholarship, fields that greatly interested him. Here too his perfect precision earned high regard from such thinkers as the genealogist and historian of ancient buildings Sir William Dugdale, a leading figure among the group of scholars whose attention to primary sources laid the foundations of modern English historiography. It was through him that Hollar met Elias Ashmole whose *History of the Order of the Garter* he illustrated, and other London historians.

During the 1650s while he was engaged on illustrating Dugdale's three books on the history of English monasteries, Hollar drew churches, castles, statues, tombstones, and ground plans and elevations of ancient buildings, many of which were already crumbling.[10] Though these documentary efforts required more geometrical exactitude than free drawing, they nevertheless echoed Hollar's predilections and deepened his appreciation of ancient monuments. When he later came to draw details and overall views of old St Paul's Cathedral, he gave one view into the nave the Latin inscription: 'Wenceslaus Hollar of Bohemia, depictor and

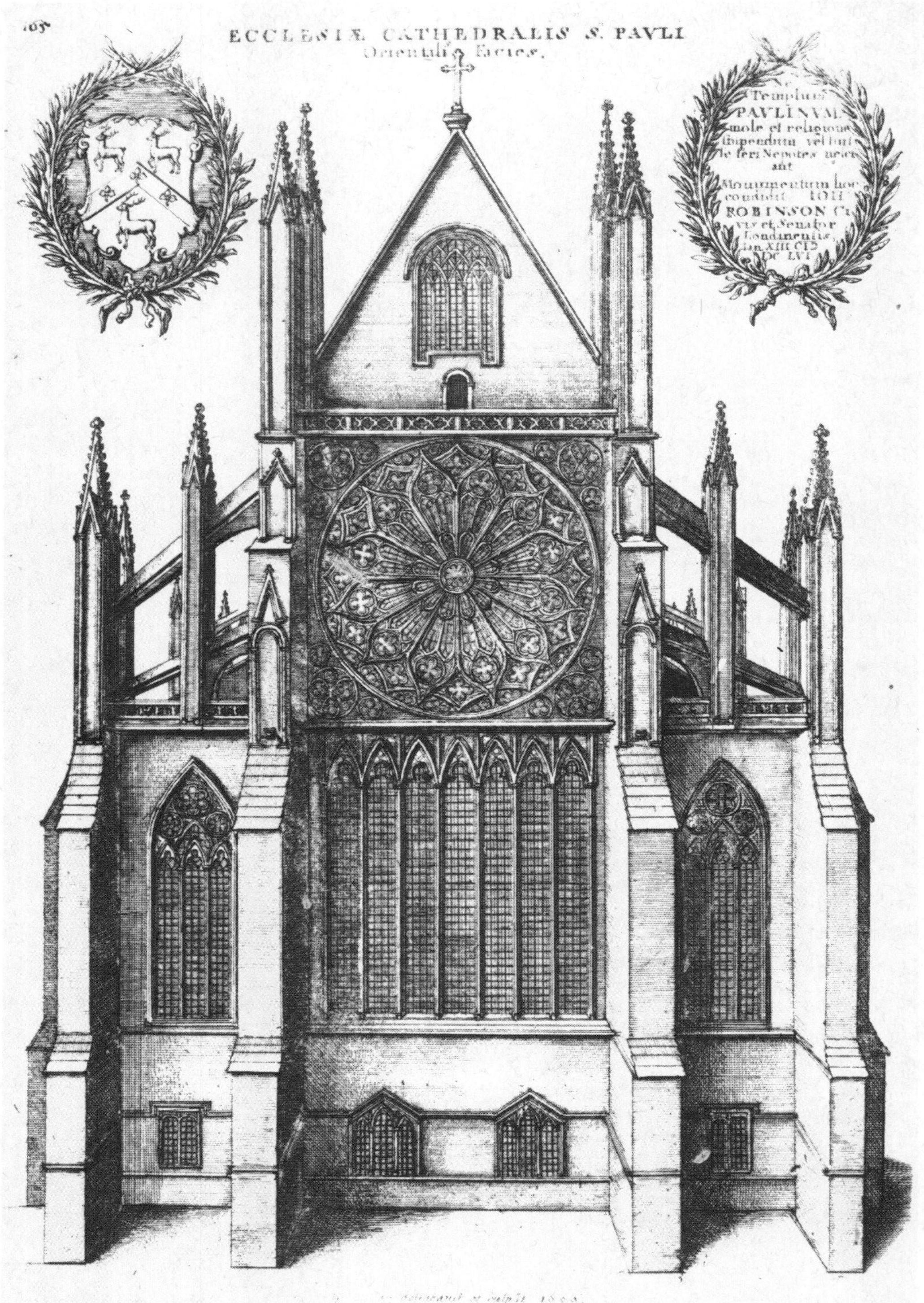

4 *Old St Paul's Cathedral from the East* Etching P 1021, dated 1656. This etching, showing the east end of Old St Paul's before it was severely damaged by fire in 1666, was one of about thirty views and plans by Hollar used to illustrate Sir William Dugdale's *History of St Paul's Cathedral* (1658). Even before the fire, the building had been in a weakened state and extensive repairs had been carried out in the 1630s by Inigo Jones; work on the Gothic choir and east end was confined to careful restoration but the outside of the Norman nave and west end were largely rebuilt in a classical style. During the fire the interior and roof were completely destroyed but the walls and central tower stood (see Hollar's *Parallel Views of London before and after the Fire*, 1666), and a decision to demolish the building was only taken after some debate. This paved the way for the erection of Wren's great masterpiece. Hollar's detailed etchings are precious records of the appearance of the old cathedral in the 1650s. (British Museum, London)

admirer of this church which every day threatens to collapse, thus preserved its memory.'

The Great Fire of 1666 brought Hollar quickly on the scene, recording it as the city continued to blaze. Afterwards he published a series of prints showing views of London before and after the conflagration, together with one of a suggested reconstruction.

Through his copies of works of art in the Earl of Arundel's magnificent collection Hollar has likewise preserved for posterity the appearance of many lost

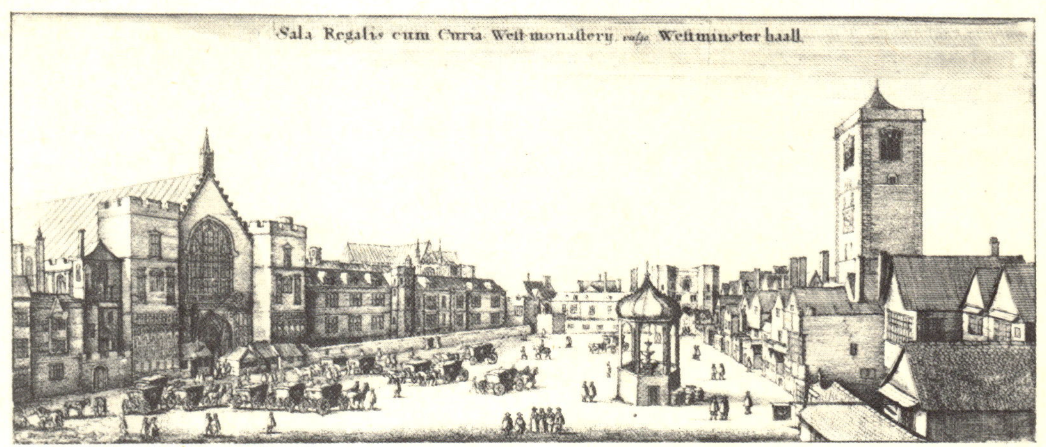

5 *New Palace Yard with Westminster Hall and the Clock House* Etching P 1040, dated 1647. The first part of the inscription, *Sala Regalis . . . Westminster haall*, refers to the Star Chamber, rebuilt in 1602, which can be seen in the range of buildings to the right of Westminster Hall; above it is the roof of Westminster Abbey, without its towers which were not built until the eighteenth century. The Clock House on the right dates from *c.*1628. (British Museum, London)

masterpieces, such as Holbein's portrait of the goldsmith Zürs. Again, his own pictures of people he knew and events he experienced and conscientiously recorded provide invaluable evidence about the world he lived in. The long series of portraits executed in the latter half of his life forms a gallery of notable figures in seventeenth-century England, while other works show him as an objective reporter of incidents he had witnessed. The title of Scenographer Royal, which he successfully requested in 1666, symbolized his attitude to the world around him. He portrayed nature, landscapes and urban views not merely as fragments of reality but as the background to human lives and the stage on which contemporary events were enacted. With an ever-ready sense of the topical he recorded such public ceremonies as the 1648 Peace Declaration in Antwerp and the coronation of Charles II, as well as dramatic scenes of court trials and public executions both in England and on the Continent. His renderings of personalities and events are equally remarkable for their precision and their reliability as historical sources. As a specialist in English history of this period Katherine van Eerde has paid particular tribute in her monograph to the inestimable value of Hollar's work in reflecting the stormy era of the English Civil War.

Hollar spent his whole life in sensitive sympathy with the artistic evolution of the age and with its ideological underpinning. He welcomed every inspiration it offered, and repaid the debt not only with the originality of his work but by bearing faithful witness to his times and earning the gratitude of historians.

Hollar's keen interest in men and nature, together with his innate accuracy, help in determining the outward circumstances of his career, for his works are often accompanied by textual inscriptions as well as information on dates and places that provide documentary evidence about his life. As Mádl puts it, 'Hollar's etchings and drawings delineate the crooked course of his long pilgrimage.' Their evidence is especially important for those obscure periods about which the writings of his contemporaries have left only fragmentary records or none at all.

The details of Hollar's first years abroad, when he was travelling in Germany, are particularly uncertain. The most interesting example of the way in which the gaps in our knowledge can gradually be filled in concerns the artist's apprenticeship with the famous printseller and engraver Matthaeus Merian in Frankfurt. It was until recently assumed on the strength of old English writings that Hollar set out from Prague in 1627 directly for Frankfurt with the aim of perfecting his skills in Merian's school. Mádl pointed out fifty years ago, however, that Hollar's works themselves provide no safe date for his association with Merian. And Eugen Dostál wrote around the same time 'Not even the best biographical sources, namely the signatures and dates on Hollar's drawings and etchings, throw any light on this most puzzling of all periods in his long life, since we do not possess any dated after the time of his departure from Bohemia in 1627; nor any dated 1628.'[11] Dostál could not know that subsequent research would bring to light many further works by Hollar, including several drawings produced during his first two years in Germany. These are not, however, marked as drawn in Frankfurt, as the English literature would have led us to expect, but in Stuttgart.

Franz Sprinzels's 1938 list of Hollar's drawings mentions two album sheets – a drawing of Mercury dated 1 January 1628 and a view of Esslingen near Stuttgart dated 23 March of the same year – and a drawing of Cannstadt in the same vicinity, which a subsequent etching also assigns to 1628. A still older drawing of Venus and Cupid, which Hollar drew for the album of Paul Jenisch, a Stuttgart theologian and musician, and marked 18 November 1627, was published elsewhere at the same time.[12] This makes it clear that Hollar was in Stuttgart at least between 18 November 1627 and 23 March in the following spring. However, it is likely that he stayed there until the spring of 1629, in view of the etching of Esslingen (P 759), which is inscribed with that year as the date of the drawing it was made from. This cannot have been the album drawing of the same subject, as suggested by critics who assume a mistake in the year quoted on the etching, since this latter carries a dedication showing that it was given to somebody in Stuttgart – where it remains to this day. The artist could not therefore have had it with him in 1665 when he was working on the etching in London. The draft for it was probably a new drawing made from approximately the same spot and can indeed be assigned to 1629.

These drawings were not the only fruit of Hollar's stay in Stuttgart. A sketch of Württemberg Castle has also been preserved, and a so far unpublished view of

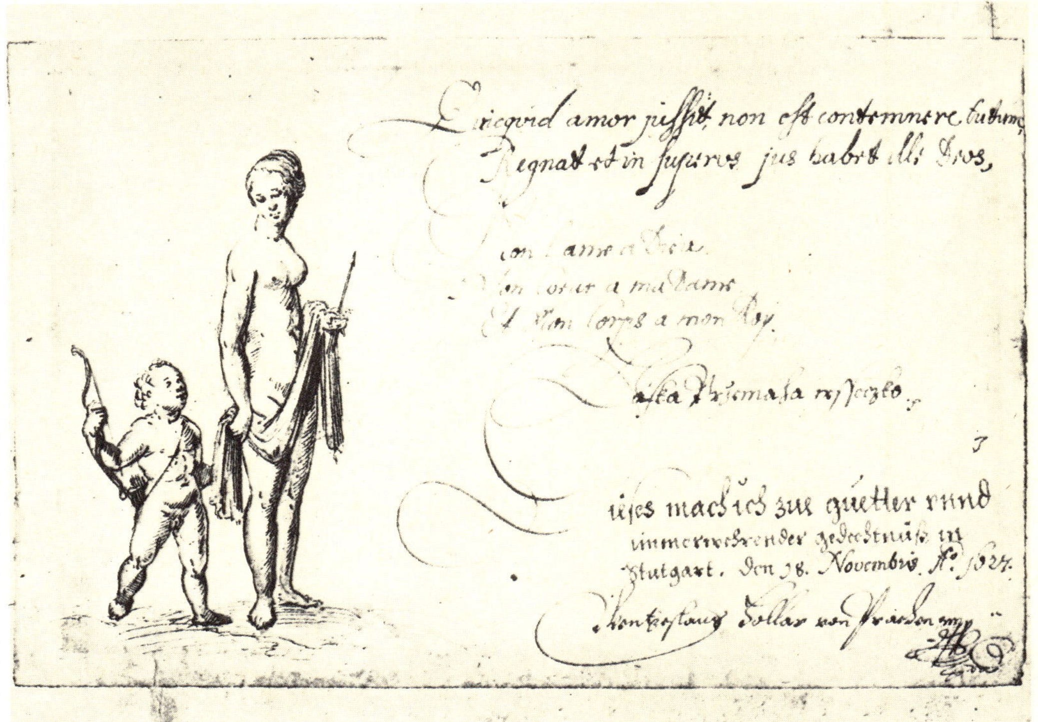

6 *Venus and Cupid* Pen, ink and wash, dated 1627. This drawing is a page from the *Album Amicorum* of the Stuttgart theologian and musician Paul Jenisch. It is inscribed by Hollar with tags in Latin, French and Czech and a note in German which reads in translation: 'I make this in fond and everlasting remembrance, Stuttgart, 18th November 1627.' The compiling of autograph albums, or books of friendship, by art lovers who got artists whom they met to make drawings for them, was a particularly German custom, and other books are known containing inscribed sheets by Rubens, Elsheimer, and many others. The style of this drawing by Hollar recalls Dürer's pupils, Aldegrever, and the artists working at the court of the Emperor Rudolf II in Prague. (Württembergische Landesbibliothek, Stuttgart, Cod. Hist. Q. 298, p. 92)

Cannstadt.[13] We must also include the lost sketch from which the P 759 etching was made, as well as drawings of subjects in and around Stuttgart on which four other etchings were based (P718*a-d*).[14] The various drawings of which we have evidence, plus other works which earned Hollar his living, presuppose that he had a permanent home in Stuttgart rather than merely visiting it occasionally from outside.

The lapse of time between Hollar's departure from Prague in the late summer of 1627 at the earliest, and his arrival in Stuttgart no later than November, was too short for him to have worked for any appreciable period under Merian at Frankfurt *en route*. In the conditions of that time to travel from Prague westwards as far as Frankfurt, then via Nuremberg and Augsburg to Stuttgart, would in itself have been almost impossible in so brief a period. The Stuttgart art historian Theodor Musper may well have been right in suggesting – though he was unaware of the November 1627 drawing and no specialist in post-White Mountain Prague history – that when Hollar left Prague he made directly for the ducal court of Württemberg. This means that his work for Merian must be assigned, not to 1627, but to a time *after* his stay in Stuttgart.[15]

In his 1973 study of Hollar's period in Germany (1627–36)[16] John Pav reached the same conclusion by a different route, revising the contemporary view current since the middle of the last century. After a critical reading of the oldest accounts of Hollar's life he found no support for the assumption that Hollar had gone straight to Merian when he left Prague in 1627. Joachim Sandrart, who himself worked for Merian in 1635–7, mentions Hollar's presence in the workshop but does not say when he arrived. In his draft notes for a book about Hollar, started in 1716, George Vertue tried to settle the route of Hollar's German wanderings, but finally gave up and omitted the passage in the published version of 1745; he mentions Merian and Frankfurt in two places but without connection or sequence. It was not until the publication of a later edition of Horace Walpole's *Anecdotes of Painting in England* in 1826 that the two facts are connected in James Dallaway's essay on Hollar and expanded into the statement: 'His first place of residence was Frankfurt, where he received instructions from M. Merian.' This then became accepted in subsequent literature.

John Pav, like Mádl and later Urzidil, resorted therefore to Hollar's dated works as the only safe guide to his travels, and by abandoning the traditional sources arrived at new conclusions. Since there are several dated works for each of Hollar's years in Germany except 1631, Pav surmised that that year, and the following one to which only a single drawing can be assigned, was the period when Hollar worked for Merian, his output appearing anonymously under the label of Merian's studio. This view is also supported by the sequence of prints in the cycle *Amoenissimae aliquot locorum effigies* ('Very Pleasant Representations of Some Places') issued in 1635. As Mádl and Pav have both established, Hollar arranged them in the order in which he had visited and drawn the various scenes during his travels subsequent to 1627. And Frankfurt appears not at the start of that cycle but in the middle, just where the 1631 gap appears in the sequence of Hollar's signed and dated works.

Pav provides further support for this view by analysing Merian's influence in particular examples of Hollar's work prior to 1631 and after 1632. However, appraisal of these arguments must be left to specialists in the history of engraving and etching. As for Hollar's drawings, the analysis in this case points to a temporary influence of Merian's studio, not – as Pav points out – in their technique or style but in certain fashions of the time, for example the composition of landscapes with large figures as accessory motifs, (as in Hollar's *View of Mainz* S 144), and these appear only from 1632 onwards, *after* Hollar's assumed stay in Frankfurt.

Pav's conclusions about Hollar's years in Germany are convincingly argued, fit in well with the analysis in the preceding chapter about the date and motives of Hollar's departure from Prague, and make it doubtful that he could have studied under Merian as early as 1627. Hollar's stay in Frankfurt can therefore be dated with considerable certainty around 1631. It was a short stay, however. Pav puts it at 1631–2, conceding that it might have begun in 1630 and ended in early 1633. But that possibility is eliminated by Hollar's extant works. The series of works from Strasbourg dated 1630, plus at least one from Cologne in the same year – the *View of Deutz and Cologne* – set the start of Hollar's Frankfurt period at the beginning of 1631 at the earliest. And the further limit of his stay cannot be much beyond the end of that year in view of the large group of signed and dated drawings executed in or around Mainz in the following year, showing that he worked there on his own account. Moreover the print entitled *The Capture of Oppenheim*, regarded by Pav as among those done for Merian's studio, carries Hollar's signature in contrast to the unsigned products of Merian's employees. As topical reportage it probably came into being, as Pav says, soon after the event that took place on / November 1631 – at least within the year. So Hollar's employment with Merian seems to have lasted less than a twelvemonth within 1631.

Closer consideration of these questions, then, justifies a reconsideration of Hollar's stay in Frankfurt and of his relationship to Merian. Hollar's drawings prior to 1631 bear no mark of Merian's influence and represent the artist's own development. This conclusion gives us a firmer base for examining the individuality of Hollar's style in his early period.

The dated drawings and prints of Hollar's early period also throw some light on obscure points in his itinerary, though less conclusively. They set the limits of his work in Strasbourg within the years 1629–30 and the date of his first Cologne trip, which gave rise, *inter alia*, to the drawing of the Drachenfels castle overlooking the Rhine (S 136), dated 1629, at the end of that year. They indicate the considerable length of his stay in Cologne (1632–6) and determine the times and destinations of journeys he undertook from there, both to nearby and distant places, including the important visits to Holland (*Harbour at Amsterdam*, 1634, and *Dutch Harbour*, recently identified as a view of Amsterdam in 1634). Finally, they help to dispel uncertainty about the exact start and finish of his period in Antwerp (1644–52), eight years of material hardship which nevertheless saw the peak of his graphic skill.

Hollar's drawings and prints therefore do constitute, as Mádl put it, 'signposts on his travels and milestones in his life'. Only by ascertaining the chronology of his journeys and the circumstances attending them can we achieve a firm basis for understanding how his art developed.

At Home

In the brief summary of his life written underneath his self-portrait, Hollar stated that from his early days he had a gift as a miniaturist and illuminator. We do in fact have several miniatures from his English period, mostly portraits, showing that this interest outlasted his youth. But he was primarily a born draughtsman and remained one all his life. There was no conflict in this dual talent, which indeed explains the very nature both of his drawing and his engraving. Only an inborn proclivity for the miniature could explain the characteristically small dimensions of his drawings, the rectangular town views and landscapes often barely ten centimetres high, the tiny representations of large views containing such incredible detail crammed into a small area that a magnifying glass is needed – and Hollar evidently used one himself – to appreciate the accuracy of the architecture and the liveliness of the figures.

The double talent of draughtsman and miniaturist was not the only advantage Hollar started out with. We have evidence of the experience he had acquired in drawing during the first twenty years of his life in Prague. Only four of his early drawings of 1625–7 have survived however. The pen and ink drawing of an allegorical subject *Fortuna* (S 83, given by Sprinzels as *Sea Goddess*) is indebted in theme and style to Dürer's pupil Aldegrever, whose winged *Fortuna* standing unsteadily on a globe Hollar copied in an early and very rare print (P 457), dated

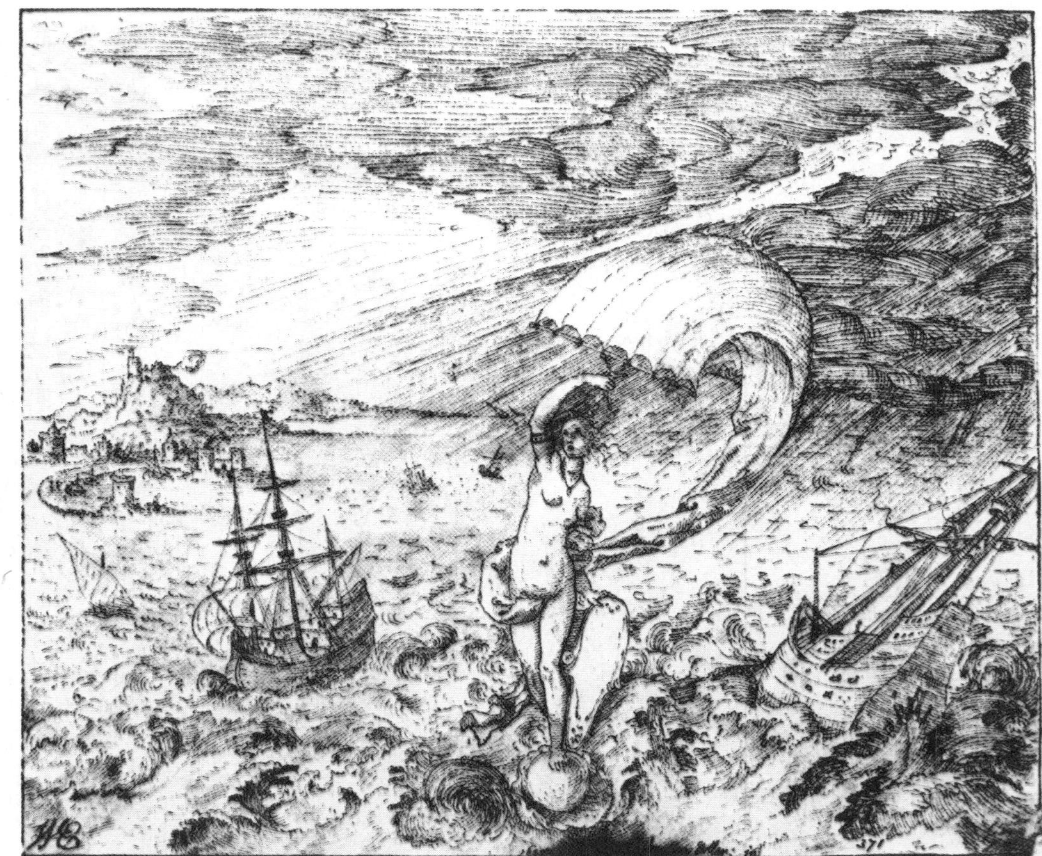

7 *Fortuna* Pen and ink S 83, dated in a later hand 1625. If the date is correct, as is likely, this is Hollar's earliest surviving drawing. In theme and style it is closely related to the work of Aldegrever, whose figure of *Fortune* Hollar copied in a print of 1626. The allegorical figure of Fortune, standing on a globe and either wearing wings or, as here, holding a sail to indicate that fortune is blown hither and thither by forces beyond man's control, is a common subject of Renaissance and Mannerist art; its application to the hazards of sea-travel is obvious. The shield, also shown by Hollar, is another common attribute of Fortune, and sometimes she is represented blindfold. (Victoria & Albert Museum, London)

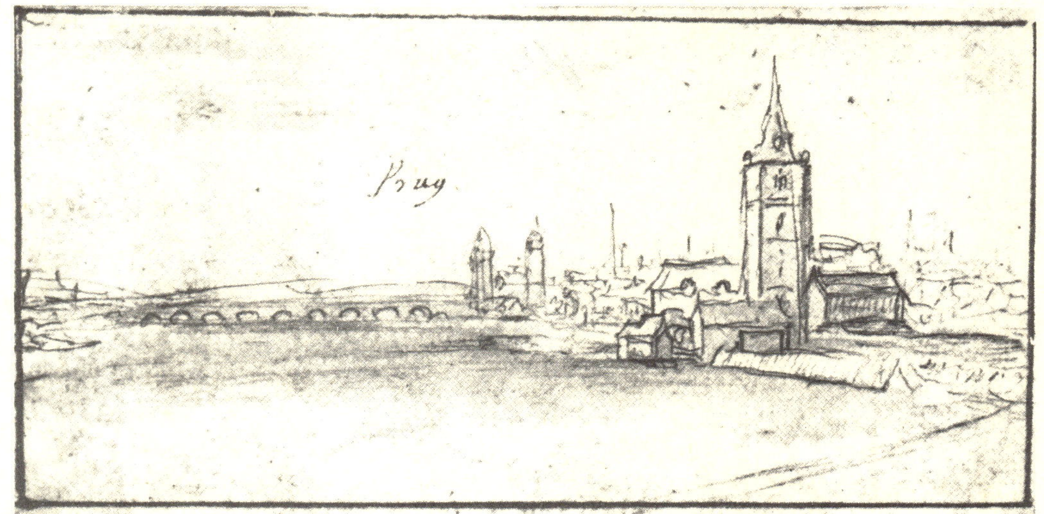

8 *View of Prague* Pencil (or black chalk) S 95, probably 1627. This view shows Prague from the south with the Charles Bridge and the towers of the Old Town in the background; on the right is the tower by the Šítkov mills. This is one of Hollar's earliest surviving topographical drawings and is thought to have been executed from nature shortly before he left his native city in 1627. (Berlin, Kupferstichkabinett)

1626. The date 1625 on the Prague drawing is in another hand, but seems plausible in view of the connection with Aldegrever's work.[17] This is Hollar's first rendering of a storm-tossed sea, something he had never seen with his own eyes. The allegoric figure stands out against a composed seascape with an imaginary coastline beyond the angry waves. There is much that suggests the intellectual climate of Rudolf II's court: the mannerist concept of the goddess with her slender, arched body, and the fashionable symbol of fickleness in the contrast between the strength of the elements and the unstable figure of Fortune.

A second drawing S 95, executed in pencil on an extremely small sheet (6.2 × 12.1 cm/$2\frac{1}{2} \times 4\frac{1}{2}$ ins) and lightly coloured, shows a view of Prague from the south in the direction of the Charles Bridge. Sprinzels dated this drawing 1628, assuming it to have been drawn in Stuttgart from memory, but it is now considered to have been done *in situ* before Hollar left Prague in 1627.[18] It is a hasty sketch, with the main lines of the towers on the skyline of the Old Town lightly roughed out and the outline of the tower by the Šítkov mills faintly indicated in the first draft and subsequently corrected. The artist already shows skill in his choice of viewpoint and even on the small sheet of his sketchbook manages to show spatial depth by varying the thickness of his lines. The drawing conveys a hint of Hollar's future stature as a landscape artist and can be safely attributed to the end of his Prague period, probably to 1627.

The remaining two drawings from this early period, neither of them listed by Sprinzels, are both in English collections and have never been reproduced so far as the author is aware, though important facts about them have been published. One is a drawing of a Prague motif, dated 1626, in the John Rylands Library in Manchester.[19] The other recently discovered Hollar drawing was shown at the 1963 exhibition in Manchester as D 2 in the catalogue, and is now in Francis Springell's collection at Portinscale. According to Springell[20] it is the draft sketch for the P 696 etching *U Prahy* (*Near Prague*), which appeared in 1635 as the second of the *Amoenissimae effigies*.

Unless a lost painting is known from old copies we can of course judge it only from the subsequent engravings. In the case of Hollar's four earliest etchings

9 *U Prahy* (Near Prague) Etching P 696, 1635. Inscribed *Beÿ Prag*, this etching is No.2 in the series *Amoenissimae aliquot locorum effigies* (Very Pleasant Representations of Some Places), etched by Hollar and published by Abraham Hogenberg in Cologne in 1635. Like the sketch shown in illustration no.8, it was probably executed in 1627. (British Museum, London)

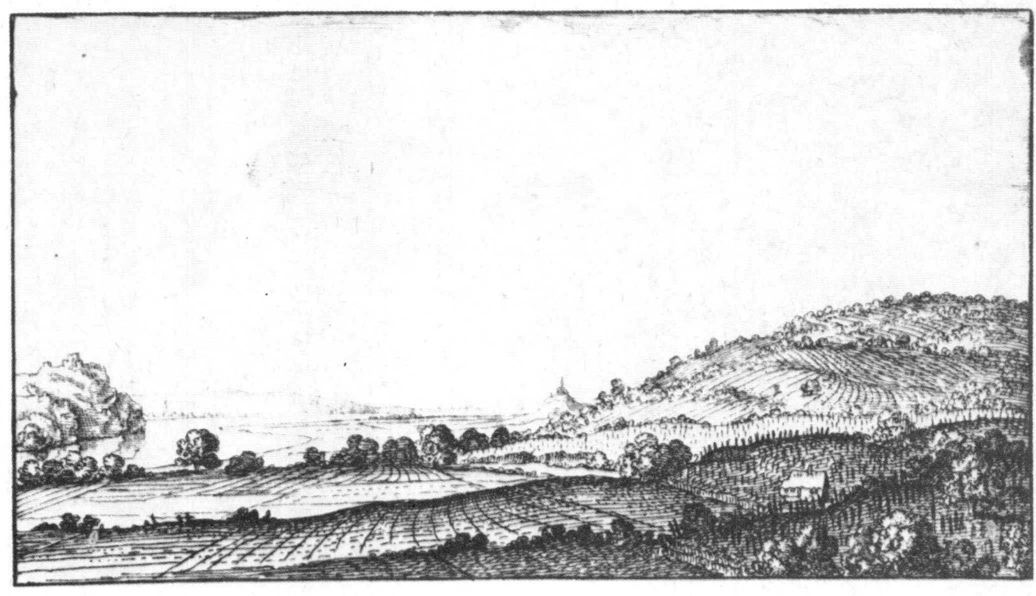

of Prague produced in 1626 (P 718 *a-d*) where there are no corresponding drawings available at all, our judgment is of course hampered by the change to another medium, aggravated in these five instances by the artist's still inadequate experience of engraving. Hollar became a good draughtsman before he was a good engraver; however, we can see from each etching the main features of the original, the choice of frame and viewpoint, the composition and in particular the artist's feeling for the landscape. On this basis we can draw the distinction between the four earlier drawings of Prague (P 718 *a-d*) and the recently discovered sketch corresponding to the *U Prahy* etching. The early views do not reflect the real Prague landscape. True, they include a number of genuine Prague motifs, their characteristic outlines or details touched in as important and even paramount elements, but they are always combined with natural features copied or adapted from other artists' work and built into an artificial scene constructed in the manner of the 'minor masters' – pupils and followers of Dürer. But there is nothing artificial about the Prague environs in the *U Prahy* etching or, one presumes, in the original in Springell's collection. This is an actual view just as the artist saw it in nature, standing with his back to the city and looking southward into the broad valley of the Vltava. The Zlíchov church stands on the rocks in the distance, the slopes above Smíchov with their fields and vineyards extend to the very edge of the paper on the right, while on the left the rock of Vyšehrad and the ruins of the castle loom over the river which forms an S-bend in the midground, disappearing in the distance towards a low horizon. This etching of the early 1630s naturally shows more experience and sensitivity of eye and hand than the more crudely executed early group; but neither the lapse of time between original and copy, nor the artist's greater command of the etching process, can disguise the realistic quality of the sketch. The objectivity of his approach, and even the choice of position, looking out not towards the city but into the open country, shows what strides Hollar had made since the early etchings and to what stage he had advanced when, in 1627, he left his native city.

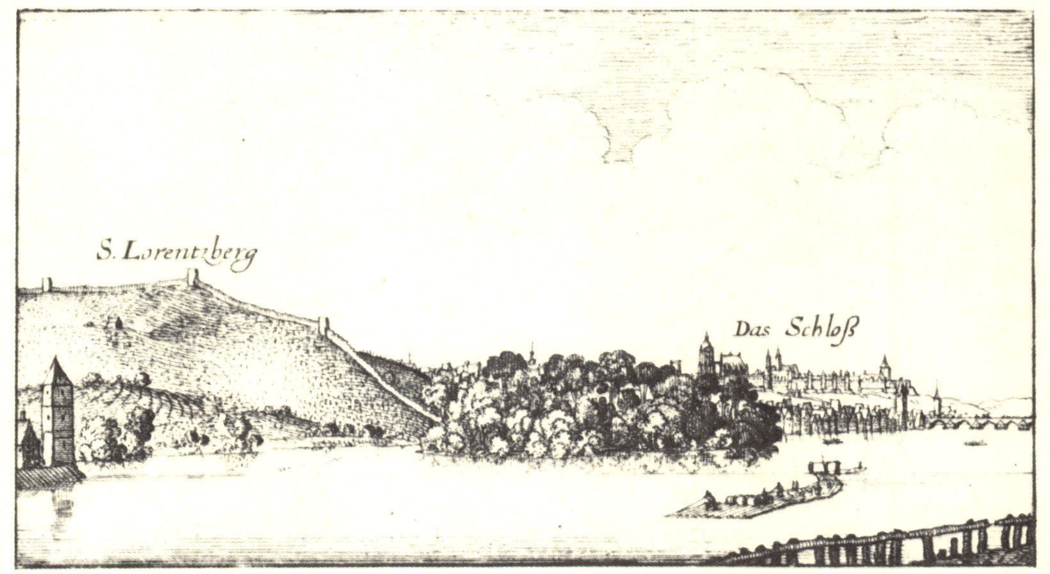

10 *View from Podskalí towards Petřín and the Prague Castle* Etching P 697, published in Cologne, 1635; it is based on a drawing in the Albertina, Vienna, S276, which Hollar probably executed shortly before leaving Prague in 1627. On the left is the St Lawrence Hill (now called Petřín Hill), with the fourteenth-century Famine Wall leading down in front of it; in the centre is the wooded Střelecký Island; in the right background are St Vitus' Cathedral, the castle and, on the extreme right, the Charles Bridge. The etching is no.3 in the series, *Amoenissimae . . . effigies* (see illustration no.9). (British Museum, London)

In all probability a fifth drawing, the original of etching P 697, the third in the *Amoenissimae effigies* series, can be added to Hollar's Prague period. Its subject, the *View from Podskalí towards Petřín and the Prague Castle*, corresponds to drawing S 276 owned by the Vienna Print Collection, the Albertina, and Sprinzels included it among the drawings done as late as 1636 on the expedition with the Earl of Arundel. However, in 1963[21] Grossman noticed the thematic link with the etching published in 1635, so that the drawing must have been still older. The coincidence of drawing and etching is close, but not complete. (In the etching the densely wooded Střelecký island is exaggerated in length, along with the skyline of the Hradčany hill in the background, evidently as a compositional adjustment of the drawn version.) There are several good reasons for believing that the drawing in the Vienna collection was done in Prague not later than 1627. Like the sketch with the Šítkov mills it is drawn with a pencil, unlike the pen and ink of Hollar's other works. It is topographically exact in outline and in the character of the terrain of the Petřín slopes, and particularly in the architectural details of the castle. The only unclear part, so far as can be judged from the tiny reproduction in Sprinzels's catalogue, concerns the Kampa embankment between the Charles Bridge and the Střelecký island, which Hollar shows built up with terraced houses. This dubious detail could be explained if the drawing were an original of the early 1630s, but derived from a sketch made *in situ* in or before 1627.

Our knowledge of Hollar's life is insufficient to tell whether his juvenilia are the product of a naturally gifted young draughtsman flexing his own talent, or reflect the guiding hand of a teacher. The progress of Hollar's art as we have traced it in the early drawings rather supports the latter possibility, but we can hardly hope ever to form a clear notion of how Hollar may have been taught. It certainly seems impossible that he should have been trained in any of the Bohemian artisan guilds. We know that his father tried to frustrate his artistic ambitions, and we have good reason to believe that he received a university education at his father's wish. He therefore could not have undergone a regular apprenticeship at the same time, since in those days this would have involved about four-years' work in a guild workshop. However, not all Prague painters went through the guild organization – court painters, for example, were exempted. Their privileged position and social prestige were further enhanced when the Emperor Rudolf II decreed in 1595 that painting should no longer be regarded as a craft, but as an art. So perhaps in the circle of court painters a way was open for the sons of noble or patrician families to embark on an artistic career without meeting guild requirements as to length of training and other matters.

Bearing in mind Hollar's remark that 'as a young man [he] enjoyed making maps', we can speculate that he may have received early training and experience by helping the painter-surveyors of Prague to draw and illuminate maps. For this skill, which so interested Hollar and became such an important part of his later output, was something that in the seventeenth century could not be learned without expert advice and training. There are sound reasons for assuming that Hollar could have obtained both while still in Prague. He might have known the Czech surveyors working for the *Land* Record Office, and indeed he had access to these circles in his own family. Pavel Aretin, his uncle Jakub's brother-in-law, was a key figure in the history of Czech cartography; in 1619 he published the third oldest map of Bohemia and was a skilled map-maker himself.[22]

We would search in vain through Hollar's early drawings for any direct reflection of the artists who lived and worked in court circles at that time. But it is quite reasonable to suppose that as he grew older the family and social environment brought him into contact with painters, draughtsmen and engravers with court connections and that once he had overcome the initial technical obstacles their work may have had a strong impact on the efforts of his late adolescence.

A number of names have traditionally been quoted in relation to particular aspects of Hollar's drawing. Among the most frequently suggested influences are the inspired views and flower and animal miniatures by the two Hoefnagels, Joris and his son Jakob, Dutch painters, draughtsmen and engravers in the imperial service; landscapes, views and in particular a sketch of Prague and its environs by Roelandt Savery, and the work of the court copper engraver Jiljí Sadeler, the author of an outstanding interior view of the Vladislav Hall in Prague Castle. Indeed, it has been proposed that Hollar learnt engraving in Sadeler's studio. In 1924 Eugen Dostál suggested that prints by Albrecht Dürer and the 'minor masters' around him, which were obtainable in Prague at that time, could have been Hollar's initial inspiration. In an article on Hollar's 'cosmography' in 1967 Luboš Hlaváček pointed to the fashion for suggestive illustrations in contemporary maps and Czech land surveyors' diagrams as a possible contributory source, and drew attention to other court artists whose work Hollar may have known.

None of these artists can be shown to have had a direct influence in steering Hollar on to his very personal artistic path. But his life in Prague certainly produced the intellectual and artistic climate in which his art was born and grew as he absorbed impulses germane to his convictions and rejected everything alien to his personal realism.

Stuttgart

The etchings in the series *Amoenissimae effigies*, which successively trace Hollar's itinerary from Bohemia to the lower Rhineland and Holland, take us – after short stops in Nuremberg and Augsburg which are not recorded in his drawings[23] – to the pleasant Württemberg countryside and the banks of the Neckar. We can see from his dated drawings that the first place Hollar stayed after leaving Bohemia was Stuttgart, where the duke had his residence. Here he lived for at least five months at the turn of 1627 and 1628, a period of some importance in his artistic development. The landscape drawings he produced in and around Stuttgart reflect a gradual release from the waning influence of Rudolfine mannerism and a steadily increasing conversion to realism.

Why did Hollar come to this particular city? He could well have been drawn to it not only by the Protestant allegiance of Württemberg in general but by the generous favour the ducal court bestowed on artists. The magnificent programme of architecture begun at the castle in the early Renaissance and continuing to the beginning of the seventeenth century, the paintings commissioned for the new buildings, the famous Stuttgart festivals and allegorical processions that became subjects for several drawings in the first decade of the seventeenth century and then, through the medium of print albums, spread the popularity of the court far beyond the boundaries of the duchy – all this meant ample work for artists and apprentices, for local talents and for foreigners invited to lend a hand. Heinrich Geissler recently calculated the number of draughtsmen involved.[24] Albums with drawings and entries by local artists and itinerant journeymen testify to the existence in Stuttgart around 1625–30 of 'a choice team of young artists such as could hardly be matched elsewhere in Germany', as Geissler puts it. In about 1628

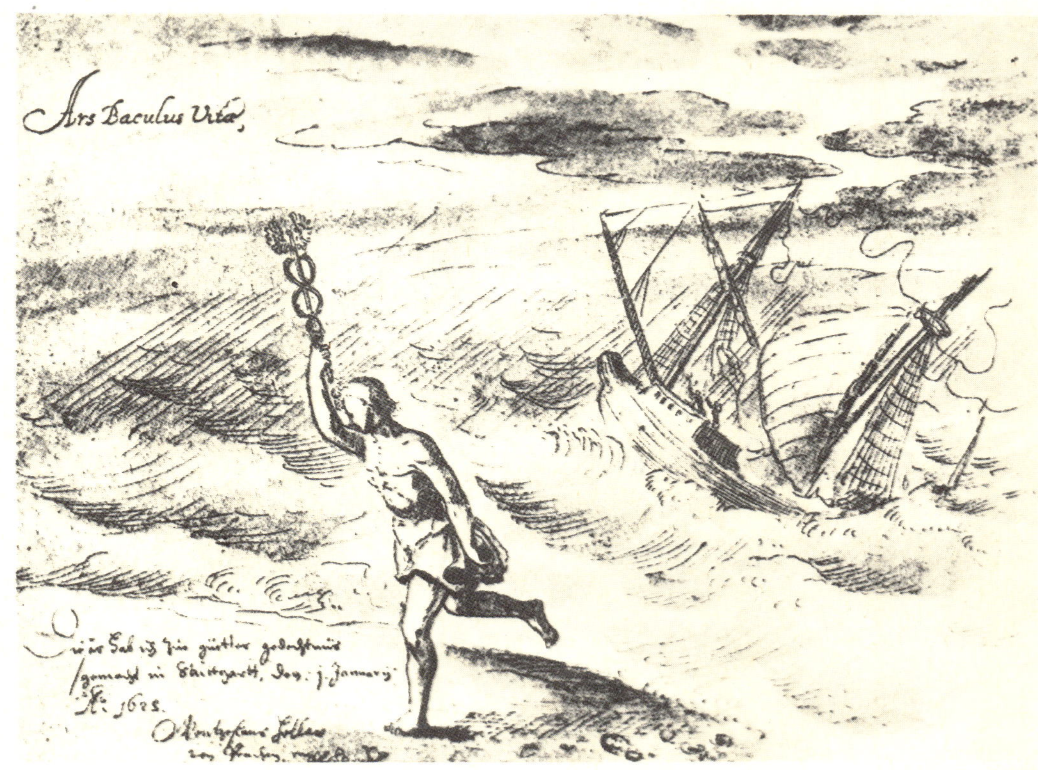

11 *Mercury* Pen, ink and wash S 81, dated 1628. It is difficult to interpret this early print exactly. The Latin phrase appears to mean 'Art is the staff of life', though in that case the last word should read *Vitae*, not *vita* (which makes no sense). The figure holding up a staff is presumably intended to illustrate this meaning, but the staff is the *caduceus*, the traditional attribute of Mercury, not a support or stay (*baculus*). On the other hand, if the figure is intended to be Mercury, he does not wear the helmet and winged sandals usual in representations of him in sixteenth- and seventeenth-century art. The German dedication at the bottom is also somewhat obscure, though it is similar in form to those in some of Hollar's other early drawings (numbers 6 and 12). The last part reads '. . . fond remembrance made in Stuttgart 1st January 1628', and signed by the artist. (Anhaltische Gemäldegalerie, Dessau)

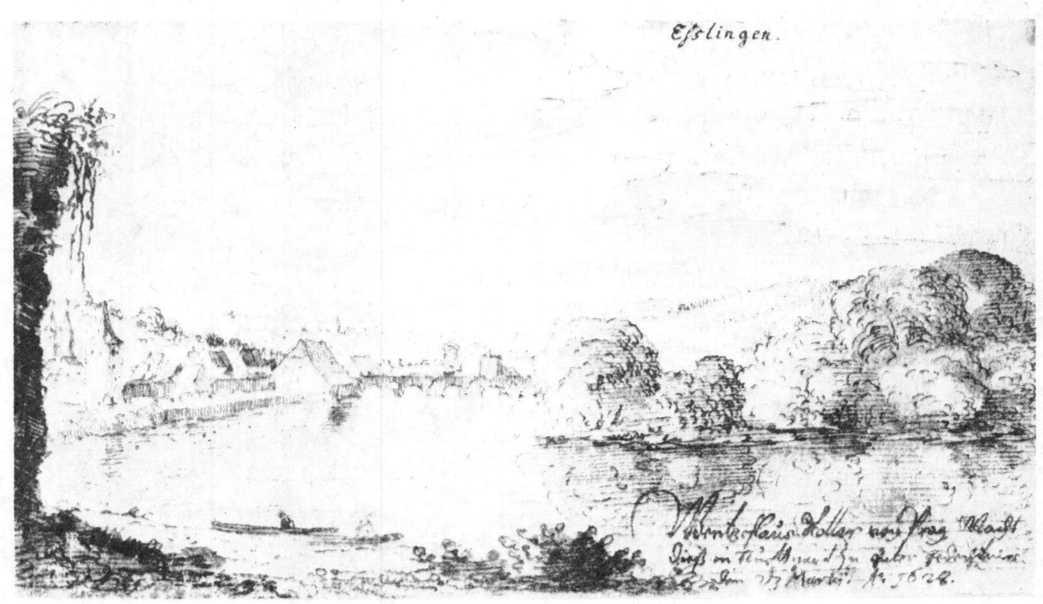

12 *View of Esslingen* Pen and ink with watercolour S 98, dated 1628. The sheet is inscribed with the placename, *Esslingen* (on the river Neckar near Stuttgart), and a dedication in German similar to that on the *Venus and Cupid* (picture no.6): 'Wenceslaus Hollar of Prague makes this in Stuttgart in fond remembrance, 23rd March 1628.' The date is important in fixing the year of the artist's stay in Stuttgart. With its overhanging rock at the left and clumps of trees neatly arranged on the far bank of the river at the right, the drawing is conventionally composed, recalling Dutch landscapes produced under the influence of Elsheimer. (Staatsgalerie, Stuttgart, Graphische Sammlung, Inv.Nr.205)

they included four names that were to attain fame in due course: Johann Heinrich Schönfeld, destined to be the leading German painter of the century; the miniaturist and engraver Johann Wilhelm Baur of Strasbourg; and two young men from Bohemia, Karel Škréta – whose presence there is known from an album drawing of 8 September 1628 – and Hollar himself. Evidence of friendship between these two comes from the important fact that in 1635 Hollar executed a print from Škréta's drawing *Bust of a Young Man*, whose date Hollar himself gives as 1627 and which he probably received as a gift in Stuttgart before the two parted company. The similarity of their early careers invites Neumann's conclusion that 'the two artists either left Prague simultaneously, or at least in concert, following the same westward route in the hope of solving their problems in a similar way'.[25]

The two album sheets – the *Venus and Cupid* of 18 November 1627 (G 4) and the drawing usually referred to as *Mercury* dated 1 January 1628 (S 81) – are only occasional improvisations. But they do testify to Hollar's ready hand and memory, as well as to an already advanced sureness of line, though his figures are still manneristic and allegorical of the kind then customarily drawn in friends' albums.[26] The *Mercury* is also characteristic for this genre (and reminiscent of the earlier *Fortuna*) with its slender running figure, holding the staff of life aloft, and the typical stormy sea and precariously tossing ship. The *Venus and Cupid* belongs to the same mental and stylistic climate, but the conception of the drawing is different. The figures are firmly outlined, with no background, the modelling is achieved by line as well as light tinting; and the calm statuesque poses almost suggest a sculptor's sketch.

Hollar's landscapes of the Stuttgart period still bear some faint signs of the Rudolfine tradition in his tendency to rearrange the features of the actual subject. The pen drawing with grey wash on the back of the *Mercury* sheet is a still-idealized Italian landscape with an ancient ruin in the manner of Adam Elsheimer, but there are two other drawings of genuine views near Stuttgart and on the Neckar.[27] In the 1628 album sketch *View of Esslingen* (S 98) there is still a fictitious addition in the form of a rock-face with overhanging turf. But the real point of interest lies clearly in the composition and in the details reproduced from the *in situ* sketch, showing the artist's fascination with the picturesqueness of the view across the overgrown banks of the Neckar towards the little town and stone bridge in the background.

The most important product of Hollar's stay in Stuttgart was the *View of Cannstadt* on the Neckar (S 97), a place that is now part of Stuttgart. This first treatment of the town, executed according to the subsequent engraving in 1628, is a portrait of the town set in a countryside panorama rather than a view of the buildings alone. Here there is no artificial composition, nothing borrowed from an alien model. The broad, open river flows through the centre of the drawing deep into the background, where the light silhouette of distant hills forms a fairly low horizon. The spatial planes are not conspicuously fixed but follow one another in smooth sequence into the distance, their intensity gradually reduced by the wash-modelling and the lines growing ever fainter. The outlines of the background forms are not blurred and softened by aerial perspective, as in Hollar's mature drawings, but their lightness looks forward to his later technique. The accurate architectural detail of the town and the settlement facing it, and the soberly deployed miniature staffages, show a definite advance on the road to realistic landscaping. This drawing of Cannstadt is all the more notable for having been done in 1628 – when the artist was only twenty-one – in the same year as the *Venus and Cupid* and *Mercury* album sketches that were so evidently related to manneristic models remembered from Bohemia. Face to face with the countryside Hollar now finds his own path in close and accurate observation of reality; to express it artistically was to become the sole aim of his life and work.

How could Stuttgart have helped Hollar along this course? In the first place, no doubt, by enabling him to practise his technique on the commissions that earned him his living, possibly under Georg Thonauer alias Donauer, for whom the young J.H. Schönfeld worked as an apprentice. There was also an opportunity of seeing the various prints collected or published in Stuttgart, the works of art in the court galleries and in other places connected with the Castle, and the cosmographic paintings in the Summer Palace, where both maps and accurately drawn landscapes of the duchy could be seen.

Hollar may have benefited from meeting and perhaps making friends with other young artists then gathered in Stuttgart – Johann Wilhelm Bauer, Schönfeld and, of course, his fellow-Bohemian Karel Škréta. It is fair to assume that these artists of very different origins not only enjoyed close contact but exchanged ideas about their common passion. Recent criticism has indeed discerned connections between the three we have mentioned, mutual influences that evidently began in Stuttgart and continued to be reflected in their work during the 1630s.[28] As for Hollar, there is one interesting motif that is common to him and Baur, that of the angry sea. The storm at sea, ships uneasily perched on the crests of foaming waves or struggling in the trough between them, broken yards, snapped ropes and tattered sails flying in the wind are all typical of Baur's etchings in the 1630s.[29]

The depiction of storms at sea in Hollar's two early drawings, the *Fortuna* of 1625 and the *Mercury* of 1628, is not yet based on personal experience and for that reason lacks conviction. The movement of waves in the 1625 essay still has no logical relation to the direction of the wind; what we see are mere chaotic masses of water in a profusion of crystal-sharp angles. The later of the two, however, shows a marked advance. It is more lifelike; the hatching and washing mould the masses producing a powerful contrast between the troughs and the broken crests of the swollen waves. The improvement is very likely due to familiarity with Baur's works. The subject reappears several times in Hollar's drawings and etchings, particularly after his Rhine journey to Holland in 1634 had brought him an overwhelming first sight of the sea. It was probably then, before he left Cologne, that he made the fine etching P 1282 that shows three-masted whaling ships fighting the elements. The etchings of both Hollar and Baur in this period include masterly renderings of natural forces let loose. Baur's have the dramatic tension of impending disaster, sometimes of nightmarish intensity; Hollar's are relatively quiet and temperate in consonance with his character and artistic personality.

It is no mere chance that this should be the sole point of contact with Baur's work or that Hollar should have nothing stylistically in common with Schönfeld and Škréta. His three contemporaries were pursuing different artistic ends and this can even be seen in the direction they took when leaving Stuttgart: Škréta and his two colleagues went south and by roundabout routes met again in Italy, while Hollar headed north via Strasbourg to the homeland of landscape realism.

Strasbourg

The Strasbourg drawings belong to an important stage in Hollar's development. The commissions he undertook for publishers – Heyden in Strasbourg and Hogenberg in Cologne – and the work of copying prints by the Dutch engraver Jan van de Velde gave him useful technical schooling. As Mádl noted, 'the shape and firm lines of the *Little Views* (*Malé pohledy*) betray Hollar's familiarity with the fascinating etchings of Jan van de Velde' whose memory was still 'all but implanted in Hollar's hand'. Dostál traced their influence in great detail in his analysis of Hollar's early etchings, for example in his way of drawing trees. More recently Pav has written of his 'fanlike branches ending in mushroom tops'. Dostál, however, also pointed out the limits of this similarity, which extends only to individual elements such as trees and figures, but not to the overall conception of the landscape, which with Hollar is realistic, not genre-based.[30] In Hollar's drawings of 1629–30 we find scant signs of van de Velde's influence, particularly in the rendering of treetops, where his engraving practice sometimes enables him to imitate complex natural outlines in a generalizing shorthand, but where the main attraction is reality itself and the task of interpreting shapes and spaces ever more truthfully and expressively.

In Strasbourg and the surrounding countryside Hollar found a wealth of varied and enticing subjects: the silhouette and substance of the city within its fortress walls, the structure of streets and squares with their richly articulated façades, the quaint garb of the townsfolk and their way of life, above all the very siting of the city near the Rhine at the confluence of two lesser rivers whose five branches with several canals criss-crossed the city itself and formed an impressive feature of the

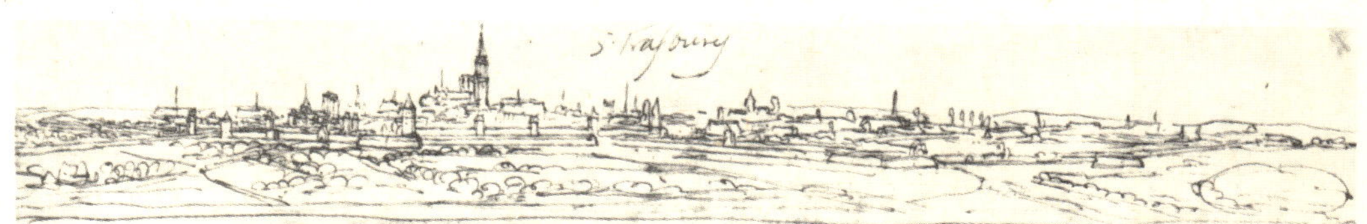

13 *View of Strasbourg* Pen and ink S 117. Dated drawings and etchings show that Hollar was in Strasbourg in 1629 and 1630, when this sketch must have been made. (Private Collection)

scenery, especially in the open country beyond the walls. All this was to extend the range of Hollar's subject matter during the years that followed.

It was in Strasbourg that Hollar's first figure studies or, more properly, costume studies appeared. Here he was attracted mainly to the variations of female attire which changed according to season, function and custom. Few of the original drawings remain and only in one or two cases can we be sure of their authorship. One of them is the rare pen and wash *Strasbourg Woman* (S 25), where the richly decorated fur-trimmed coat is drawn with a microscopic accuracy that makes its attribution certain and points forward to Hollar's famous drawings and etchings of fur muffs.

Hollar gave an overall view of the city in the hasty sketch *View of Strasbourg* (S 117), something fairly unusual among his extant drawings. The main outline of the city with its walls and other dominant features is caught with a sure but light and lively hand; its position on a plain with a low skyline is suggested, and the roads leading up to it are sketched in. No final version or resultant engraving have been preserved. This Strasbourg draft is the earliest of Hollar's overall city views. It bears neither date nor signature, but the subject proves that it was done in 1629 or 1630, since so far as we know this was the only period in Hollar's life when he could have drawn Strasbourg from nature. As regards authorship, a comparison with drawings of Strasbourg details done at this time provides the evidence.

There are four drawings in which Hollar directed his eyes at the centre of the town. The grand conception and architectural detail and decoration of Gothic cathedrals tempted him on more than one occasion to reproduce accurately a wealth of fine points without detracting from the monumentality of the whole: he drew Strasbourg Cathedral no less than three times. The extant drawing S 110 shows a view almost exactly from the west. Two other renderings, approximately from the north-west, are preserved only as etchings – P 892, which gives the date of the original drawing as 1630, and P 893. In the life sketch the massiveness of the cathedral is emphasized by its contrast with the tiny scale of the attendant figures and the aerial view of burghers' houses on the town square.

The *View of the Monastery Church of St Thomas* (S 112) takes in additionally the picturesque nook of the monastery wall, the bridge over the river and the embankment from which spectators are gazing up at the crowded nave. It is thus thematically related to two further drawings, drafts for the print series called *The Four Seasons* in which Hollar, with his feeling for the reality of both whole and detail, used specific glimpses of town life to express the symbolism of his subject. The *View of the Barefoot Square* (S 111) is probably only one of several drafts for a portrayal of a sleigh ride and other winter amusements in the snow-covered city. It shows a partial view of one corner of the city square where the event was to be depicted; the restricted area was only a portion of the projected composition.[31] The only extant drawing of those made for *The Four Seasons* etchings is the *Strasbourg Shooting-range* (S 113). Here Hollar chose as a symbol of spring the shooting-match with musketeers firing at a target, an event the townsfolk organized with great enthusiasm after Easter every year on the range outside the walls. Hollar managed to include natural scenery in his composition by opening a view into the countryside on the right of the sheet. He filled the grass-covered range with groups of figures whose diminishing scale gives depth to the scene. As this was the prototype for an engraving rather than a sketch he imposed a few corrections on reality. The picturesque tree growing out of the low strip of terrain in the foreground and theatrically framing the right-hand edge of the picture is a concession to the traditional requirement of a foreground feature contrasting with the rest – a *repoussoir*. In the rendering of the treetops we can detect the clear influence of Jan van de Velde, which is even more conspicuous in the etching. On the whole, however, the conception of the drawing is realistic in respect of scenery and human figures, in accordance with the spirit of the cycle.

What attracted Hollar most, however, was the fringe of the city where nature and human habitation came into contact. In the fine drawing of 1629, *View of Strasbourg* (S 114), two distinct glimpses of the town in the background are separated by vegetation: a left-hand view of the cathedral and a right-hand one of a more distant part dominated by the Judentor and the castellations of the tower. The main theme, however, is nature itself at the approach to the city and the picturesque confluence of the rivers. In the centre is the broad river surface with a typical Strasbourg covered-cabin boat on it. On both sides of the scene and in the middle-background are overgrown banks and tall deciduous trees with single branches overtopping their ramified crowns. This sketch was drawn with a pen dipped in *bistre*, held lightly in a hand supremely confident of its technique. The subject matter is rendered all the more impressive by the use of watercolours for tonal discrimination between the brown soil, the green vegetation and the lighter blue and grey shades of the buildings and clouds, while variation of colour density is used at the same time to model the masses and provide spatial depth. This chromatic harmony, typical of some of the aquarelle drawings of the Strasbourg period, echoes the Dutch landscape tradition of the late sixteenth century in which the triad brown-green-blue was used to organize space into foreground, middleground and background. However, Hollar's consistent realism blurs the artificial boundaries between spatial zones, uses successive transitions to give an impression of continuity in depth, and also achieves aerial perspective by progressively softening shapes as the distance from the observer increases.

We have two more drawings of Strasbourg seen from a distance. One of them, *View of Strasbourg from the South-West*, is not mentioned in Sprinzels's list, but we know from the catalogue of the Manchester exhibition that it was drawn from a point beside the river I11.[32] The second, *Near Strasbourg* (S 116), was produced in 1630. The lightly sketched outline of the city recalls the remarkable general view of Strasbourg described previously. It is extraordinary through the very ordinariness of the subject chosen. Somewhere outside the city, part of which forms the distant background, Hollar had caught sight of a bend in the river, but his notice was chiefly attracted by a long stretch of riverbank with a clump of rushes and a garden fence beside it. The subject is simple and characteristically suburban. But Hollar's sketch, washed with rapid brushstrokes, gives a convincing portrait of an aspect of Strasbourg's surroundings which is quite different from those romantically picturesque riverside picnics with pollarded trees and bushes amid the meadows. We must admire the keen eye Hollar must have cast round him on his walks outside the city and the progress this sketch demonstrates in comparison with the artificially composed landscapes of a few years before.

There are some twenty etchings of the Strasbourg area to testify to those strolls with the sketchbook. One of them (P 703) was probably based on the wash drawing *View of Wikhäusl* (near Strasbourg)[33] since its central subject is the medieval watchtower, the Wighaus, with surrounding buildings among a group of trees. What the sketches for the rest were like we can guess at least from the engravings. For the most part they depicted large and small water-bridges on the outskirts of the town, a bridgehead with customs and guardhouse, weirs and water-barriers, a mill outside the city wall, boatyards, groups of cottages, courtyards and isolated towers. Nature is present everywhere, not as a picturesque backcloth but as an authentic and indispensable component of town life.

Stylistically and chronologically the Strasbourg period includes a number of drawings of quite distant places, which were produced on Hollar's first Rhine journey to Cologne, probably around the turn of 1629 and 1630. In addition to the ink and brown wash *Drachenfels Castle near Bonn* (S 136) of 1629 there is a fine undated drawing *View of Mühlheim-on-Rhine* (S 115), showing land owned by the Archbishop of Cologne. This last represents a transition from the Strasbourg to the Cologne periods in Hollar's stylistic development. It is linked to the 1629 works by the denser watercolour and more expressive hues, reminiscent of the S 114 view of Strasbourg at the junction of the rivers. The grove of trees still displays the fan-branching motif, while the tradition of the *repoussoir* lingers in the dark-brown foreground whose sharp and almost silhouette-like outline contrasts with the bright surface of the Rhine. On the other hand the clay soil with its strongly modelled surface shows a deliberate choice of natural reality – anything but an artificial proscenium. A new feature is the Rhine valley to the left, opening out wide into the plain, bounded in the far background by a fairly low horizon. Hollar opens up the view into the distance, not through narrow slits, but with a broad prospect full of light and air, a harbinger of the Rhineland and Dutch landscapes of his maturity.

A third drawing that was probably produced on the same journey (finished off with watercolour and dated 1630) is the *View of the Rhine near Cologne and Deutz* (S 122). The right-hand half is taken up with the riverside fortifications and gates of the Cologne perimeter, while the centre of gravity lies on the left-hand side with rowing boats and yachts sailing along the river. In the distance, close to the low horizon, is the lightly touched-in outline of Cologne's guard tower, the Bayernturm, along with the sails of a windmill and a forest of masts in the harbour. Hollar redrew this scene three years later, this time from the other bank, where a Swedish army had in the intervening years occupied Deutz and converted it into a fortress. But this belongs to a later stage of Hollar's work.

Hollar and Merian

Pav has reason to set Hollar's stay in Frankfurt-on-Main, at Matthaeus Merian's studio, in the year 1631. This may have been a temporary paid assignment to help in preparing Merian's volumes of prints, but even this form of employment at the studio of a famous publisher and printseller, under the guidance of the expert Merian himself, could have given the young artist valuable practice and useful ideas for his original work.

There is interesting evidence that Hollar enjoyed good relations with Merian, who was fourteen years his senior. In 1647 Hollar etched, signed and dated a fine portrait of the goldsmith Zürs after a drawing of Holbein's original in the Arundel collection. The print was published by Henrik van der Borcht, Hollar's young friend from the days when they worked together at the earl's London residence. (Borcht was the son of a prominent Frankfurt publisher and himself an engraver trained under Merian.[34]) The print is dedicated by its publisher to his former patron with the respect of a pupil. But constituting as it does a double masterpiece of Hollar's skill as draughtsman and engraver, the print may also be seen as a joint memento of the Frankfurt artist who was then already a very sick man.

Commentators agree that Hollar's work for Merian enriched his knowledge in several ways. He perfected his graphic techniques, acquired a more thorough knowledge of cartography and topography, learnt about aerial perspective and enlarged his open-view repertoire by increasing his skill in urban panorama composition. These techniques, however, still involved a number of time-honoured landscapists' tricks: the prominent, over-emphasized *repoussoir* carried over from the old bird's-eye perspective method and the motif of large foreground figures drawn to a different scale from the rest of the composition. Merian still clung to this last mannerism and Hollar several times applied it likewise to outdoor subjects, especially views of towns, even in his English period.

In his own field of draughtsmanship, particularly in his ability to show landscape three-dimensionally, Hollar had little to learn in Frankfurt. From the rapid progress and range of his drawings during the years 1627–30 we have already seen what a thorough command of the means of expression he had by this time. As early as his *View of Cannstadt*, and particularly in the clean and delicate sketches of his Strasbourg years, Hollar's sensitive and total mastery of techniques was self-evident. But the basic contrast between Hollar and Merian lay not in technique but in artistic expression, in the aim and concept of a creative approach to objective reality.

In his monograph on Merian's drawings[35] Lucas Heinrich Wüthrich dealt primarily with eighty works that display Merian's stature as a draughtsman. Over half of the items in Wüthrich's list are landscape and figure drawings for engravings in which the landscape features are blended into an artificial composition with a theatrical foreground – striking tree forms, withered trunks, stone and plank bridges with accessory figures; middlegrounds strewn with quaint cottages, mills, wells, pole-fences and other paraphernalia of the old Flemish school; backgrounds consisting of steep hillsides and peaks surmounted by towered castles. But the real proof of Merian's ready gift as a draughtsman is furnished by his quick landscape sketches where the main features of the subject are caught in

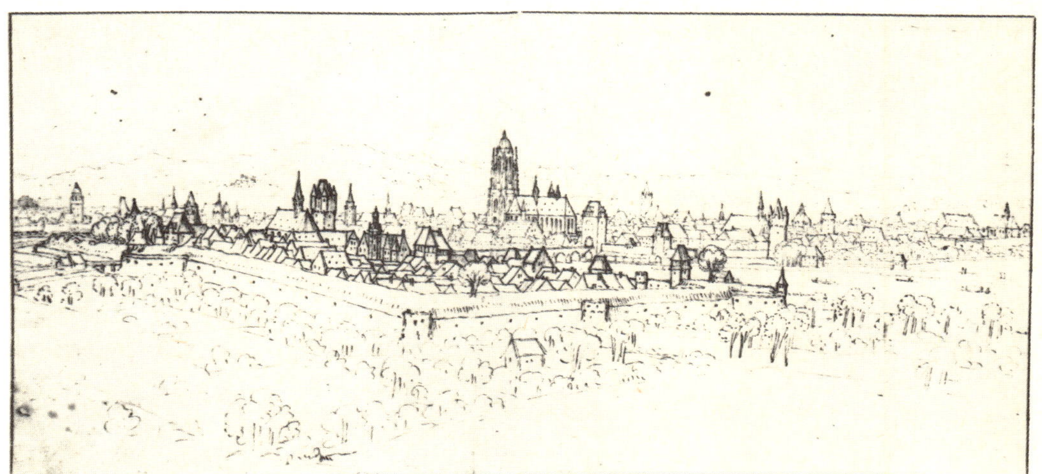

14 *View of Frankfurt-on-Main* Matthaeus Merian the Elder. Pen and ink, about 1625. The Swiss-German graphic artist, Matthaeus Merian the Elder (1593–1650), was the leading designer of views in Frankfurt in the second quarter of the seventeenth century. Hollar worked under him there probably in 1631. See illustration no.15. (Städelsche Kunstinstitut, Frankfurt)

free and flexible lines, usually finished off with a wide range of wash colours. In his sketches from around 1620 there is a marked style, the main subject strongly modelled while areas of the foreground are left blank or merely articulated with a few hasty lines.

Wüthrich justifiably holds up two particular sketches as prime examples of Merian's characteristic style in his best period: a view of Basel and a view of the Church of St Clare in Little Basel, both probably dating from 1620–1.[36] They display Merian's virtuosity and realism, but they also show his tendency, even in sketches made on the spot, towards a theatrical exaggeration of spatial and light values that was at root a legacy of the old emphasis on distinct planes.

In his other works Merian moves on from this habit of sharply contrasting successive depths and placing unnatural emphasis on dominant features to simply graduating the intensity of the lines, without the aid of washes. His *View of Frankfurt*[37] from around 1625 is an example. Some ten years later Hollar drew his *View of Frankfurt-on-Main* from the same viewpoint (the sketch S 213 is a draft for S 214, signed and dated 1636). In these Pav finds evidence of Hollar's indebtedness as a pupil to Merian. But, if we compare the two drawings we see that all they have in common is the identical angle from which the town is portrayed (allowing for some changes in the fortifications made in the intervening decade), while the basic concept of the subject is quite different. In Merian's version the actual foreground

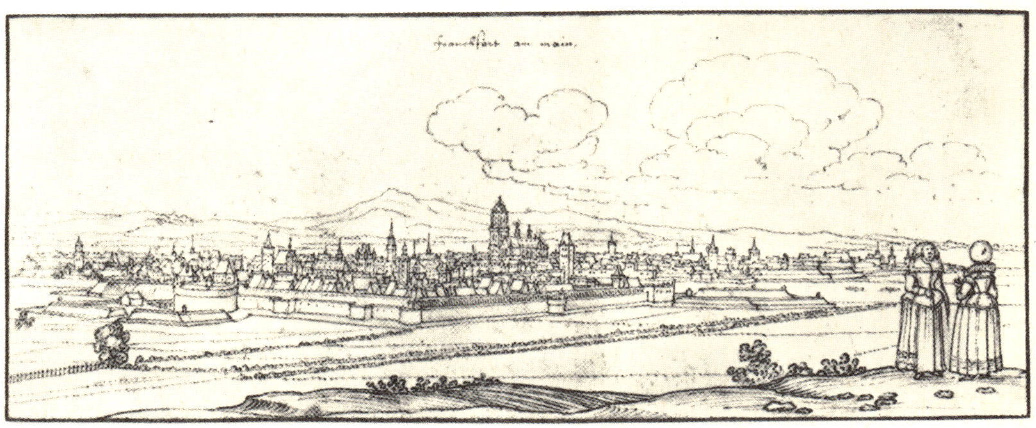

15 *View of Frankfurt-on-Main* Pen and ink S 213, probably 1636. This drawing was probably executed during Hollar's journey down the Rhine and the Danube in 1636, rather than in 1631, when he first stayed in Frankfurt; a finished drawing based on it, dated 1636, is now at Chatsworth. Compare Hollar's treatment of this subject with Merian's illustration no.14. Hollar's style is more refined, revealing a stronger sense of atmosphere. (Städelsche Kunstinstitut, Frankfurt)

is almost empty while the near part of the town is rendered with strong strokes of a broad-nibbed pen and the houseroofs and churches are seemingly imprisoned in their stiff outlines. Even the cathedral and several minor features in this part of the picture are drawn with lines only marginally lighter, while the rest is but faintly indicated in the background. Hollar's version has no such sudden transitions. The intensity of the lines tails off very gradually towards the background, the clarity of detail diminishing progressively as the space-gap expands and the veil of intervening atmosphere thickens. There is also a different way of indicating the relationship between dominant features and the rest. In Merian's drawing the disparity of scales is conspicuous, as is the exaggerated size and mass of the cathedral and other dominant architectural features, while the other buildings are merely suggested by a few groups of tiny roofs. In Hollar's version there is a natural relationship between the parts. The dominant features are not out of scale with the remainder; they do not tend to squeeze out their surroundings and make the houses look irrelevant. Hollar's Frankfurt is fuller and more detailed, a truthful picture of the city. Only in the figures (evidently put in with a view of the subsequent engraving) does Hollar follow Merian's example in the large scale of the two women standing on a narrow strip of ground in the foreground. But they differ from the traditional *repoussoir* in being authentic costume studies of Frankfurt women and so illustrative of the city in question.[38]

So it is not merely the ten-year gap between the date of the two works, nor the difference in the artists' ages, but a contrasting artistic attitude that distinguishes these drawings. While Merian's virtuosity remained tied to the fading tradition of 'composed' landscapes, Hollar at the close of his Strasbourg period was already solving problems of space, air and light by realistic observation and reproduction, just as his Dutch contemporaries were. Wüthrich may argue that Hollar's drawings are like the best of Merian's,[39] but a closer examination shows that not even the finest of Merian's drawings are as convincing as Hollar's. Hollar was all his life a consistent searcher after realism. In his study of Merian's contribution to Hollar's technical development Pav reaches the same conclusion as the author – that though in his formative years Hollar was continually exposed to the stylistic influence of other artists, none of these left a permanent mark on him nor deflected him from his adherence to his own personal expression and his realistic selection and treatment of subject.

Conclusive evidence that the year 1631 – when Hollar most likely worked for Merian – was no particular milestone in the artist's development as a draughtsman, nor in his approach to nature, comes from the two variants of his *View of Cologne and Deutz*. One dates from 1630, the other from 1633 or soon after,[40] since in this drawing Deutz is already shown on the opposide side of the river as a fortified settlement. The two versions therefore mark the beginning and end of Hollar's stay in Frankfurt. Like the earlier drawing (S 122), the later sketch (S 120) also affords a glimpse of the broad surface of the river. On the left is a tower with the fortress wall in front of it; on the right, on the far bank, we see more of the southern part of Cologne than in the earlier drawing. But the chief point of interest is the Rhine itself. It follows its wide course through the centre of the picture far away to the low skyline, while above it clouds sail across the sky in misty nuances of grey wash only lightly touched in with the pen here and there. Here too we feel the spatial breadth and depth of the Rhine valley. Both views speak the same stylistic language – and were therefore assigned to the same period by Sprinzels. In almost equal degree, Hollar displays in both an impressive treatment of reality with all the skills of a mature draughtsman. There is nothing to suggest any external stylistic intrusion during the brief years that separate them.

There is however one genre – the large town panorama – well represented in Hollar's drawings and etchings, in which immediately after 1631 we can discern Merian's influence, or at least of the cosmographic tradition he belonged to. The first example of this is the large view of Mainz whose date can be fixed by the stage of construction of the Gustavus Burg,[41] as well as by the detail sketch of one area on the left-hand side which is labelled 1632. The *View of Mainz*, the first of a series of celebrated city panoramas, thus occupies a key position in Hollar's development as a specialist in depicting views.

By the beginning of the 1630s Hollar was already well established as a draughtsman. His formative years had ended; he was now a mature master developing rapidly as an artist and displaying astounding range and thematic variety. In Cologne he produced further studies of female costume and his first drawings of a portrait character. And from Cologne he embarked on his first journey to the Netherlands, where the Dutch landscape and the sea he had never seen before added to his store of impressions. It was in Cologne, moreover, that he met the Englishman Thomas Howard, Earl of Arundel, who was to play such an important role in his subsequent life and work. Hollar's residence in England, which he finally made his home, was to be interrupted only by the eight years of intense concentration on engraving in Antwerp. New contacts and a new environment gave Hollar fresh inspiration and expanded his thematic world.

In the second half of Hollar's life we find the proportion of time he devoted to drawing and to etching greatly altered. His graphic work, highly esteemed in society, grew and came to predominate; it also conditioned his drawing. The landscapes he had concentrated on in Germany now gave way to portraits and other subjects sought after for engraving. There was now no time for country walks in search of impressive motifs; in place of extempore sketches Hollar had to devote himself to finished drawings for reproduction, drawings that could not be based on on-the-spot drafts. But the drawings were often executed with a new aim in view, equally serious in terms of Hollar's realism, namely the need to transfer to a copper plate a faithful copy of another artist's picture, not by way of superficial imitation, but by reproducing the qualities of an oil painting through the medium of drawing and engraving so that the final effect corresponded to the artistic character of the original. It is impossible to trace the evolution of this vast and varied output in a single summary. The various strands of interest and subject matter in Hollar's supreme late period spring from the common basis of artistic realism and sometimes follow parallel paths, sometimes appear alternately or intermittently; each develops independently, however, according to its own theme and purpose and the methods employed in expressing it. It will therefore be easier to find our way through the interconnections and idiosyncrasies of the different genres – town prospects, landscapes, portraits and figure subjects – if we follow each in turn, using characteristic examples to plot the artist's progress.

Town Prospects

Urban panoramas, published by the major printsellers either in separate sheets or as illustrations to travel books and cosmographies, were a popular and widespread source of information in the sixteenth and seventeenth centuries. They had developed mainly from three sources. Maps drawn or painted – or later reproduced by engraving – with small-scale bird's-eye views of important buildings added in, led in the sixteenth century to a type of vista-drawing that showed whole towns seen in perspective from above. Then the Renaissance fashion of painting buildings and ruins objectively and in accordance with the theory of linear perspective lent a geometric character and standard method of composition to townscapes. Finally, Dutch landscape painting in particular encouraged interest in the spatial resolution of subjects and its expression in the plane of the picture. These three traditions affected one another and produced a varied and complex differentiation in the technique of drawing town prospects. It was under the influence of landscape paintings that artists moved on from merely portraying a town within a landscape to showing a landscape-panorama where the town is an organic component rather than the dominant feature.

Book printing and engraving contributed to the popularity of prospects. But hasty publication and utilitarian aims combined with the publisher's preference for stereotyped models to lower standards and to shackle artistic creativity with traditional conventions. But a few individual workers stood out and their originality set an example to the younger generation. The most important in the Hapsburg court circles of Prague were Joris and Jacob Hoefnagel, who drew *inter alia* views of European cities for engraving series. The young Hollar must have known their work, notable as it was for its minute documentary accuracy and three-dimensional excellence, along with the views of Prague by older masters and the works of the court copper engraver Jiljí Sadeler, who in 1606 produced his famous large view of Prague based on a drawing by Filip van den Bossche. Hollar was also familiar with the paintings of Czech land surveyors and their *Trompe-l'oeil* technique for depicting dominant features on plans and maps.

Drawings of views first appear in Hollar's Strasbourg period. The view of Cannstadt near Stuttgart is a landscape motif – a river valley – containing a small town. Not until the *View of Strasbourg* sketch (S 117) do we find Hollar portraying in sure and rapid pen strokes a town not merely as a whole, but as a single motif filling out the entire frame. In its format too – drawn on a long, narrow strip of paper 4.5 cm by 28 cm ($1\frac{3}{4} \times 11$ ins) – this little work belongs to the prospect genre; it is an initial draft, giving only the main outline and anatomy of the town. No finished version or subsequent etching have survived, so we cannot reliably judge to what extent Hollar followed the traditions he was familiar with in the final composition. But this virtually miniature sketch, done between 1628 and 1630, was the beginning of a long line of vistas in which the panoramas of major European towns, from Mainz to London, were to represent his peak achievements.

The *View of Mainz* (S 144), with somewhat elevated perspective, was drawn in 1632 from a high point above the confluence of the Main and Rhine rivers. The slightly exaggerated altitude of the viewpoint and the high-contrast modelling of the terrain produce in the central and right-hand two-thirds of the picture a foreground which the artist, under the influence of contemporary fashion and probably of Merian's compositions, converted for the first time into a *repoussoir* with tree stump and large-scale figure staffage. In the left-hand third there is no foreground; the view here drops down from the observer's level to the waters of the Main and the confluence, where the Gustavus Burg (the fortress was almost finished at the time) appears on a broad promontory from a high perspective.

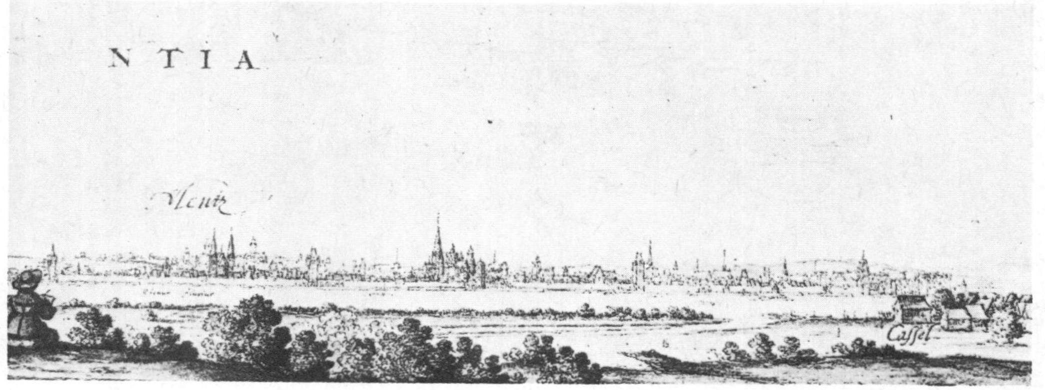

16 *View of Mainz* (right half) Pen and ink with watercolour S 211, 1636. This is part of one of the finished drawings dating from Hollar's Rhine journey in 1636. Mainz is seen from the east from across the river; in the foreground to the right is the small town of Kastel (called *Cassel* by Hollar). The Latin name for Mainz – *Moguntia* – is written in capitals across both halves of the work. (Devonshire Collection, Chatsworth, Derbyshire)

Hollar views the city across a river that intersects the picture diagonally – an effective device which he was to use on several subsequent occasions, particularly in his views of London. The portrait of the city is full of Hollaresque touches: the breadth and depth of the space enclosing the city; the diminishing sharpness of outlines towards the sides and background; the Rhine scene with its ships and boats, and the busy movement of tiny figures on the construction site.

Four years later, on his journey with the English diplomatic mission, Hollar drew another *View of Mainz* from the same place (S 211). Here there is no sign of conventional devices, no hint of artificial composition. The viewpoint has been lowered, the line-of-eye likewise; in the foreground is a simple hill with its natural scrub, in which, in place of costumed staffage figures, there sits the painter himself with his back to us, sketchbook in hand, The aspect of the town has changed too. It lies further off and nestles naturally in the folds of the gently rolling countryside, lightly veiled in a sunlit haze. The passage of time had also brought a change that contributes to the harmony and tranquility of the picture: the fortress had been rased to the ground.

The contrast between these two masterpieces, separated by a mere four years, testifies to the intensity of Hollar's artistic effort. But it does not constitute any violent watershed in his development. For several years to come we can still detect both advances and reverses in the marginal features of Hollar's townscapes, though these do not detract from the overall evolution. For some time, along with his personal and fundamentally realistic qualities, we can trace the effects of contemporary fashion and demands, particularly in the large works with their slightly official tone. But even then the external influences that tended to hold him back are outweighed and finally transformed and eliminated by his own creative personality.

Almost all the townscapes were executed in the single year 1636 on the journey undertaken by Lord Arundel's party along the Rhine and Danube and overland. Its starting point is portrayed in the monumental etching *Large View of Cologne* (P 859), consisting of ten sheets and probably published in 1656. It was in all probability done from a number of drawings from the end of Hollar's stay in Cologne prior to 1636. However, the preparatory sketches would hardly have included the *View of Cologne* listed as S 180, since the portion of Duetz shown there is in a different stage of construction from that of the great etching. It has recently been suggested,[42] quite plausibly, that Hollar drew S 180 to prove his skill to the earl and secure his attachment to the mission. The character of the drawing is consonant with this explanation. It is not a sketch for engraving, but a double-sheet pen drawing finished with watercolour. Again, the sober foreground with the roofs and tower of Deutz in no way suggests a draft for a major official work. What it is, however, is a fine drawing with every characteristic of Hollar's maturity – masterly in its delicate penwork, grandiose in its breadth of panorama, sensitive and precise in its wealth of detail, sometimes almost too minute to see. This is a city-portrait faithful not only in externals but in its appreciation of all the immanent qualities that give warmth and life to it. It was a picture on which Hollar must have concentrated all his creative energies – and which may well have been decisive for his career.

On his journey through Germany Hollar drew views of the great cities wherever the mission's programme enabled him to stop long enough to make a sketch or even a finished draft for an engraving. Thus in the middle of May, during a pause of about a week, he was able to produce vistas of Frankfurt and Nuremberg. The sketch of Frankfurt we have already discussed in comparing it with Merian's treatment of the same subject (see page 37). The finished version, *View of Frankfurt-on-Main* (S 214) with its firmer drawing and watercolour intonation, added not only colour harmony but solidity of modelling in both the main bulk and the details of the town, while retaining from the first sketch the spatial relations and the costume details of the two Frankfurt women in the foreground. The viewpoint for the finished drawing *Large View of Nuremberg* (S 221 – we do not have the first sketch) was lowered to the level of the town itself. The artist stood in this case among the fields in front of the fortifications, drawing the town from a low perspective where the outlines and external appearance of the place count for most. Instead of an elevated *repoussoir* we have the deep folds of the ground in front, an intensity of shading and colouring. The group of figures, which dominated the centre of the foreground in the first Mainz vista, is now, as in the first and final Frankfurt drawings, sited on the very edge of the sheet, thus losing its rather 'official' axial role in the composition.

In Austria the mission was due to visit two major cities, Vienna and Prague, both of which certainly merited major drawn views. Of Vienna we have no panorama, only three sketches of individual parts. On his way across Moravia to Prague Hollar drew a *View of Znojmo* (S 272) in watercolours; this is not one of his greatest works, but it has its place in this section. It captures the character of the town with its dominating position in the south Moravian countryside. Drawn from a hill facing the town – a dark strip of the hill forms the foreground – it looks toward Znojmo across the river Dyje, which itself lies hidden in a deep gorge between steep banks. Perched up high, the town's silhouette completely dominates and occupies the plane, almost totally hiding the horizon. Hollar's spatial feeling effectively distinguishes the two parts: on the left the expressive outline and moulding of the old settlement on the castle promontory stand out in front, whereas on the right the heart of the city, dominated by its high tower, appears in the remoter plane only as a series of dim outlines with a wealth of lightly drawn structures. This spatial gradation is also reflected in the watercolour nuances

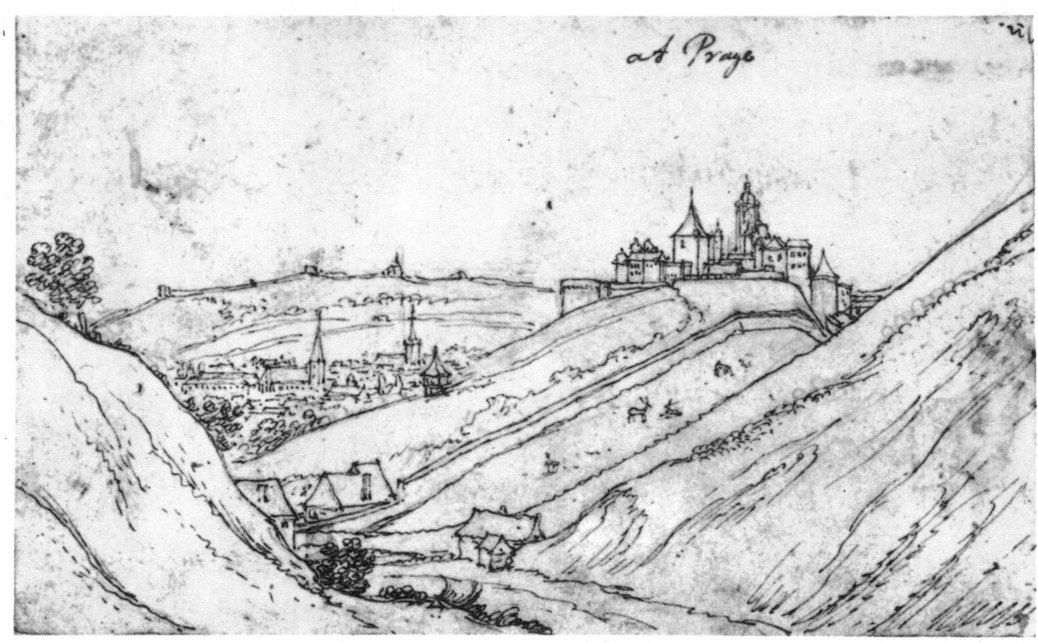

17 *In Prague* Pen and ink S 275, 1636. This was drawn in Prague while Hollar was staying there as part of the Earl of Arundel's expedition 16–23 July 1636. In the foreground is the part of the Castle moat known as the 'Stags' Moat', which was used as a deer-park in the seventeenth century (some deer are seen grazing in it). At the top of the slope to the right is the eastern end of the castle itself. Through the gap centre left is the Little Side (*Malá Strana*) and, beyond that, the Petřín Hill. (Private Collection)

whose harmonization, particularly in the red roofs, lends this drawing a rather warmer colour than is usual for Hollar.

While staying in Prague from 16 to 23 July, Hollar drew not only studies for a general view of his native town but close-ups of street scenes too. Evidence of this is the interesting S 275 *In Prague*, affording a rare – though in later, romantic times popular – view from the sunken way above Klárov and to the hill of Petřín, the eastern part of the castle and the slope of Jelení příkop (the 'Stags' Moat'), where at that time deer really did browse. Street architecture details appearing in the magnificent 1649 etching with its panorama of Prague (P 880), but not present in any of the extant overall drawings, indicate that alongside the Jelení příkop sketch there must have been others done by the artist as he wandered along the streets of his youth, taking in every detail, his pencil and sketchbook ready for a quick impression at every step.

Views of Prague from the Petřín hillside are preserved in two draft studies and in one finished pen drawing of the whole city, washed in watercolours. Until recently only one study of the right-hand area of the panorama was known – the *View of the New Town* (S 274) now in Springell's collection. In 1964 Franz Winzinger discovered the central part, *View of the Old Town, Little Side and East Part of the Castle*, in the collection of the École des Beaux-Arts in Paris, but the remaining, left-hand part with its view of the left side of the castle and the Hradčany hill has never turned up.[43] The two extant sketches correspond to the appropriate parts of the great P 880 etching, and were evidently initial drafts – the final ones are lost.

The coloured pen drawing *General View of Prague from the Petřín Slope* (S 273) in the Prague National Gallery collection is a good deal smaller than the etching, covering only about a quarter of the area. At first glance it appears to have been drawn from a point rather lower than either of the draft sketches of the etching, for on the left side the tops of the castle towers show above the skyline, while on

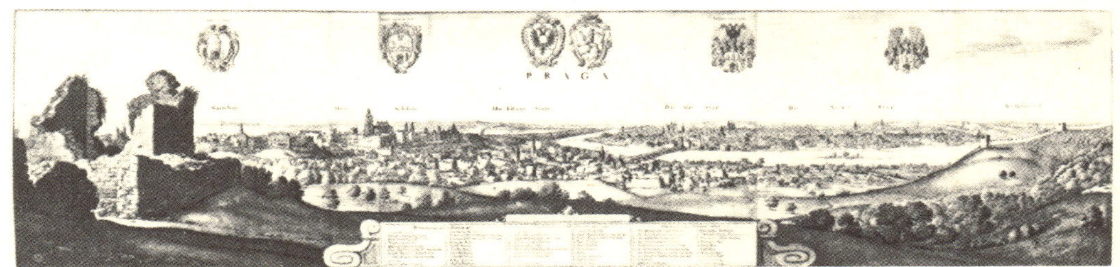

18 *Study for the General View of Prague from the Petřín Slope* Pen and ink with blue-grey wash, 1636. This study and illustration no. 19 were used both for the superb finished drawing in the Prague National Gallery, S273, dated August 1636 (see plates 54–7), and the etching, P 880, of 1649. (British Museum, London)

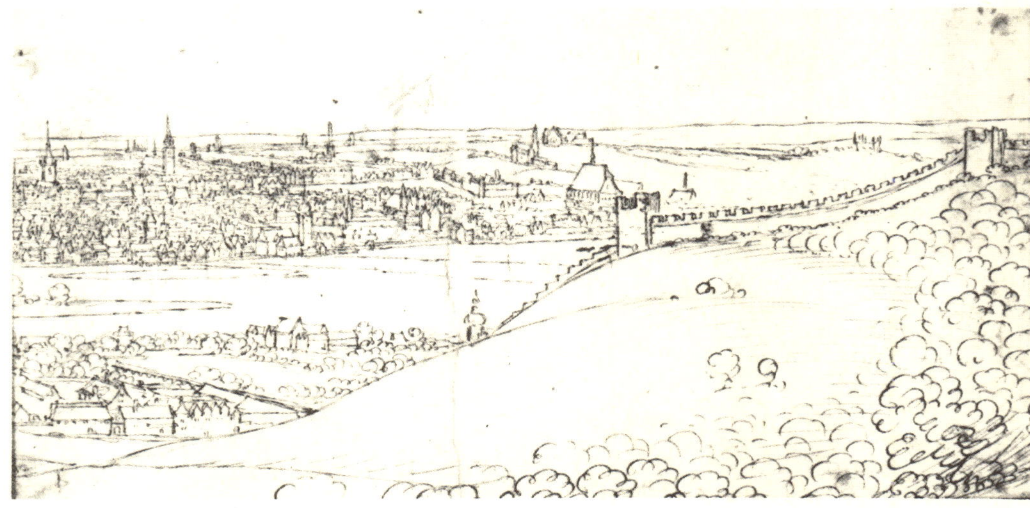

19 *Study for the General View of Prague from the Petřín Slope* Pen and ink S 274, 1636. Like illustration no. 18, this is a study used for both the finished drawing, S273, dated August 1636, in the Prague National Gallery (plates 54–7) and the etching, P 880, of 1649. It corresponds to the right part and shows the New Town on the far side of the river and, in the right foreground, the fourteenth-century Famine Wall. No study is at present known for the left part of the composition. (Private Collection)

the right the Hladová (Famine) Wall rises up more steeply and conceals the Vyšehrad Gate. Winzinger has pointed out that these differences arise not from a different choice of viewpoint but from an adjustment of the horizon. However, the same is true of the right side, where in composing the foreground the artist has raised and lengthened the wall to counterbalance the picturesque ruin on the other side. At the same time he left the extent and direction of the view unaltered, so that the viewpoint is the same in the coloured drawing, the two draft sketches and the etching. The Prague National Gallery drawing is dated August 1636; it was probably done during Hollar's long stop in Regensburg and was based on the same sketches as the later etching. It was not itself, however, the basis for the etching, which is considerably larger and more detailed, has a different resolution of the foreground, without recourse to staffage, and shows some parts of the town which in the drawing are concealed behind the invented details of the foreground.

The Prague National Gallery drawing probably had a different purpose from the outset. It is one of the finest existing general views of Prague and one of the pinnacles of Hollar's achievement. In its composition it makes skilful use of the effective natural motif of the fortress ruins and the Petřín slope along with the wall. Between them a majestic vista of the city spreads out, affording views of the royal castle and the Vltava basin, with the three constituent cities of Prague stretching along both banks. Carefully elaborated with a wealth of detail, this masterpiece combines objective precision with a sense of spatial depth. It lacks the spontaneity of a sketch, but its soft texture and harmony of transparent tints preserves the (same) quality of vision as the artist experienced when he roughed out his first sketch and engraved an enduring picture of Prague in his memory. We sense in the drawing an intense remembrance of that July evening with its lucid veil of haze cast over the city, the reddish roofs set among the turret tops and the azure shades of a sky tinged with rose in the fading light. In recalling this impression in August Hollar added a casual group of figures to enliven the foreground. Perhaps, not for the first time, he depicted himself as one of the couple who are gazing at the splendid panorama, maps in hand.

The remarkable technique of this picture, and the fact that no engraving was made of it, raise the question of why Hollar devoted such care to its drawing. It could be that this is, as has been suggested, that 'careful and exact view of Prague' which according to Hollar's first biographer, George Vertue, gave the Earl of Arundel such pleasure. The fact that it passed into old English collections would support this explanation.

This was the last great townscape Hollar was to draw on the Continent. As an engraver in England he executed many large views of London and other places which made his name. These are great works of graphic art, portraying whole towns with miniature-like detail. Those done from an elevated or bird's-eye view are closely akin to his many meticulous maps of England and its individual counties. Of his townscapes from this period we possess a general view of London – one of five watercolour pictures on the margin of the great 1662 map of London,[44] and several close-ups of the major buildings or house fronts along the riverside; in their accuracy and quality of draughtsmanship these are among the greatest treasures of London iconography and history.

The 1637 *View of Greenwich*, Hollar's first town view produced on English soil, is also known only through the print P 977, but the drawing from which it was made clearly formed a link, compositionally, between the great views of Hollar's earlier years and the panoramic-engravings he was to make in his new homeland. Hollar observes the scene through a broad opening between two elevations, just as he did in the Prague pictures. On the left hand we see in the foreground a staffage of figures – now for the last time, and only as a natural feature of the countryside.

The misty background to a landscape, or by the sea, is a feature that often recurs in Hollar's mature work. We find it for the last time in the large views executed during the final adventure of his career, the drama-filled expedition to Tangier, in which he took part as official draughtsman. The S 393 *View of Algiers* is in form and concept only partially to be classed among the panoramas. The city, fortress and minor bastions, rendered with his usual truth to life, form something of an oriental backcloth to the stage on which a naval battlescene is being enacted.

A sober contrast is presented by a fine group of twenty-four large drawings, the *Views of Tangier Fortress*. Hollar executed these pictures of the African shore of the Straits of Gibraltar in his capacity – as he styled himself in a memorandum to the English monarch before leaving – of 'scenographer royal and designer of prospects'.[45] The nature of his assignment dictated the precisely descriptive rendering of the fortress from various points of the compass, seen from above and below, from the sea and from land. The Tangier drawings show that Hollar's ability to attend to significant detail and reproduce it with a light but sure touch had not diminished during his last years. Even in this bespoke documentation

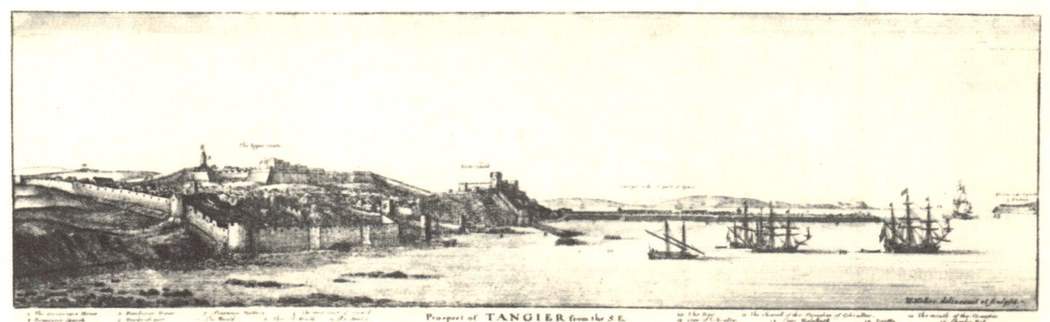

20 *View of Tangier from the South-East* Etching P 1201, published after 1669. Tangier was the dowry of Charles II's Queen, Catherine of Braganza. One of Hollar's last commissions as Scenographer Royal was to accompany the English fleet on its unsuccessful expedition to take possession of the fortress from the Portuguese in 1668–9. (British Museum)

of a military structure he was able to express the nature of the terrain on this bare promontory opposite the southernmost tip of Europe and enliven it with an appropriate human element in the form of groups of soldiers and countryfolk. The most effective of the drawings are those of the straits themselves with three-masters sailing on the water both near and far, the barely discernible horizon of the sea merging with the sky in what we can sense as a boundless volume of space. These views, evidently so dear to Hollar's eye and heart, verge upon true seascapes – portraits of marine scenery and life at sea.

The classification 'prospect' implies, of course, not merely a wide view but a spacious setting free from the specifications of official panoramas, though some of the latter may well rank as town prospects, such as the *Large View of Passau* (S 247), and a smaller version of the same subject (S 248); or the overall *View of Regensburg* (S 226). But like many of the smaller townscapes produced during the Arundel expedition these show such an immediate relationship to the surrounding country that they are both town prospects and wide-angle nature panoramas. The second element sometimes so predominates that in composition and conception we are left with a landscape drawing. From this it is only a step to choosing open country as the sole and independent theme of the work, as in Hollar's genuine landscapes.

Hollar's stay in Cologne provides an important link in the story of his landscape work, whose first steps appear in drawings of the outskirts of Prague, Stuttgart and Strasbourg. His contact with Holland on his journey north from Cologne in 1634 left a particularly deep mark on him. Where his scenery up until then had been strictly inland, we now find colourful and picturesque seaside themes: piers, harbours, and low, flat shores with drawn-out horizons between sky and water. Clearly enthralled with these novel sights and shapes, the grandeur of wide spaces and boundless distances, Hollar drew his first harbour sketch in the drawing *Delfhaven near Rotterdam* (S 154). In Amsterdam it was not the quaint old parts of the city that caught his eye, but a corner of the harbour. In the *Harbour at Amsterdam* dated 1634 (S 157), the line of vision runs past the harbour railings and boatyard in the foreground to the barely visible spiderweb of masts and on to the misty skyline of the open sea. Another drawing with blue and brown wash, *Dutch Harbour* (S 155), recently identified as the 1634 view of Amsterdam, concentrates on the same motifs.[46] On the right, a part of the town is summarily outlined behind the forest of masts, but the real centre of interest is the vast expanse of space separated from the sky by a narrow strip of sea and land, the low-set horizon being in places scarcely drawn in at all. The effect is conditioned by the diagonal, left-inclined view, reminiscent of a similar tendency in the early pictures of Jan van Goyen in the 1630s, where the vanishing-point of the perspective lines is shifted to the very edge of the design.

On this journey Hollar cannot have failed to see works by the Dutch masters. He paid tribute to Rembrandt by including a mirror-image copy of the artist's portrait-etching of Saskia, which was published that year, in the gallery of heads which he himself compiled a year later – the *Reisbüchlein* ('Little Sketchbook') intended for young draughtsmen. But Rembrandt's painterly solution of the problems of light remained alien to the draughtsman in Hollar. As far as means of

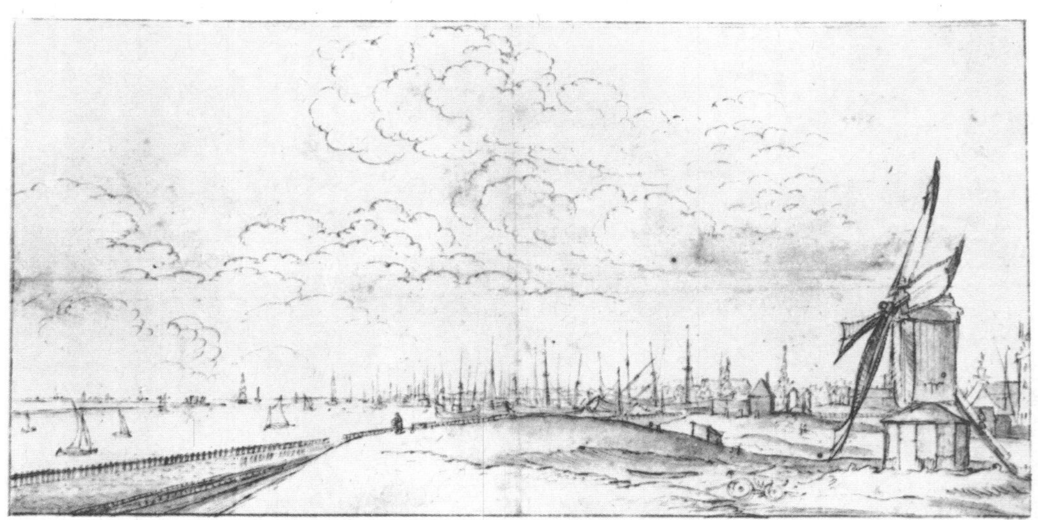

21 *Dutch Harbour* Pen and ink with light brown and blue washes S 155, 1634. This drawing, inscribed *Amsterdam*, was executed during Hollar's visit to the Netherlands in 1634, when several views of Dutch scenery are dated. In keeping with the Dutch approach to townscape at this time, it shows the city from a distance, with the stress on the water, the vertical accents of ships' masts, spires and windmills, and the sky. (British Museum, London)

expression were concerned he borrowed nothing from van Goyen or any other contemporary Dutch landscape artist. What he did have in common with them was an identical aim in solving spatial questions and in employing aerial perspective. The best evidence lies in Hollar's treatment of space even prior to his Dutch trip. There are three drawings of Wesel-on-Rhine which Sprinzels, arguing from Hollar's dated works, persuasively assigns to the beginning of the journey from Cologne to Holland. Two of these are finished designs for engraving: one dated 1634 showing a general view of the town across the river (S 159), the other a partial view in which cathedral and windmill dominate the middle background (S 161). The starting point for both was the S 160 view of Wesel-on-Rhine, a fine sketch testifying to Hollar's masterly draughtsmanship and his ability to express the relationship of space and atmosphere. The row of boats at anchor is drawn with such delicate hair-lines that the very breadth of the Rhine seems to have made their shape uncertain. A long way behind them rises what looks like a dream-town rather than the real thing. An atmospheric veil, made denser by the distance, hangs between the artist and the background and blurs the sharp outlines of the

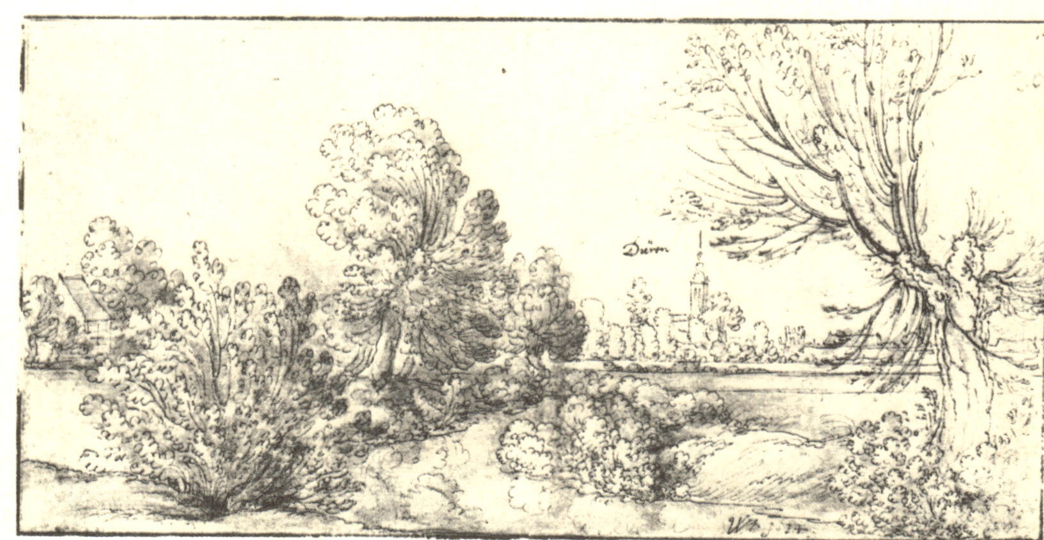

22 *By the Mill-Pool at Düren* Pen and ink with watercolour washes S 174, dated 1634. Düren is on the river Rur between Cologne and Aachen, and Hollar went there in 1634 to draw and etch a view of the town (see plates 10–11). While in the vicinity he made several less formal landscapes, of which this and the drawings reproduced in the three following illustrations are examples. (Kupferstichkabinett, Berlin)

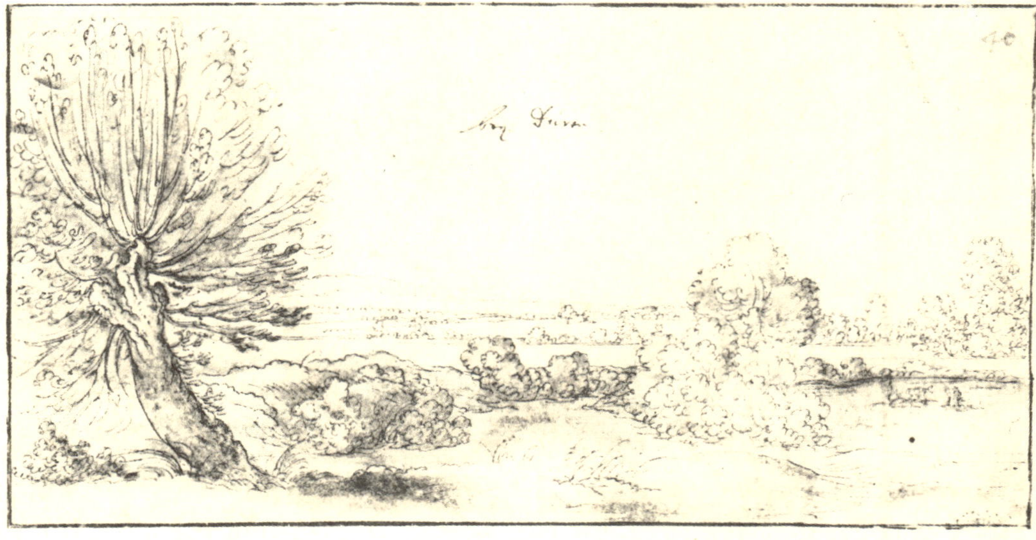

23 *Landscape near Düren with a View of Distant Hills* Pen and ink with watercolour washes S 176, 1634. See illustration no.22. (Kupferstichkabinett, Berlin)

town like breath on a mirror. With its filigree drawing this is one of Hollar's most emotionally impressive works. But he had long ago demonstrated his ability to suggest space retreating over the broad surface of a river. Back in 1633, in his *View of Deutz and Cologne*, he had based his composition on the eclipsing of the view at the very margin of the sheet. So perhaps he was guided not so much by the example of Dutch landscape painting as by his own feeling for the optical values of locale and time of day, or indeed by the intrinsic quality of the Lower Rhine scenery and, later on, by the spatial boundlessness of the Dutch seashore.

After he came back to Cologne Hollar's memory of the broad Dutch scenery was put to good use in the rustic panoramas of 1635, for which the Lower Rhine valley around Cologne afforded him ample scope. In the same period that he drew the view of this valley from the foot of the Bonn walls (S 132) he put on paper a wider prospect from the hill above the hamlet, the *Rhine Near Bonn* (S 133). The precision of the topographical information written in over the various important features betrays the habit of the draughtsman of views, yet the drawing in no way belongs to the category of townscape. The surrounding countryside, which in earlier works had formed nothing more than an accompaniment to the town when

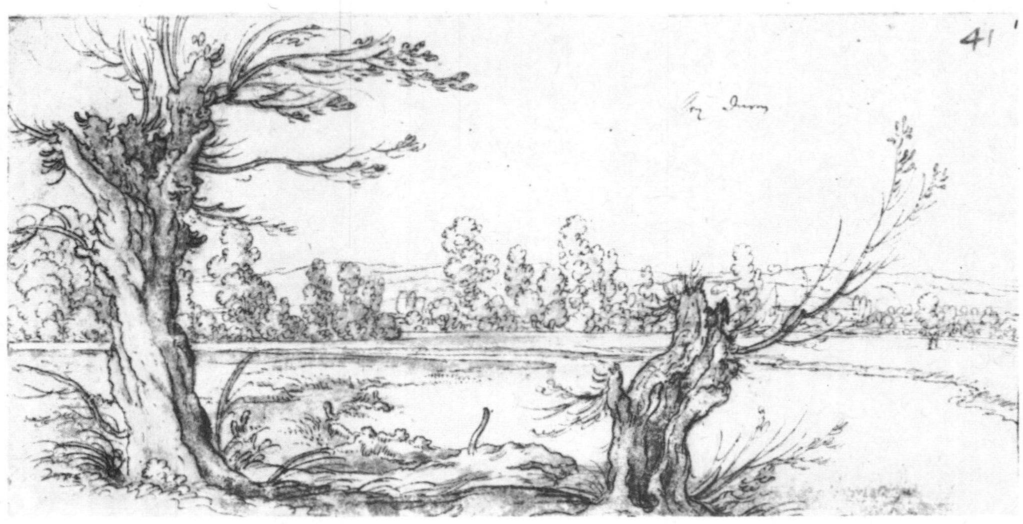

24 *Willows by the River Rur near Düren* Pen and ink with slight watercolour washes S 177, 1634. See illustration no.22. (Kupferstichkabinett, Berlin)

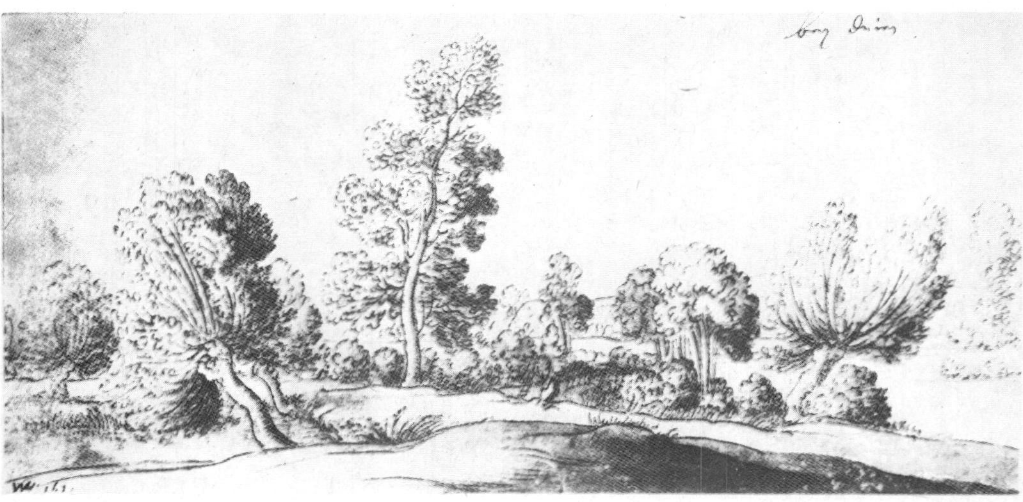

25 *Trees on the Banks of the River Rur near Düren* Pen, ink and wash S 175, dated 1634. See illustration no.22. (D.L.T. and Armide Oppé Collection, London)

a wide frame was chosen, now becomes the principal theme, giving a broad view of a country scene full of light and air. In another drawing from the same region, and probably the same period – the slight sketch in long format called *Rhine Valley* (S 135) – Hollar opened the curtains on a truly panoramic area of gently rolling plain. The view dips deep into the distance as far as the drawn-out hillcrests on the skyline, where the lightly sketched parallel lines, like crowded contours, dictate the spatial rhythm in depth.

The last time we notice a Dutch accent is in the fine drawings from Düren near Cologne, unique in Hollar's output and showing the depth and immediacy of his artistic feeling for nature. They are dated 1634 and Sprinzels assigns them with good reason to the period immediately after his Dutch experience. The reason for his stay in Düren was a commission for a detailed perspective plan of the town (P 841), which took him a considerable time to prepare – possibly several months. In addition to the *View of Düren* across the river (S 286), Hollar used the opportunity to sketch a number of country sights he found attractive, We possess twelve such drawings in the original, and two engravings derived from them. Some portray the picturesque features in front of the town fortifications, but the most interesting are drawings of the open countryside round about. There was no lack of subjects in this riverine scenery. In one case the outline of the distant town can be glimpsed between the trees, but generally what attracted the artist was the watery terrain amidst the woods, showing the occasional glint of light from a bend or hollow in the river. With its dense scrub cover and ancient willow trunks the landscape is romantic only in terms of the points and directions of view that were selected: the observation and interpretation of nature in details of form and surface is completely realistic. These Düren drawings (S 174 to 177) are among the most exquisite examples of Hollar's pure landscape work. They were drawn in moments of leisure when Hollar was not weighed down by engraving tasks and could abandon himself to the sheer charm of his environment.

Hollar's seven-month journey with the Earl of Arundel produced a rich harvest of drawings, as he recorded in his sketchbook the course of their expedition up the Rhine from Cologne to Mainz and thence along the Main to Frankfurt. The party travelled in a covered boat hauled on a long rope by nine horses walking along the bank in single file. The lively movement of these beasts provides a mere marginal accent – albeit a demonstration of remarkable optical memory – to pictures whose *raison d'être* lay elsewhere, in the combination of a conscientious chronicler's duty and the private enthusiasm of a landscape artist before whose eyes a series of towns, great and small, appeared and vanished in succession. Some of these Hollar had never seen before; others, such as Bonn, Drachenfels, Koblenz and Mainz, he knew from previous travels. But he could not resist drawing them a second or third time from a different angle that revealed new facets of architecture or natural features. Sketches accumulated in his book, later to be touched up with ink and watercolour as finished drawings or filled out as designs for engraving. This he would do wherever he made a long halt, and in many cases at a later date, even after the lapse of several years.

In addition to the towns, which were always carefully identified by name over the principal building or natural feature, we see recorded an ever-changing strip of

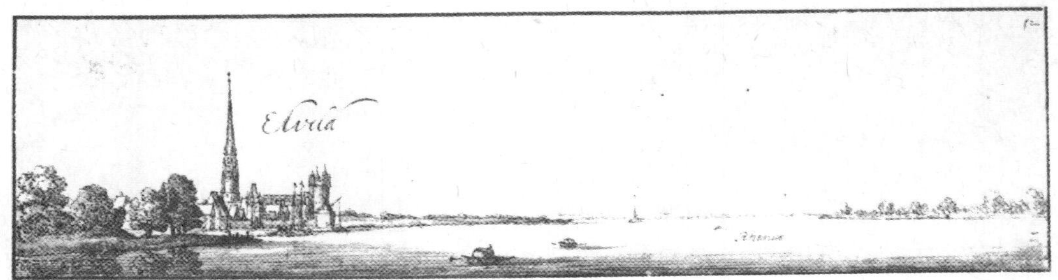

26 *View of Elfeld-Eltville* Pen and ink S 149, probably 1636. Eltville (also known as Elfeld) is on the Rhine west of Mainz. The drawing, with its thin wedge-shaped composition and its view of the river receding diagonally into the distance, is very Dutch in style. (Kupferstichkabinett, Berlin)

countryside. Here too there was a mingling of impressions recalled from earlier encounters with fresh sights and intriguing discoveries. The broad Rhine valley, previously observed from high vantage points, now afforded close-up views of overgrown banks, deep hillsides topped with tufts of groves, gentle slopes among whose folds village houses and churches descended to the river, and almost eye-level reflections in a surface spreading out like a lake with distant vistas. One sketch that catches the breeze-blown, rippling water almost hauntingly is the *View of Boppard* (S 196). Echoes of Hollar's recent journey in the north appear in the *View of Elfeld-Eltville*, whose high tower surrounded by a tiny group of buildings on a wide point of the Rhine was drawn twice – in S 149 and S XXXII. Most critics have judged that the former, which has a more distant viewpoint, is the older and belongs to the Mainz drawings of 1632,[47] but a reconsideration of this has been suggested in view of the identity of frame and concept.[48] Probably both variants with their Dutch flavour were produced during the 1636 journey.

Hollar found a different kind of scenery when, after travelling overland through Frankfurt, Würzburg and Nuremberg, the mission arrived at Regensburg and embarked on the Danube, bound for Vienna. In this hill country the upper reaches of the river are often locked in narrow gorges, sometimes taking sharp and strenuous turns, widening out again into basins lined with towns and villages and churches, only to pass through more rock-strewn rapids before reaching another plain and spreading out broader than ever as more tributary streams flow into it. In Passau Hollar drew two contrasting versions of the town, so captured was he by its dramatic site at the confluence of the two rivers that carve up the rocky terrain into steep-sided limbs of land and so determine the outlines of the separate parts of the city. Beyond Linz he portrayed the romantic scenery of the notorious Strudl rapids with their grotesque rock formations. At Neuhaus Castle his eye lingered closely on a forest slope and he produced a foreground of minutely drawn spruce trees. He drew valley towns and castles old and new, and the monumental pile of Melk monastery on its rocky perch, beyond which the Danube flows through the beautiful ruin-lined Wachau valley as far as Krems before breaking up into several streams as it flows slowly on to Vienna.

The charm of this journey inspired Hollar to record some views of the open countryside along the Danube – this time without identifying labels. At one point he drew a view down the Wachau valley, with only a little church among the trees to hint at nearby habitations; at another he simply sketched a bend of the Danube between gentle, grassy slopes with scattered clumps of trees. But, not even in these purely rural subjects did Hollar forget his official task; he drew the convoy of three

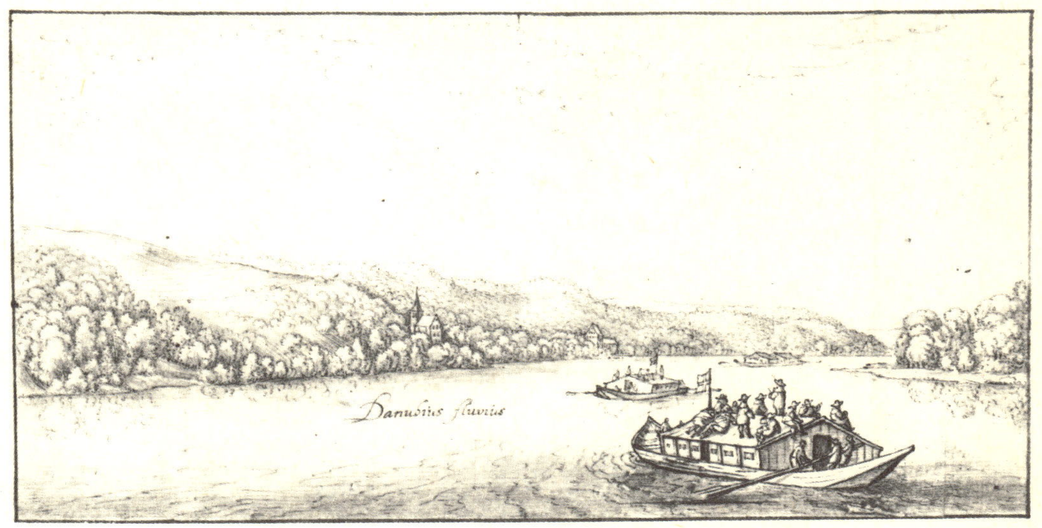

27 *Wachau Valley of the Danube* Pen and ink with slight watercolour washes S 264, 1636. The Earl of Arundel and his entourage left Linz (Upper Austria), where they had met the Emperor, for Vienna on 23 June 1636, travelling by boat on the Danube. Here they are seen passing through the picturesque stretch of the river valley, between Melk and Krems, known as Wachau. The two boats in the foreground carrying the earl and his party fly the flag of St George. (Kupferstichkabinett, Berlin)

covered boats, their crews gazing at the landscape from their cabin roofs. In one of these drawings, the *Wachau Valley of the Danube* (S 264), he also preserved himself for posterity in the shape of an artist, sketchbook in hand, standing among a group of seated travellers.

However great the contrast between the two river voyages and the subjects that Hollar was therefore able to draw, his personal style remains consistent throughout. The works executed at this time attain a peak of mastery from which there is little falling off in the years that follow. His conception and interpretation represent the combined effect of his experience and his creative striving, spurred on by the example of those European artists whose inspiration lay close to his own feelings and convictions. The drawings of the Lower Rhine have a Dutch flavour in their wide river surfaces and low-lying distant horizons, but in the nearer planes the same technique is used to portray nature motifs as in the Danube pictures. Similarly aerial perspective to define spatial relations in the smaller river basins of the romantic Danube valley is used just as effectively as in Hollar's flat seaside expanses or in his drawings of the wide vales of the region of the Lower Rhine.

This monolithic quality in Hollar's mature work is accompanied in his landscape work by a highly personal means of expression and a perfectly co-ordinated use of every technique of draughtsmanship. It was Hollar's aim and vocation to be an engraver. This to a great extent determined the linear, non-painterly character of his drawings, especially of that majority intended, whether or not the intention was fulfilled, to serve as designs for engraving. Hollar was able to project the space and mass of real objects on to a plane by pure draughtsmanship, not rendering every complex detail but simplifying, selecting the characteristic feature, such as the shape of a tree's crown, always striving in whole and part to discover and express the truth about a landscape. By graduating his lines from hair's breadth thickness to bold strokes of a broad-nibbed pen he could situate an object in its spatial depth; using a wide range of line-shading, varied density of hatching, and cross-hatching for the deepest shadows, he could model a shape and bring out its three-dimensional values and its structure.

Hollar used pure draughtsmanship, then, to express those relationships of light in nature whose role in the structure of a picture was of such concern to the painters of the Baroque. But he did not use sharp contrasts of light and shade to achieve a dramatic effect, either as a compositional element or for its emotional impact. What he aimed at was to express as accurately as possible the three-dimensional quality and mass of every detail in the subject at hand. He never drew like a painter; he was a draughtsman first and last.

It is important to distinguish between Hollar's sketches and his finished drawings, which were usually intended for engraving. The sketches, hasty records of things seen, done usually with a pen, less frequently with leadpoint or pencil and often washed with watercolour, have the strength and immediacy of a personal confrontation with the landscape. Hollar's sketches are not intended to be works of art. He had the ultimate engraving in mind all the time he was drawing and never hesitated to write in the name of a place, or even the type of terrain, to jog his memory when he came to do the finished version for engraving. Nine years after he left Prague he was still writing in such words as *les*, *pole* ('wood', 'field') in Czech on some of his drawings. (In later years these labels were usually in German, and later still in English.)

This openly utilitarian motive does not detract from the spontaneity of Hollar's sketches. They reflect a primordial artistic experience of the country, the way its surface is articulated, its interpenetration by light and air, its co-ordinates in space. They are truly impressive drawings, whose 'picturesque lyricism in many cases, especially in the lowland and seaside views, strikes the chord of Dutch landscape-painting at its very best' (Mádl). Choice of viewpoint and direction play a large role, though not usually determined by exigencies of composition. His sheer feeling as an artist elevates the choice of angle, even in what may be a strictly descriptive study, into a major constituent in that aesthetic outcome.

The finished drawings, including those ready for engraving, retain all the topographical precision of the initial sketches, but differ in the drawing technique and in the use of washes or watercolours. Firmness of line in the drawing assists the process of reproduction, expressiveness of line predetermines its character, graduated intensity of line produces the impression of spatial depth. Increased thickness of line in the foreground characterizes the shapes of trees and bushes and the folds of the land. Sharpness of line diminishes towards the background but it is never as the distance increases, altogether lost: the boundary between earth and sky is defined by a hairline that is nevertheless clearly discernible.

Line modelling is supplemented in drafts for engraving by a wash – usually deep-coloured in the foreground – or by delicate, translucent watercolouring, commonly in the brown, green and blue triad of colours. A pale red may also be added for towers and roofs in a town panorama, passing to pink if there are white clouds on a pale azure sky. Hollar's use of watercolour is not a mere local tinting, but is related to the plane boundaries established by the drawn outlines or the inner anatomy of the forms. Only in sky colour, and on water surfaces in some of his mature drawings, does Hollar relax the rules and produce a watercolour painting. Then we find areas where the lacy edge of a cloud is only partially defined by line, or not at all, and then broad horizontal brushstrokes are used to create pale blue and pink stripes and these, washed with water in pure painterly fashion, express the play of varied colours in a changeable sky.

The chief role of watercolour, however, is to supplement the drawn shadows and model the shapes by differential saturation. Washes and watercolour thus help in the construction of spatial depth which has already been determined in the main by linear means, deep tones being applied in the foreground and paler ones in the middleground; while in the background they have no place at all, contours being shown by light, unshaded lines with aerial perspective. Colours stop short of the drawn outlines in every area of the landscape apart from the sky, never crossing or replacing them. Hollar's strict adherence to this procedure sometimes enables his authorship of a disputed work to be tested.[49]

Some of Hollar's drawings have survived only in the form of a draft sketch; with others there is only a finished version for engraving. But in a few cases we have both. When such doublets are present in the same collection they provide an ideal opportunity for contrasting the impulsive initial sketch with the drawing and colouring of the definitive work. There are three such pairs in the Prague National Gallery collection – the views of *Lahneck – Lahnstein* (S 195, 194), *Grein* (S 262, 261) and *Püssingen – Dillingen* (S 282, 281). Often however we have several sketches of the same subject, or alternative designs for engraving; sometimes these differ in viewpoint, sometimes – in the second category – in the degree of completeness, making the simple classification into two categories difficult to sustain. Springell, who has studied Hollar in depth, continuing and completing Sprinzels's pioneer work, was able to investigate many of Hollar's drawings in private as well as public collections and to discover complex relations among some of the sets of versions based on the same subject.[50] One of the Prague doublets, for example, the wash drawing and watercolour drawing of Lahnstein, turns out to have another predecessor in Springell's own collection, S XVI, a wash drawing made *in situ* with a different motif in the foreground.

The Arundel expedition drawings represent the culmination of Hollar's landscape work, and indeed of his draughtsmanship in general. It is also a peak period in terms of size of output and of concentration on the landscape genre for its own sake. In Strasbourg and Cologne Hollar's landscapes were simply precursors to engravings; on the Rhine and Danube journeys only the topographical notes recall the ultimate engraving, which was evidently remote from the artist's mind at the time. During those months the drawings themselves were the sole focus of his interest. But during his years in England landscapes occupied a smaller portion of his time and became once more a stage in the production of engravings.

There are a few extant drawings of the English landscape by Hollar, and their attribution is disputed.[51] The ones that have survived – views of parts of London, and of Windsor and other castles – deserve all the more appreciation for this reason. Drawings of individual buildings and suburbs, or of stretches of the Thames embankment seen diagonally across the broad river, are not strictly landscapes at all. There is such a sense of spaciousness, so many accessory motifs in the form of ships plying on the water or boats moored to the little harbour bridges, so much air and a hint of the sea beyond the wide river as it tails off to the

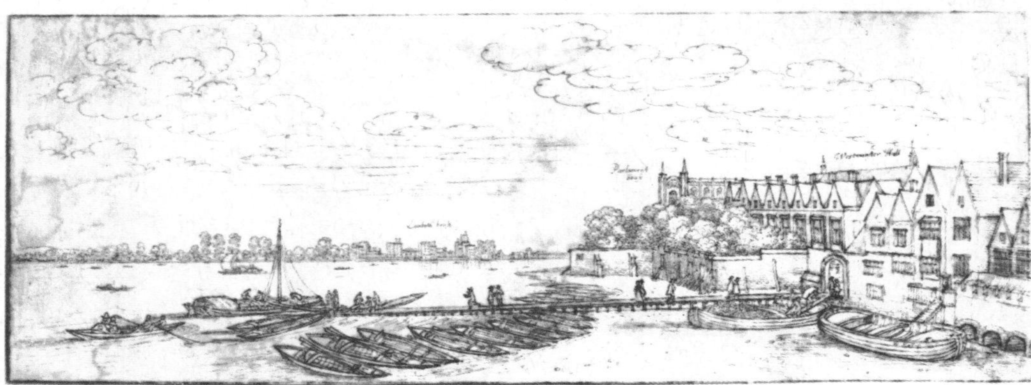

28 *The Thames Embankment near Westminster Pier* Pen and ink S 326, 1637–44. This is one of Hollar's comparatively rare surviving drawings, as opposed to etchings, of English scenery. The view is taken looking upstream. The buildings marked are: on the far side of the river, *Lambeth house*, the residence of the Archbishop of Canterbury; on the near side, *Parliament house* and *Westminster Hall*, the latter still surviving (Barber Institute of Fine Arts, Birmingham)

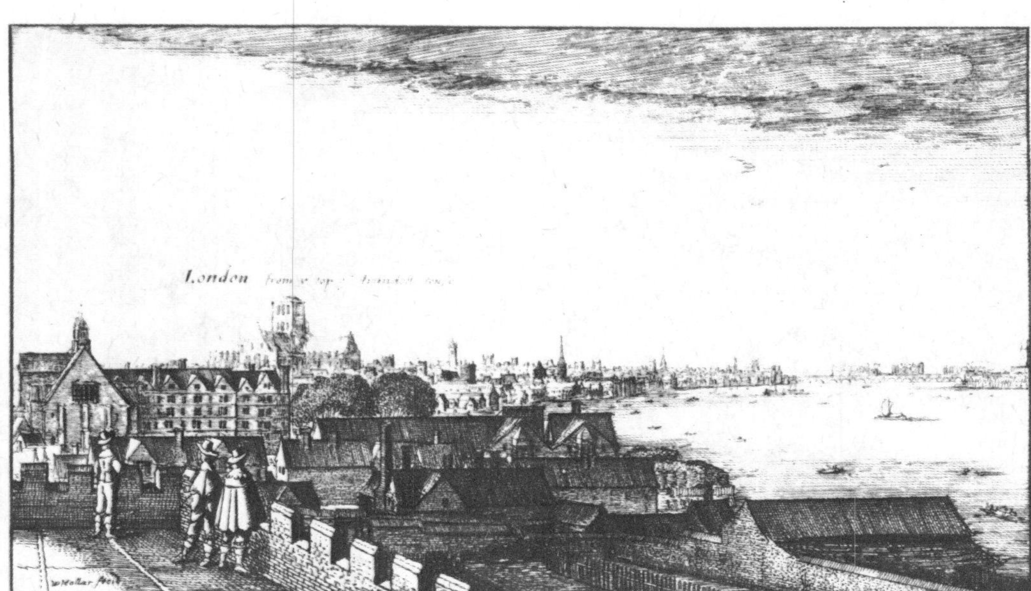

29 *View of London from the Roof of Arundel House* Etching P 1011, *c.*1640. Arundel House, situated on the north bank of the Thames just to the east of Somerset House, was one of the great London houses of the period. It was chiefly a fifteenth- and sixteenth-century building but had early seventeenth-century additions by Inigo Jones; it was pulled down in the eighteenth century. Immediately beyond it in this view can be seen the Inner Temple and beyond that, dominating the skyline, Old St Paul's Cathedral. London Bridge is in the right background. (British Museum, London)

right towards a notional horizon, outside the frame, that these drawings come closest to the Dutch seashore and Rhine valley views. Examples are the *Thames Embankment near Westminster Docks* (S 326), *View of the Thames near Westminster* (S 328) and *The Thames near Westminster – View towards the East* (S 332). Here we find sea and land – both shot through with diffuse light and veiled slightly in a translucent haze – joined together in the distance with no discernible boundary separating their different structures. Hollar no doubt felt for these views the belated affection of a man from a landlocked country; he was to return to them again and again in works that sound a chord of sympathy with those of the Dutch seascapists. London gave him plenty of scope for such encounters, even in the Earl of Arundel's palace on the Strand where he lived and worked during his first stay in England. In *Arundel House* (S 364) we see the façade of the palace on the river, viewed from the opposite bank, while an engraving he made in the 1640s from one of his own drawings shows the splendid view from the terrace across the Thames as it winds slowly into the distance.

Hollar was to hit upon pure landscape subjects on his trips out of London to the earl's country seat at Albury in Surrey. Though only the engravings he made from them later in Antwerp have survived, it is not difficult to guess the quality of his

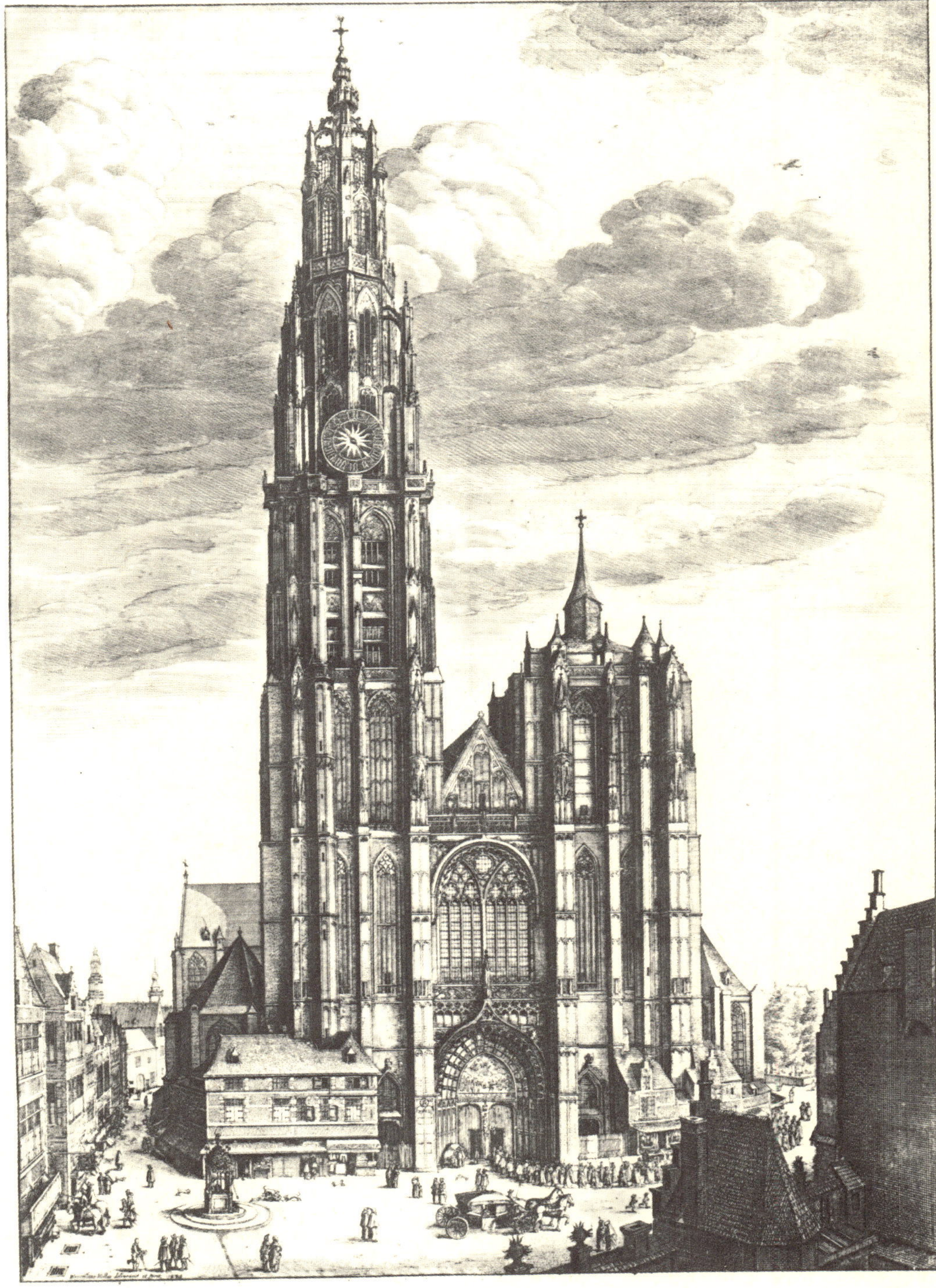

30 *Antwerp Cathedral from the West* Etching P 824/I, dated 1649. This, one of Hollar's finest cathedral views, is less diagrammatic than his etchings of St Paul's, since it was designed to stand on its own as an independent print, rather than to illustrate a book. The great Gothic cathedral, with its 300-foot tower, is almost unchanged today. It was no doubt the tower which chiefly impressed Hollar but, while he would have shared the common seventeenth-century admiration for the structural marvels of Gothic architecture, he seems also to have had a fondness for its details, which was much rarer. (British Museum, London)

original drawings of the English countryside and the Albury park. Some charmingly intimate etchings of motifs from around the estate were no doubt also sketches *in situ* in the first place.

There are also a few drawings from the period of eight years that Hollar spent in Flanders between his first and second stays in England. They include the fine *View of Antwerp Cathedral* (S 345) and detail studies of the cathedral which Hollar used for the superb engraving of this subject; a portrait of the old town square in Brussels and two overall city views of Antwerp and of Deventer on the Yssel. The watercolour drawing of Deventer (S 349) – one of Hollar's favoured views of a town from across a river – does not aspire to be much more than a townscape but it

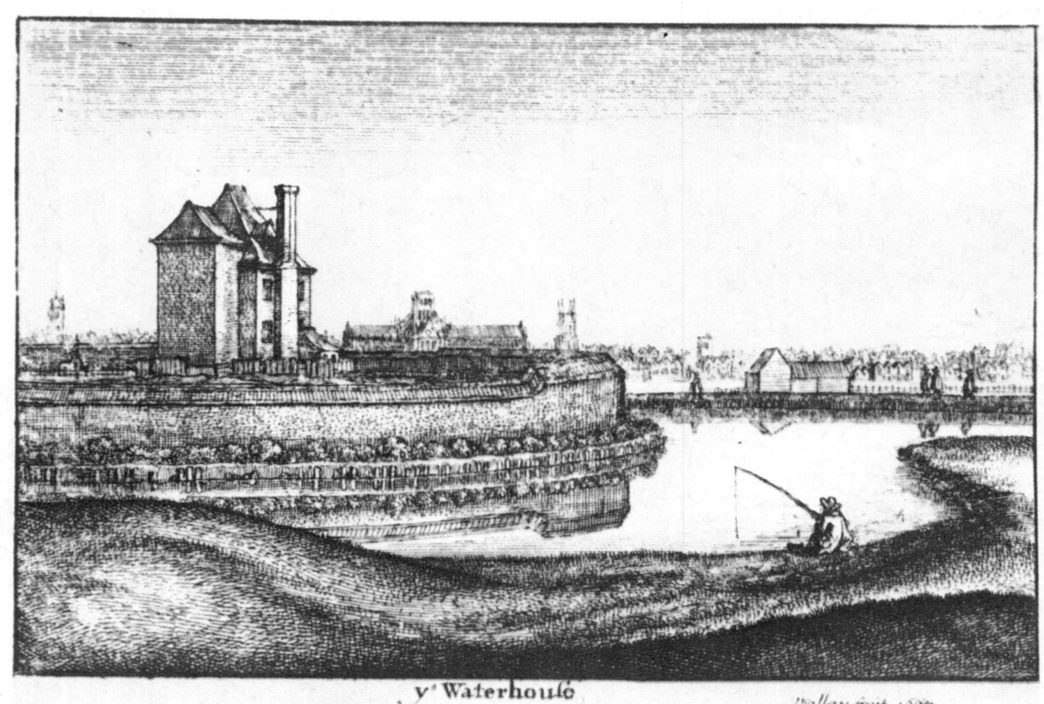

31 *The Water House and New River Head in Islington, North London* Etching P 920, dated 1665. This etching shows the first major scheme for bringing water to London by man-made means. An artificial river – the New River – was constructed in the early seventeenth century to flow from springs in the Hertfordshire countryside to a reservoir – the New River Head – in Islington. Its location was near the present Sadlers Wells Theatre. From there the water, controlled by stopcocks under the water house, was piped to customers in the City of London. Old St Paul's Cathedral and the roofs of the City can be seen in the background of the etching. (British Museum, London)

illustrates Hollar's mature manner of around 1650 in the freedom of line that so flexibly seizes on the essence of a shape, and in an atmosphere that is Dutch in interpretation as well as subject. A seaside landscape of this period justifiably attributed to Hollar is entitled *On the Coast* (S 347). Here the boats at anchor and houses strewn along a flat beach express the spaciousness and character of the Dutch shore. The uniqueness of this subject, however, confirms how rarely during his hard struggle to make a living in Flanders Hollar was able to tear himself away from the engraving bench to travel in the countryside in search of landscape themes.

It was the same during Hollar's second English period up to the time of his final journey to Tangier. Fully taken up as he was with drawing and engraving for Dugdale's instructive volumes on English monuments and other works of history and natural science, and oppressed by the demands of publishers and financial strains, Hollar could hardly have found a spare moment for landscape work. He nevertheless included among his graphic subjects what he could find in the immediate vicinity of London, by the Islington water tower. The folds of bare ground did not offer the romantic picturesqueness of the scenes he had strolled through in the outskirts of Strasbourg. But even here there was an occasional glint of water in a canal, reflecting a lonely house or branchy tree, with a pensive fisherman sitting on the edge in place of the artist with his pad (P 920). Even in suburban simplicity Hollar could feel out the charm of a place and express its idiosyncrasy.

Apart from his magnificent views of the bare fortress of Tangier, this was Hollar's last essay in the landscape genre – that genre which constituted the centre and peak of his achievement as a draughtsman and upon which he had lavished so much of his creative attention.

Figure Motifs and Portraits

Hollar's figure drawings are closely related to his engraved work. Except for his youthful contributions to other people's albums, they are all sketches or finished designs intended for engraving. In contrast to the landscape drawings, however, they were not usually done from life. In his allegorical, mythological and sacred illustrations Hollar often worked from memory, combining his own knowledge of human form, movement and gesture with figures and scenes recalled from other works of art – sometimes directly copied.

We have very few of his figure designs based on other artists' pictures. However, they do happen to include *in toto* the two early allegoric cycles *The Four Seasons*

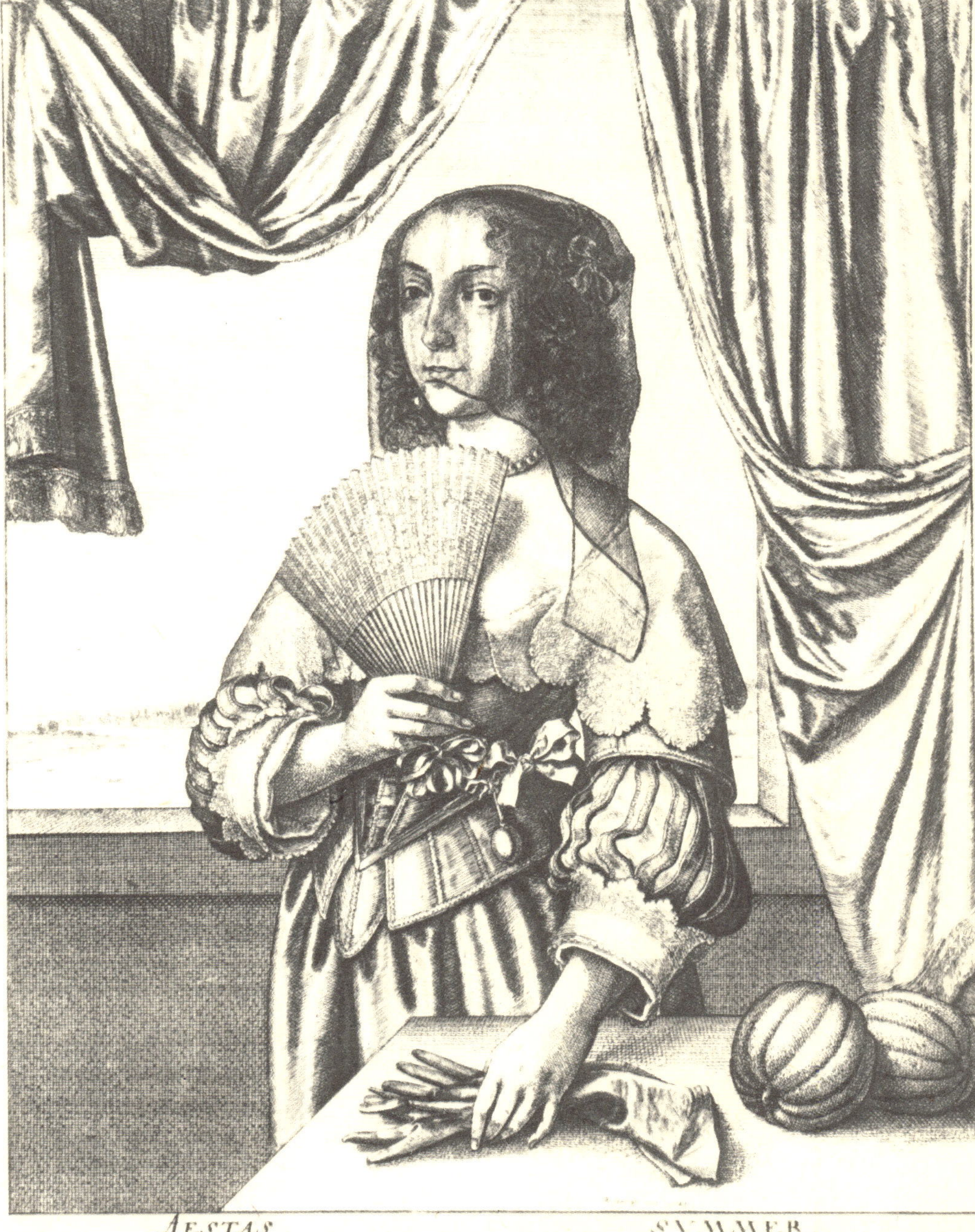

32 *Summer* Etching P 611, dated 1641; from a series of *The Four Seasons* in three-quarter length figures. This was the first such series which Hollar produced. The idea of representing a subject from everyday life in allegorical disguise was typically Dutch. Both the Four Seasons (often represented as landscapes with figures performing the appropriate rural tasks) and the Five Senses are common. In the present etching the idea is conveyed by the woman doing all she can to shield her delicate complexion from the sun. (British Museum, London)

and *The Months* drawn from originals by Jan van de Velde (S 60 to 74). Even as a draughtsman Hollar gained from the exercise of copying these during his stay in Strasbourg. Otherwise we have only isolated examples of figure scenes from Hollar's later years.

These include for example the drawings of *Knights of the Garter* (S 42 to 45) done to illustrate Ashmole's history of the Order and inspired by Gothic illuminations; the black-chalk and red-earth drawing of *John the Baptist in the Wilderness* (S 51) copied from Correggio; and above all the *Christ Attended by Angels* (S 49), after an original by Adam Elsheimer,[52] a drawing of the early 1640s

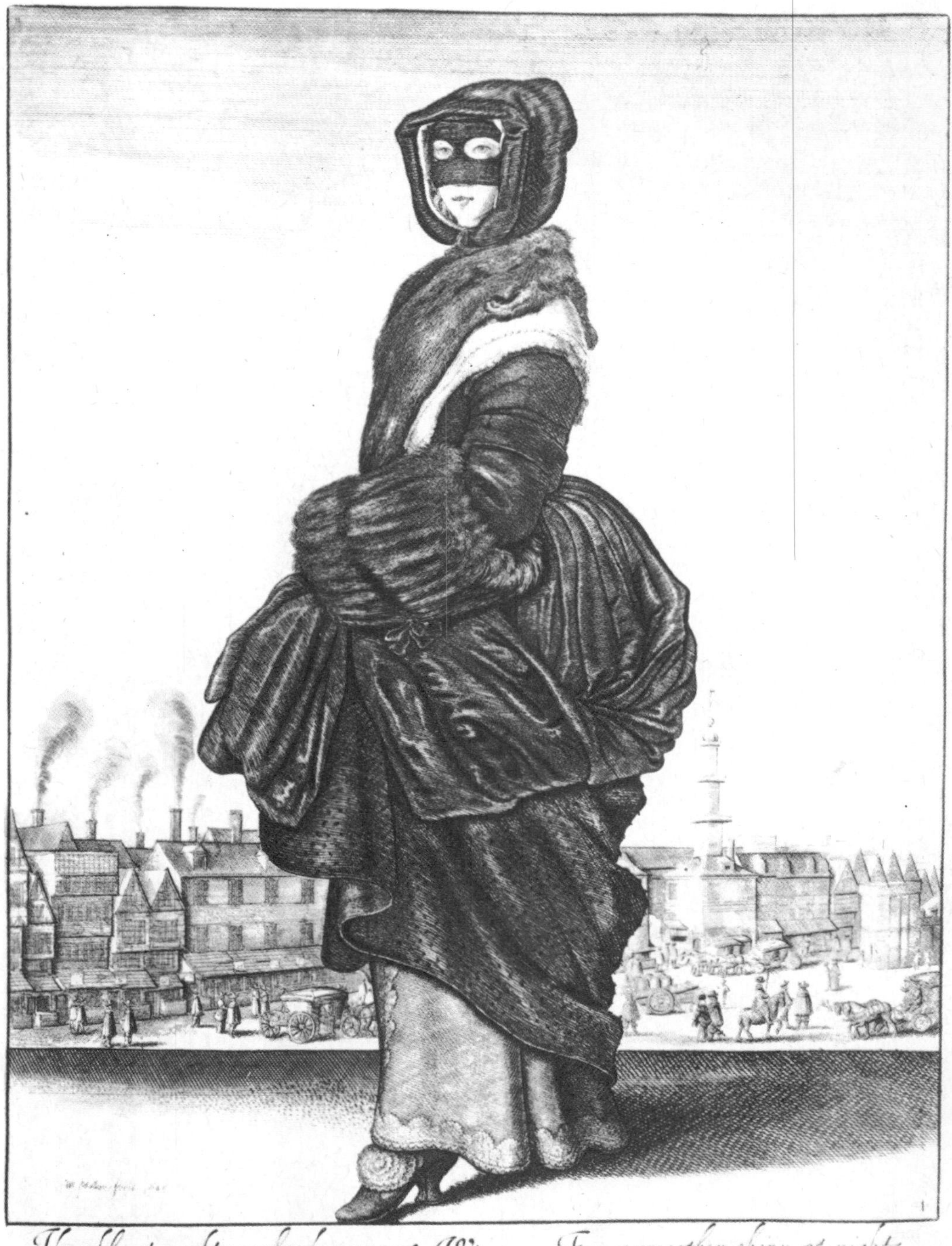

33 *Winter* Etching P 609, dated 1643; from a series *The Four Seasons* in full-length figures (see illustration no.32). This is perhaps the most appealing and famous of all Hollar's costume etchings; the frankly suggestive lines of verse at the bottom, in keeping with the spirit of the black furs and mask worn by the figure, only add to its charm. Cornhill and the tower of the old Royal Exchange (see illustration no.34) can be seen in the background. (British Museum, London)

which is characteristic of Hollar's manner of composition in his early and middle years.

In some cases the source of historical or reportage compositions was Hollar's own fantasy. We just have the etchings of these, but the drawings they were taken from can be imagined, and did not always adhere to the same principles. In his scenes of the struggle between King and Parliament, such as the trial of Archbishop Laud or the public execution of the Earl of Strafford, Hollar adopts the manner of old woodcuts with regular, close-packed rows of spectators whose stiff and stereotyped stance contrasts sharply with the dramatic occasion at its moment of climax. In contrast the assembly of Antwerp citizens in his *Declaration of Peace between Spain and the Netherlands in 1648* and the lively crowd on the *Courtyard of the London Stock Exchange* was depicted in a deliberately complex grouping. The force of these scenes from recent or contemporary events no doubt owes much to Hollar's own experience as onlooker or participant, and the same personal involvement must have contributed to the scale on which he depicted the beginning of the Thirty Years' War in Prague. In his *Civil War* engraving (P 543) we find alongside the English revolutionary scenes in the margin glimpses of the Defenestration of Prague and the execution of the Czech nobles on the Old Town Square; while one half of the inner area is taken up with a map of England, the other is entirely devoted to a bird's-eye view of the Battle of the White Mountain and a miniature panorama of Prague. The relative weight given to the two subjects, and the very attention paid to those fateful days in Czech history and in Hollar's own life, must surely reflect the depth of the artist's feelings even after so many years had elapsed.

Intermediate between the figures derived from pure invention and those drawn from life, are the staffages in Hollar's landscape drawings. The horses hauling the

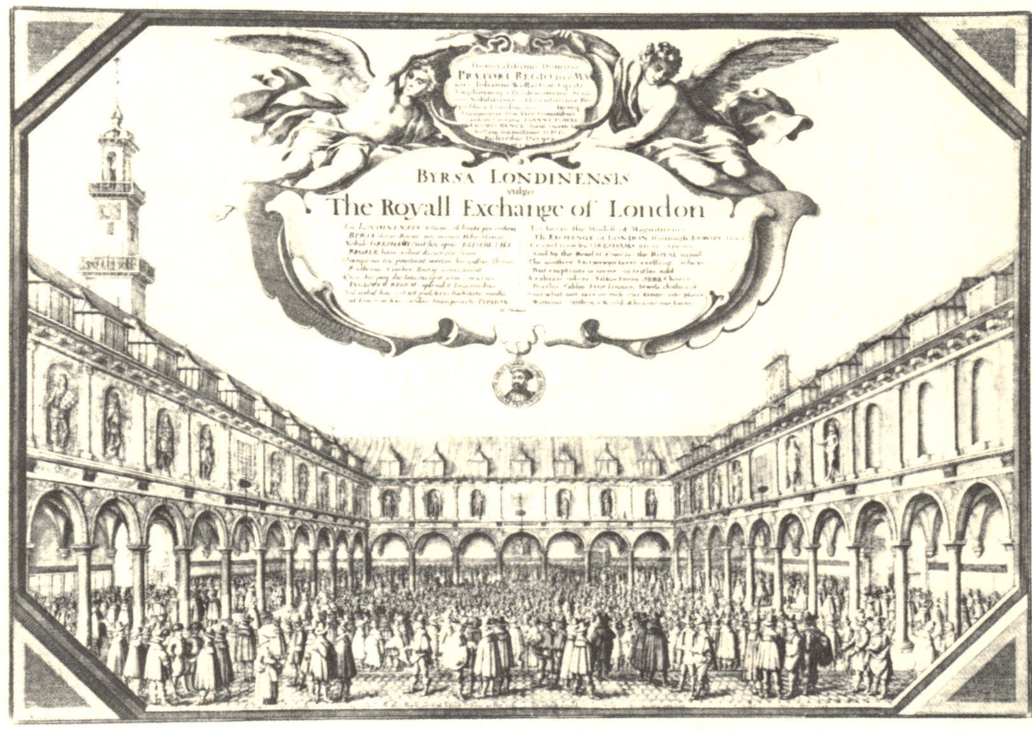

34 *Courtyard of the Royal Exchange, London, facing West*
Etching P 1036/I, dated 1644. This etching shows the old Exchange, built by private enterprise in 1566–71 and destroyed in the fire of 1666. Designed under strong Flemish Renaissance influence, it was one of London's finest civic buildings of the Elizabethan era, and Hollar's etchings are the best visual records of it. The Exchange was a general mart, where dealings in commodities of all kinds were carried on. (British Museum, London)

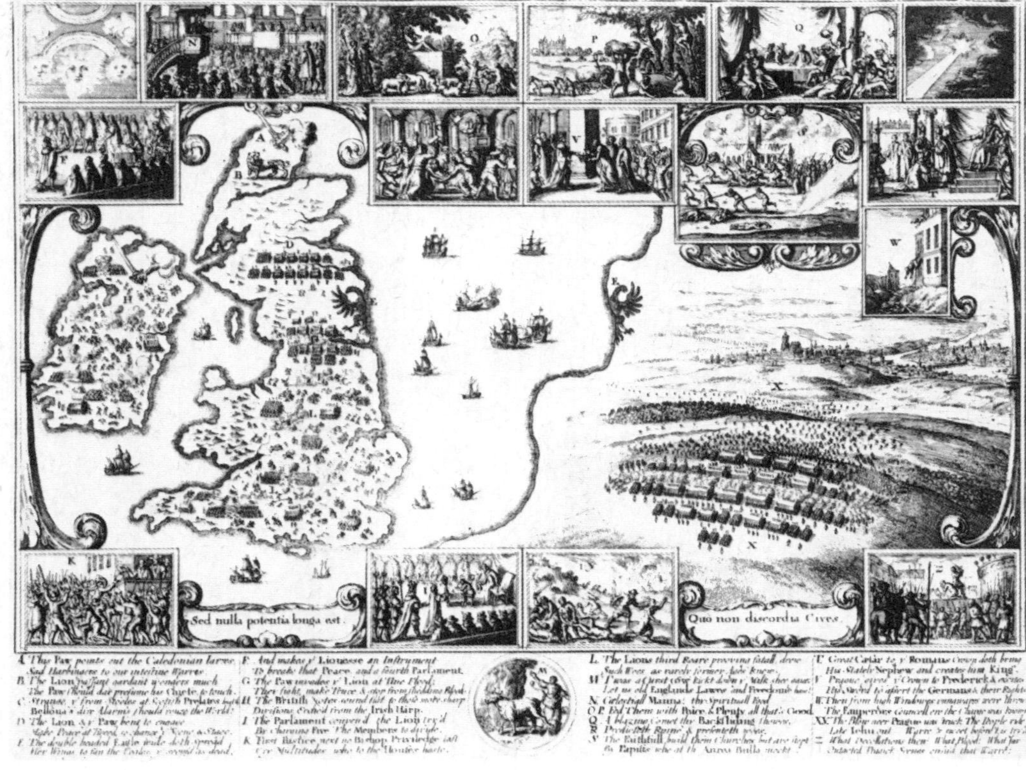

35 *Civil War* (detail) Etching P 543, published after 1650. This etching, executed during Hollar's years in Antwerp (1644–52), is a kind of parallel representation of the English Civil War and the rebellion of the Czech nobles in Bohemia. Episodes from the two events appear in scenes in the margin, while the centre of the plate is occupied on one side by a map of England and on the other by a bird's-eye view of the Battle of the White Mountain (1620) outside Prague (shown in this illustration). At least indirectly, Hollar was made an exile by both disasters. (British Museum, London)

boat upstream appear frequently in both sketches and finished drawings of the Rhine journey. Their lifelike portrayal may reflect sketchbook records as well as the accumulation of impressions in Hollar's memory. Personal experience no doubt lay behind the busy shipyard scene in *Hull of a Ship* (S 90) and the building site on the fortifications in *View of Mainz* (S 144). The staffages in the panoramic drawings, and the costume studies for these and other engravings, are of a different character. The costumed figures stand casually and show a natural physique, but their faces are devoid of expression – as are those of the monks in Hollar's studies of the habits worn by the various orders. The draughtsman's attention is concentrated entirely on rendering the costumes down to the last detail with an objectivity that seems to anticipate modern ethnographical illustrations and makes these drawings virtual studies of external appearances only. That Hollar's dryness of manner here stemmed purely from the purpose the drawings were designed for, and not from any inability to portray the women of his time in a forceful and suggestive way, is amply demonstrated by two fine genre drawings of 1635 and 1636, which survive in engravings. *The Lacemaker* (P 595) shows a woman in profile, absorbed in the crochet work on her lap, while *Woman at a Keyboard* (P 594) is a rear-right diagonal view of the subject playing a virginal. These glimpses of a townswoman's life, quiet and redolant of well-being, have a perfection of form and depth of feeling that suggest many lessons learnt from the Dutch genre paintings that Hollar may have seen on his 1636 trip, and which were to achieve their supreme success in this very field – the poetry of everyday life – through the works of Jan Vermeer who lived and worked in Holland during the middle of the seventeenth century.

Hollar must have had more frequent occasion to portray the human body artistically than the extant drawings reveal. In 1635 he worked on a female seated nude – a copy of a Rembrandt painting (P 603). Two years earlier we find a coloured pen drawing of a reclining nude (S 12) to which a narrow slip of paper is attached bearing Hollar's dedication. This work is unique in Hollar's output, and somewhat mysterious, not because of the needless conclusions about the artist's private life in Cologne that the subject and the clumsy dedication have prompted, but because of serious doubts about authorship. These spring from the absence of other similar works in Holler's output; from the shaky evidence of the label, which bears every sign of Hollar's handwriting but is only pasted on to the drawing; and from considerations of style. Karel Guth, and following him Franz Sprinzels, have also objected that the painterly treatment is inconsistent with the linear character of Hollar's work, concluding that the draughtsman was some other seventeenth-century artist influenced by Dutch models.[53] However, the modelling of the body, with hatching and cross-hatching in the shadows, is purely that of a draughtsman; the watercolour wash, applied in deeper tones to the prominent areas of the body, is used merely to supplement the penwork. A more serious point is the stylistic inconsistency with the rest of Hollar's work. All these arguments cast doubt on Hollar's authorship but by no means disprove it. Again it is possible that what we have here is a copy by Hollar of someone else's work.

Apart from a few drawings that have survived only in their engraved versions, the great bulk of Hollar's extensive portrait work consists of likenesses derived from other masters, whose names are always conscientiously and modestly appended. They are not mere copies, however, and the results are truly creative works of art, especially when the prototype was a painting whose quality had to be expressed in terms of drawing and engraving.

Where we possess the drawn versions they testify to the virtuosity and strength of Hollar's methods. The fine pen drawing *Portrait of the Goldsmith Hans von Zürs*, done prior to 1647 (S 1), interprets in linear terms a painting by Hans Holbein which belonged to the Arundel collection but has been lost. Hollar's drawing for the etching of the same subject (P 1411) is an outstanding achievement in its own right, as well as providing an important piece of information about the vanished Holbein. With a light but sure hand it accurately traces the subtlest nuances of the original's modelling – the softly sagging beret, the rich drapery of the cloak, and especially the face with the furrows round the mouth and the sunken cheeks: a face bony and no longer young, but firm and virile. Hollar's skill enables him to express in a quite different medium the inner truthfulness of Holbein's art and to preserve the subject's character through the expression of the eyes. The drawing is a creative transportation of a kind that, at this level, it would be unjust to dismiss as 'portrait reproduction'. Nor is this the only such example of Hollar's skill. Others are his *Portrait of Edward VI as a Child* (S 2), again after Holbein, and the *Portrait of Johannes de Reede* (S 5), from an engraving by Meyssens.

We are lucky to have the original versions of three fine portraits drawn by Hollar from life – the *Two Studies of a Woman's Head* on a single sheet (S 10) and the little *Girl's Head in Profile* (S 9). These are similar in style to the heads in

36 *Two Studies of a Woman's Head* Pen and ink S 10, early 1640s. It has been presumed that this drawing, like plates 68–69 and illustration no.37, represent Hollar's first wife, formerly Mistress Tracy, who had been a lady-in-waiting to the Countess of Arundel. They were married in London on 4 July 1641. (Private Collection)

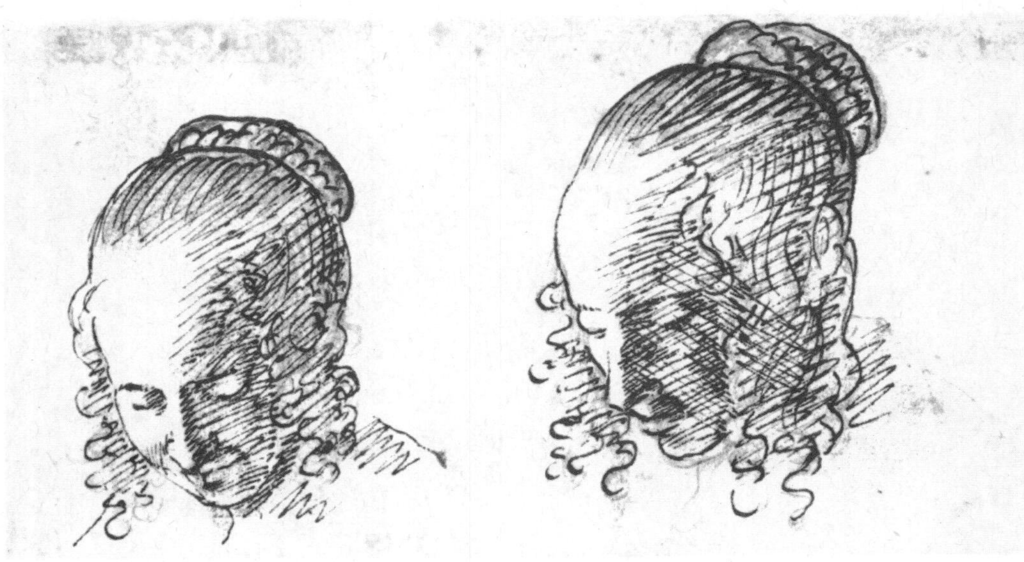

37 *Hollar's Wife with Downcast Eyes* Etching P 1716, early 1640s. This etching is self-evidently close in style and subject to illustration no.36. That the person portrayed is likely to be Hollar's wife is borne out, not only by the intimacy with which the facial expression is depicted, but also by the angle of the head. In a commissioned portrait, the sitter would be shown with her head more nearly upright and with her eyes, if not her whole face, turned towards the spectator. (British Museum, London)

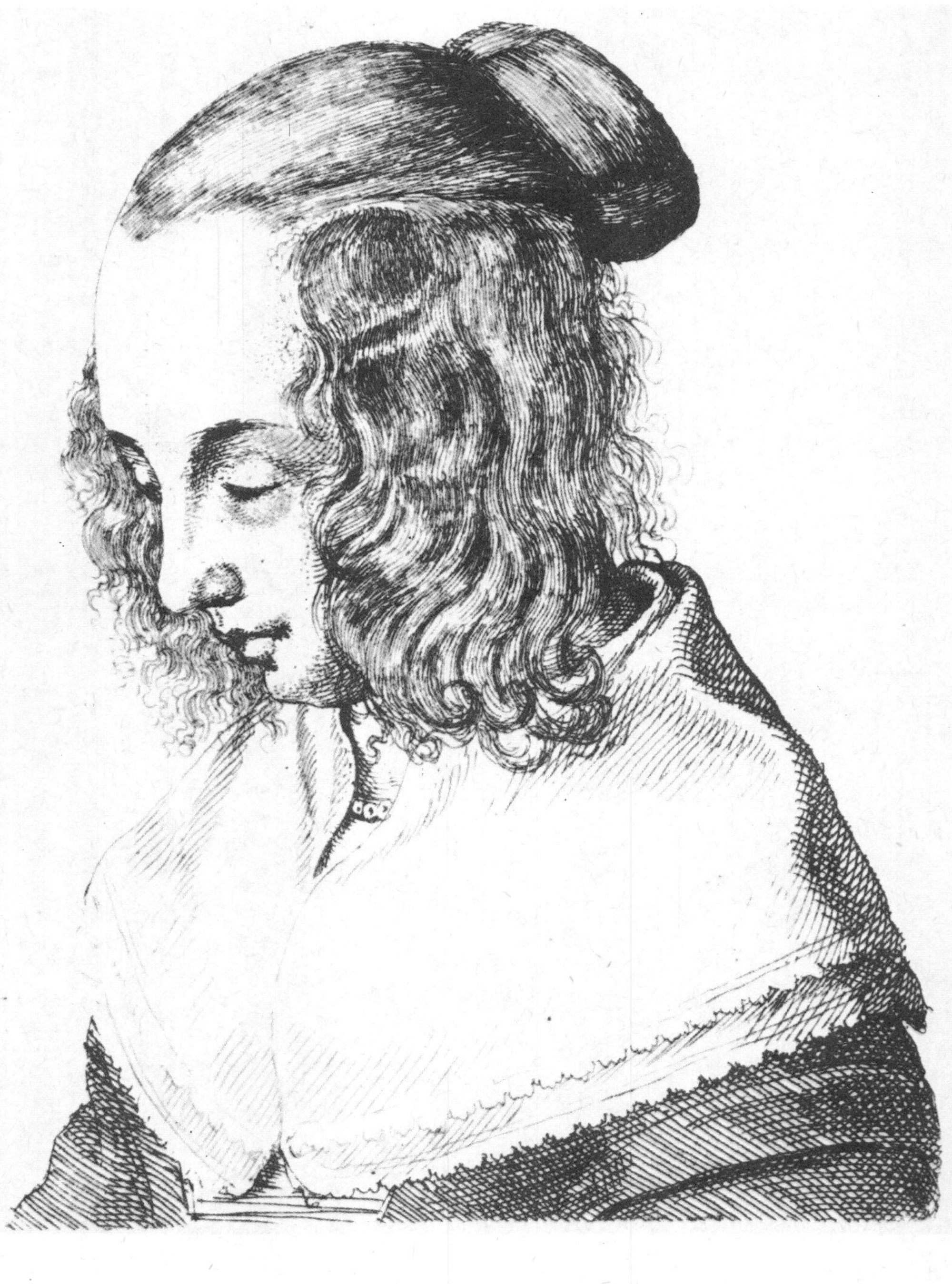

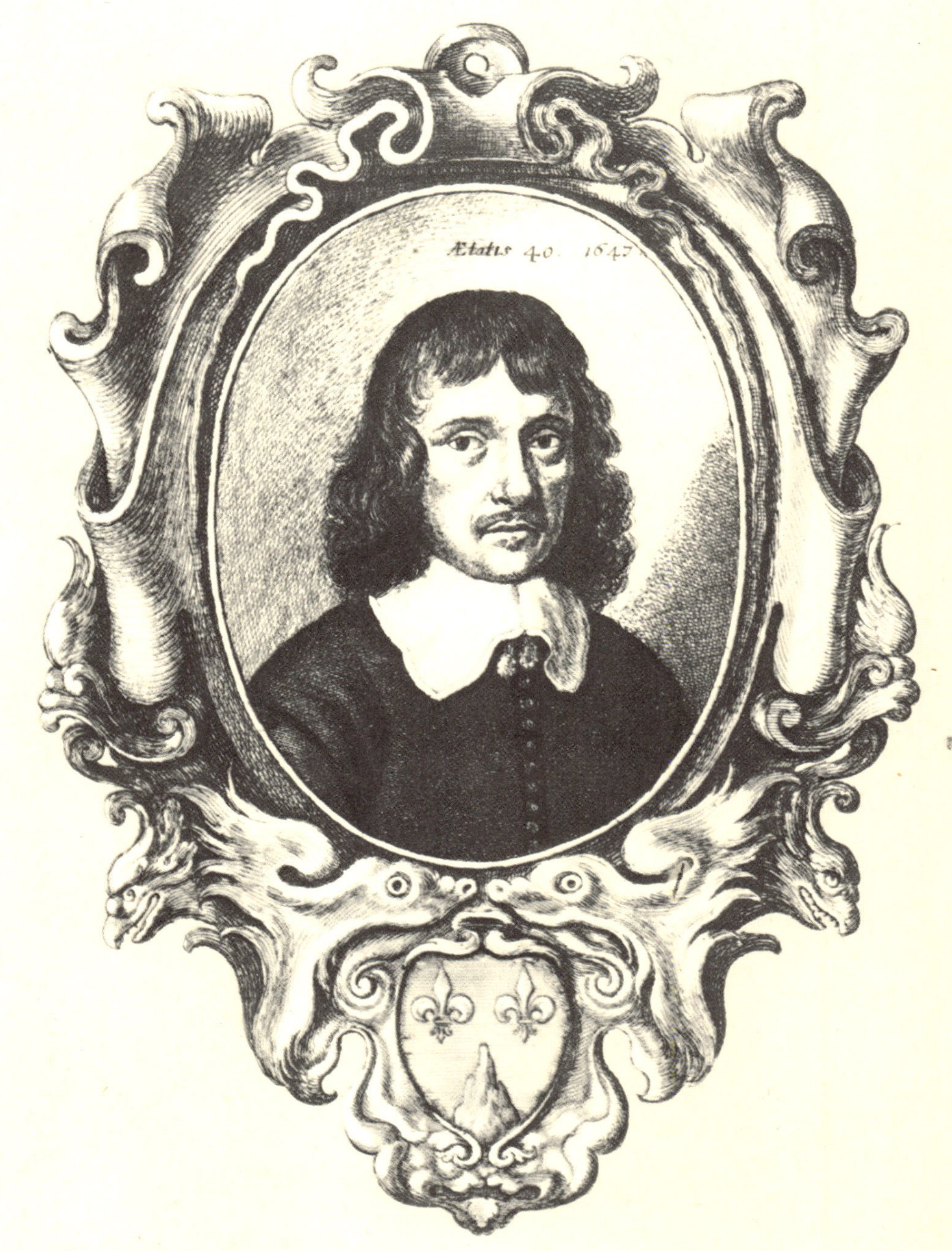

38 *Self-portrait of Hollar*
Etching P 1420, dated 1647. This portrait was executed while Hollar was in Antwerp (1644–52) and may be compared with the portrait of him by Meyssens (illustration no.1) published in the latter's *Images d'hommes d'ésprit sublime*, Antwerp, 1649. In the present portrait he looks distinctly more melancholy, and, while too much should not be read into that, it is a fact that his years in Antwerp were marked by considerable hardship. His coat of arms with an escutcheon showing a hill and two fleurs-de-lis appears set into the bottom of the elaborate baroque frame. The hill refers to Domazlice in Southern Bohemia where a castle was traditionally said to belong to the Hollar family. (British Museum, London)

Hollar's *Reisbüchlein* of 1636. Sprinzels casts doubt on Hollar's authorship of the *Two Studies*, but recent English criticism regards them as likenesses of Hollar's first wife and assigns all three to his first stay in England.[54] They are clearly indebted to Dutch portrait painting. In the depth of expression, in the bowed heads of the girl and the wonderfully light and certain lines of the twin sketches, catching three-dimensional and light values as well as outlines in swift touches, they are consummate examples of portraiture. Two further sketches of the same model, which have not survived, were used in 1645 for the two engravings *Hollar's Wife with Downcast Eyes* (P 1716) – almost in profile, with a broad white collar over the shoulders – and *Hollar's Wife Seen from Behind* (P 1717). The 1646 *Portrait of William Oughtred* (S 7), a mathematician, rector of the academy at

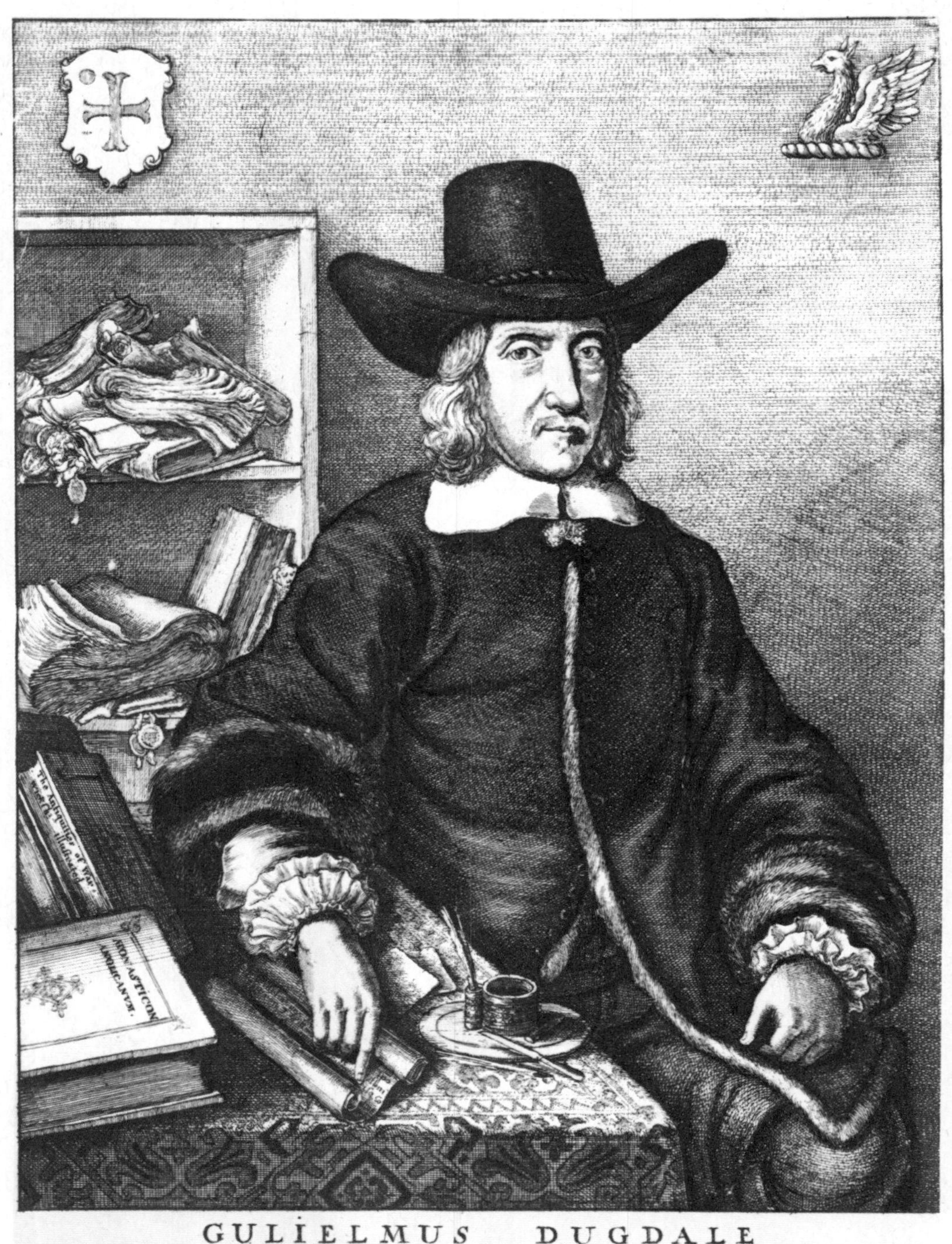

39 *Portrait of Sir William Dugdale* Etching P 1392, dated 1656. The antiquarian Sir William Dugdale (1605–86) was Hollar's chief patron during the 1650s. Hollar engraved numerous detailed illustrations for his three principal publications: *Monasticon Anglicanum*, covering the 'Cathedral and Conventuall Churches of England and Wales' (3 vols., 1655–73, the first two with Roger Dodsworth); *The Antiquities of Warwickshire* (1656); and *The History of St Paul's Cathedral* (1658; see illustration no.4). The volumes already published of the first two of these books appear in Hollar's portrait of Dugdale – a portrait which is very Dutch, almost Rembrandt-like, in feeling. (British Museum, London)

Albury and sometime tutor in the Arundel family, completes the list of likenesses from life. This last drawing was one of the designs for the P 1477 engraving.[55]

Quite a number of other life portraits have failed to survive as drawings, but exist as engravings signed 'Hollar delineavit', 'Hollar invenit' or '. . . ad vivum delineavit'. They are likenesses, as Dostál puts it, 'full of truth and realism, devoid of affected pose – simple portrayals of more or less important personages'.[56] They include Hollar's *Self-portrait*, drawn in 1647 for his fortieth birthday. A good later example is the *Portrait of Sir William Dugdale*, that enthusiastic connoisseur of English history and antiquities, executed in his study in 1656 (P 1392). It appeared as a frontispiece in both of Dugdale's volumes which Hollar illustrated. This is the likeness of a man whom the artist knew well, and his character and interests are convincingly depicted. For all the care he took over the scholar's features, Hollar seems to have been even more fascinated by the objects around him, not only because they include historical works in which Hollar had invested so much of his own energy as draughtsman and engraver, but by dint of the picturesque shapes and details that could not fail to inspire Hollar and to bring out the miniaturist in him.

The portrait of Dugdale brings the series of Hollar's portraits and figure drawings to a worthy close. Though this category accounted for much of the creative effort of his later years, it represents only a relatively small fraction of his total output. In public esteem it is overshadowed by his topographical work and especially by his landscape drawings. But it must not be overlooked that by sheer misfortune only a small fraction of Hollar's original drawings in this genre have been preserved, as the engravings prove. The finest of those that have survived, such as the sketches of female heads or the Zürs portrait, show that Hollar's draughtsmanship was fully able to cope with this kind of task.

The Microcosm of Forms

Hollar's interest in the shapes of small objects appeared as early as his costume studies. But it was not until he started his engraving work in London that he made full use of the drawings of women's clothes that had been accumulating in his sketchbooks since 1630 and had been only partially exploited in the figures in some of his townscapes. Soon after his arrival in London in 1637 Hollar started drawing the dresses worn by women from various strata of English society, and in 1640 he published a complete collection of them. The success of this series, due in part to the attention paid to details of clothing in seventeenth-century figure painting as well as to the fashionable obsession with costume, encouraged Hollar to publish further series with wider terms of reference, using earlier drawings that he had made on his travels. He had similar success in using his English costume studies for the main allegorical figures in the three versions of his *Four Seasons*, which were published in London in quick succession between 1641 and 1644.

One of the English works that survived is the pen drawing *The Wife of the Lord Mayor of London* (S 24), from which the P 1892 etching was made. According to Grossmann the title relates rather to the costume than to the actual individual.[57] Hollar's interest in this subject stemmed from his miniaturist's love of detail in female costume, from the delicate weave and variety of decoration to local and social variations in cut. The artist in him also responded to the technical difficulty of the task. To reproduce with convincing accuracy the glint of silk, the softness and fine down of fur coats, or the profile of a face concealed by, and yet showing through, the delicate network of a veil – all this was a challenge to Hollar's technical command of drawing and engraving, and to his ability to use them for artistic ends.

40 *Wife of a Prague Merchant* Etching P 1808, probably after 1637. The title appears on the etching both in German and Latin. Hollar's interest in women's fashions seems to have begun about 1630 and he must have made the drawing on which this etching is based while he was in Prague in 1636. However, he did not begin making etchings of this type of subject until after his arrival in London the following year. He became one of the most effective 'costume illustrators' of the seventeenth century, less aggressive than Goltzius, less mannered than Callot, wittier and more stylish than Bosse. (British Museum, London)

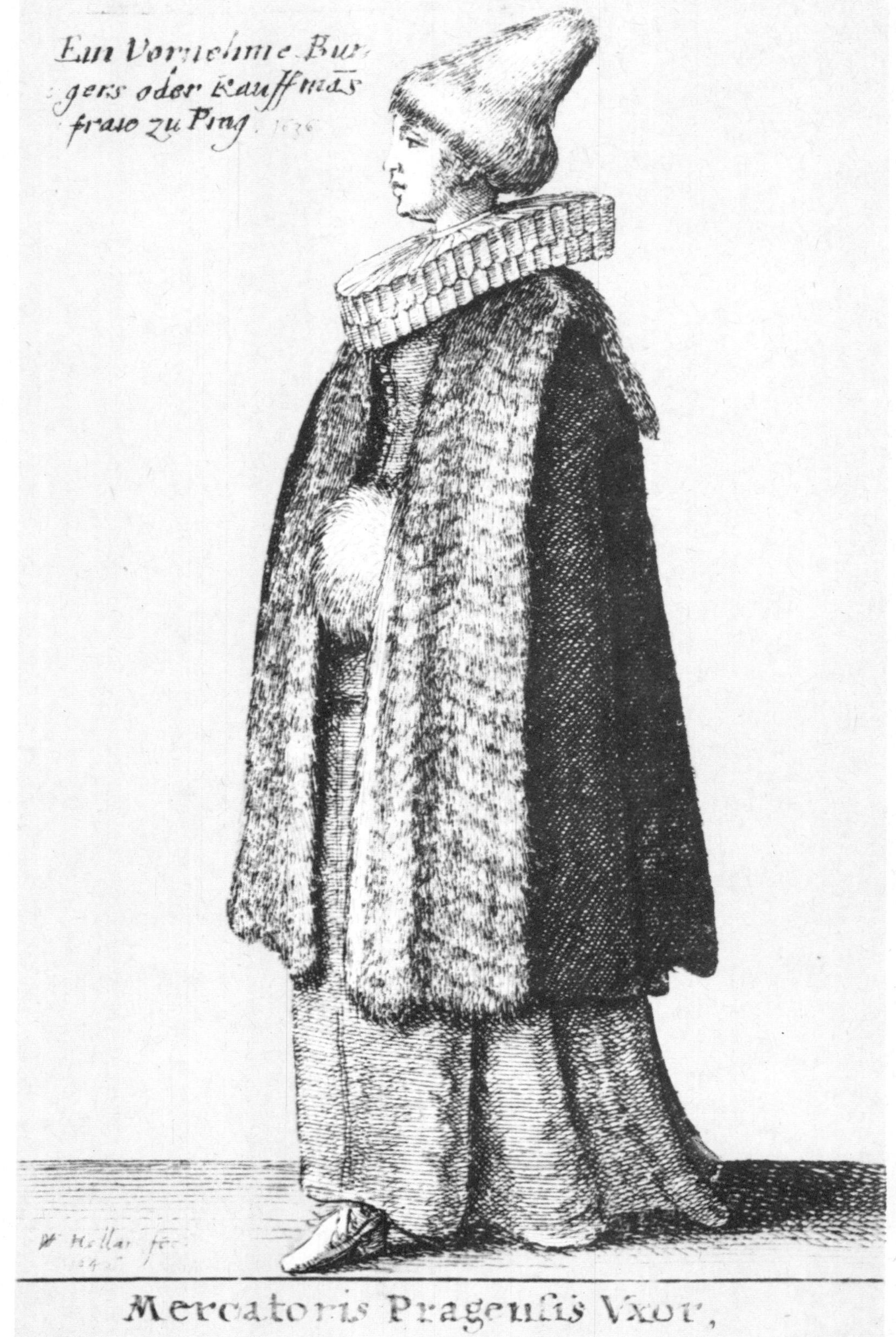

Hollar's alertness to detail led him on from the general appearance of costumes to the accessory items – muffs, sleeves, fans, carnival masks and other fashionable miscellanea. The social context of Arundel House, where Hollar's wife had been a lady-in-waiting, no doubt gave him opportunity enough to study and record the forms and textures of every luxury in season. The memoirs of Hollar's friends confirm the social esteem that his precise rendering of all these modish items

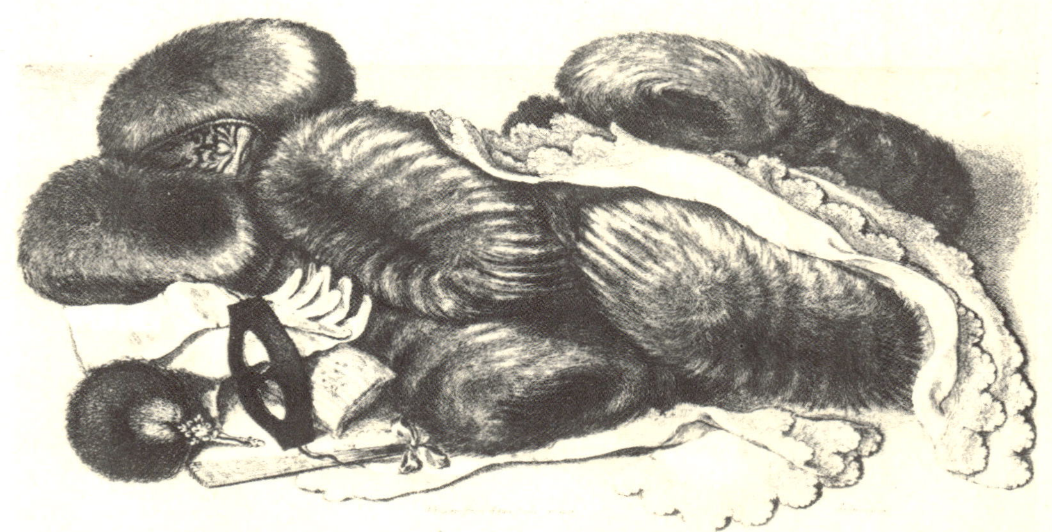

41 *Muffs and Finery* Etching P 1951, dated 1647. The eight etchings of fur muffs which Hollar produced between 1642 and 1647 form one of his most celebrated series. While related to some extent to his meticulous illustrations of natural objects (see illustrations 42 and 43), they also have something in common with Dutch illusionistic still-life paintings (for example, crosses resting on books, in such a way that the long arm of the cross appears to swivel as the viewer moves his eye across the picture). Coincidentally, Hollar's highly convincing method of representing fur by means of etching was developed at exactly the same time as the invention of mezzotint. (British Museum, London)

conferred on him, and indeed these remain among his best-known works. Of all the drawings from which the etchings were taken only one has survived. This is *The Muff* (S 21), a superb piece of draughtsmanship that wonderfully reproduces both the surface of the fur and the nuances of reflected light. Some time ago there was speculation that it might itself have been copied from the 1647 etching (P 1946), but Grossmann recently dispelled these doubts by drawing attention to the image-reversal of the etching and the high quality of the drawing.[58]

Occasionally Hollar would group together various costume accessories on their own. Such groupings are never casually or artificially arranged; they form a sensitively composed whole, harmonious in content and appearance. The total effect is enhanced by the sensual charm of the individual components – objects of simple beauty that add to the pleasure of life. The compositions are clearly indebted to the development of the still life as a distinct artistic genre, particularly in Holland. But Holland was not an exclusive inspiration. Hollar's etchings in this category were all, it is true, produced in Holland just before the middle of the seventeenth century but, as so often, he used older sketches that he had drawn in England. Possibly, however, Hollar had the idea from older Dutch still lives that he remembered seeing at the Hapsburg court in Prague.

The same models may have influenced his drawings of small natural objects. In this area of his work, of which only etchings remain, the most celebrated subjects are the mollusc shells (not signed, but traditionally ascribed to Hollar) and the butterflies drawn from nature for the inventory of Lord Arundel's collection. Good examples are the etchings of the *Shell, Conus imperialis* (P 2195) and of *Butterflies and Dragonflies* (P 2177). Probably the idea for this illustrated catalogue came from the imperial collections in Prague, still fresh in Hollar's mind from his visit in 1636. These were designed, in the mannerist spirit, to present an encyclopedic picture of the whole world through an assemblage of natural objects and artistic and technical artefacts, an aim that must have greatly appealed to the collector's spirit of the earl. It is quite possible that the two men, naturalist and artist, saw some of the pictorial documentation attached to these collections,

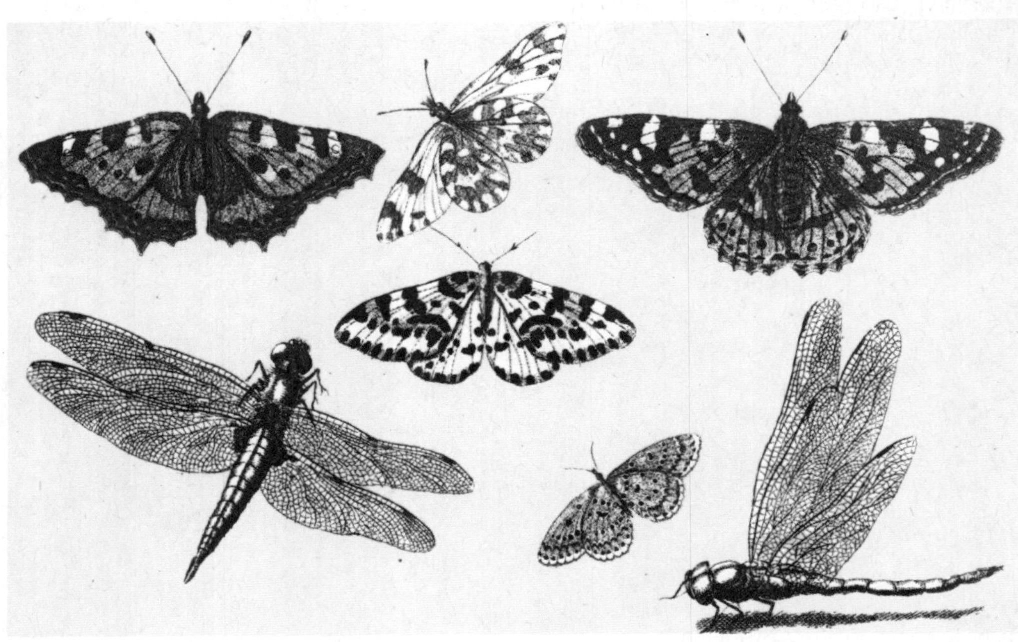

42 *Butterflies and Dragonflies* Etching P 2177, about 1646. This etching is closely related in type and style to the series of twelve which Hollar produced in Antwerp in 1646 after a group of coloured drawings (which he may also have made) in the Arundel collection. They all represent insects of various kinds. Similar drawings were in the imperial collections in Prague, and Jacob Hoefnagel had produced a series of insect etchings there in 1630. Hollar and the Earl of Arundel almost certainly saw these drawings and etchings on their visit in 1636. (British Museum, London)

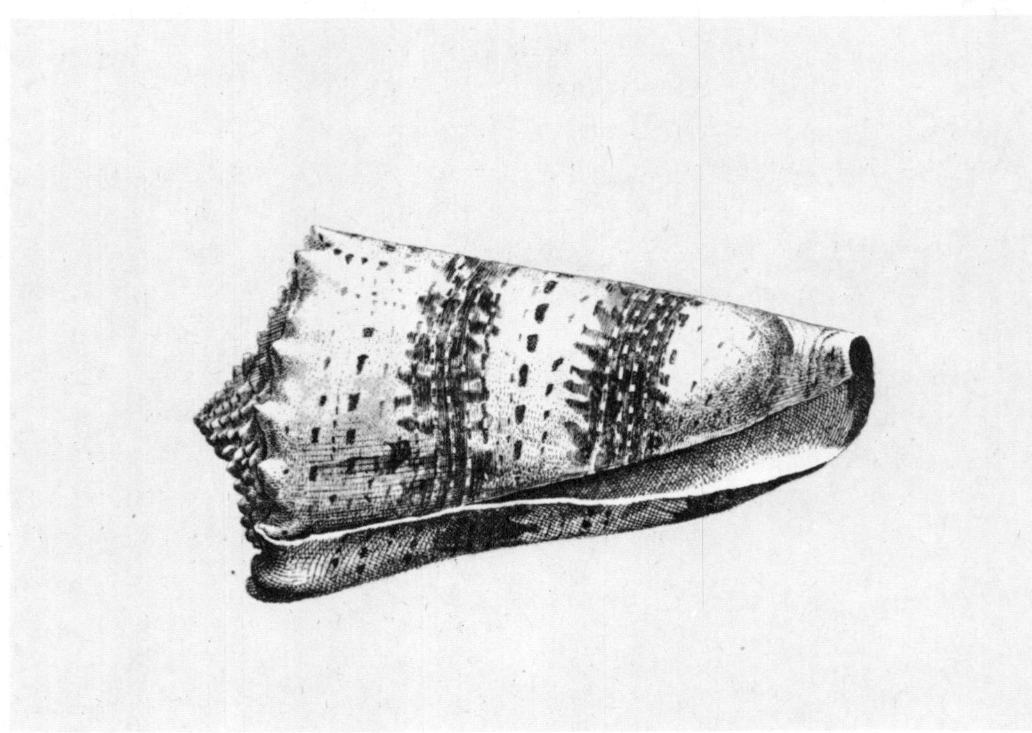

43 *Shell, Conus imperialis* Etching P 2195, *c.*1646. This is one of a series of thirty-eight etchings of shells which Hollar is assumed to have made in Antwerp in or about 1646, though none is signed or dated. Illustrations of shells, like those of insects, appealed to learned collectors of the period. They were part of an encyclopedic documentation of the whole world, in which natural objects and living things formed a continuum with artistic and technical artefacts. (British Museum, London)

particularly the series of insect etchings by Jacob Hoefnagel published in 1630.

In his biological studies Hollar was attracted chiefly by beauty of shape, line and colour. By masterly artistic means, yet without loss of scientific accuracy, he was able to reproduce on a plane surface in black and white the amazingly complex structure of a specimen with all its colour and the 'ornamental' delicacy of its surface grain – an achievement that must fascinate any lover of drawing and engraving. One such admirer seems to have been his contemporary Rembrandt, who did in fact own some Hollar engravings. A.M. Hind[59] suggested some years ago that Rembrandt's own shell etching of 1650 was inspired by one of

Hollar's works, which he copied with remarkable fidelity, though of course he used his own technique of contrasting light and shade.

Among all these studies of natural objects that balked so large in Hollar's English and Dutch periods we rarely come across drawings of large animals. Horses frequently appear in vigorous movement, but only on a small scale as elements in a landscape. Again, his animals were not always drawn from life, particularly in his travel illustrations. There is some uncertainty about the extant drawings, of which the group consisting of *Eight Waterbird Studies, Stag Lying Down* and *He-goat* (S 53 to 55) are merely attributed to Hollar. The only one signed by him, and dated 1646, is the *Study of Two Dogs* (G 114). According to Grossmann this is in the style of the Antwerp artist Pieter van Avont, whose work

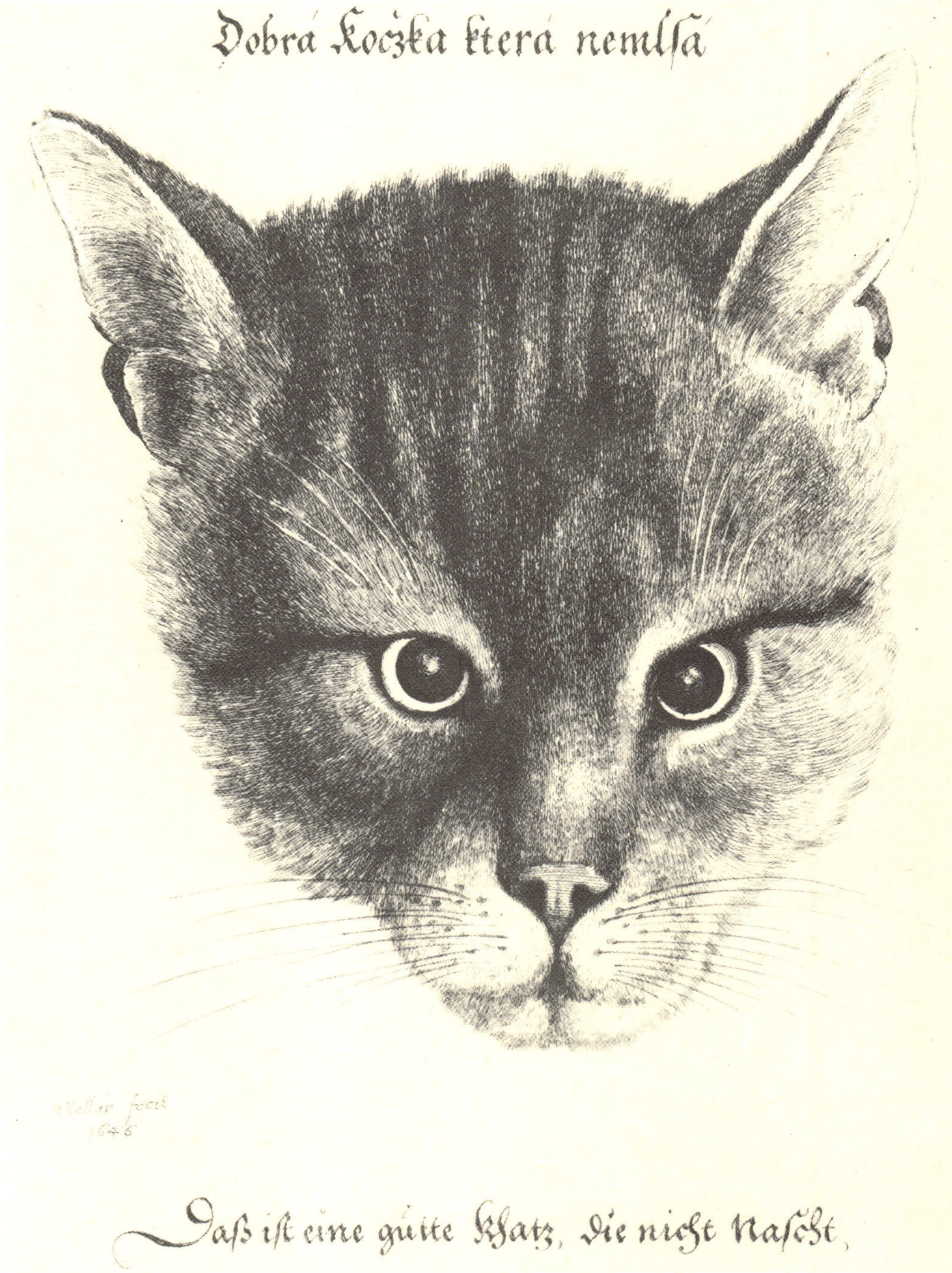

44 *Dobrá kočka, která nemlsá*
Etching P 2109, dated 1646. The inscription, repeated in Czech and German, means: 'It's a good cat that doesn't beg for titbits between meals.' This was no doubt a proverbial saying at the time. Hollar's sensuous love of fur is expressed here as in his etchings of muffs, and a somewhat similar mood seems to underlie both this cat's head and the allegorical figure of *Winter* (illustration no.33). (British Museum, London)

Hollar copied in several engravings. The drawing cannot be matched with any etching by Hollar, so it is impossible to say whether it was done from nature or reproduces a drawing by van Avont.

One item that deserves special notice – a quite unique one in Hollar's output – is the front view of a cat's head with an inscription by the artist in Czech on top – *Dobrá kočka, která nemlsá* – repeated in German below – *Das ist eine gutte Katz, die nicht nascht* ('It's a good cat that doesn't beg for titbits'). There are three variants of this engraving in different sizes, of which the middle-sized one bears the legends. This and the small head are dated 1646, the large version 1661, the portrait being the same in each case. The heading on the last one makes it clear that they were based on a life drawing of a cat belonging to the Grand Duke of Muscovy. The rendering shows every sign of Hollar's skill, not only in the perfect portrayal of the fur, with its distinctions of colour, density and direction of growth in different areas, but in the expression of the eyes, which seem to peer out from some mysterious depths of animal emotion. The drawing is a quite outstanding example of live portraiture.[60]

The Czech inscription is evidently a popular proverb that Hollar had heard at home, implying metaphorically that those serve well who serve honestly. Folklore students are thus indebted to Hollar for this evidence of the currency in the early seventeenth century of a piece of Bohemian folk-wisdom. Hollar had unwittingly provided a useful fragment of historical information.

CONCLUSION

While Hollar's drawings and etchings have become an intrinsic part of the heritage of European art, their affinity to the culture of the artist's own countrymen gives them a prime place in the history of Czech art as well. Their roots lie deep in the native soil and mental climate of Bohemia. The basic traits of Hollar's work are linked to the traditions of the Czech Renaissance and Reformation and of the realistic stream of Bohemian art.

Wenceslaus Hollar died in London on 25 March 1677. Only a year before he had recalled his native city in the Prague motif of his P 879 etching, showing the Petřín hill in the background. He always considered himself a Czech artist, never forgetting his home or denying his origins. He spread the fame of Prague and of Bohemia by signing his engravings *Wenceslaus Hollar Bohemus* or *de Bohemia, Pragensis* or *de Praha.* He put Prague in first rank among the European cities he portrayed, executing a simple sketch of Prague Castle in 1649 for Jan Meyssens so that he could insert it symbolically in the window-view at the rear of his Hollar portrait. Above his fine panorama drawing of Prague in 1636 he put, instead of the usual placename, a monumental calligraphic inscription to denote the city's prestige: PRAGA BOHEMIAE METROPOLIS. Years later in 1649, when publishing his great prospect-engraving of Prague, he stressed his personal attachment to the subject by adding, in the Latin legend, that he had 'drawn this metropolis of the Kingdom of Bohemia, his own fatherland, in 1636 from the top of the Petřín hill as accurately as he was able'. Such was the artist's own evidence of his loyalty to his native country. Years after Hollar had left Bohemia he still wrote Czech words on his works.

England, which had received him hospitably at a critical moment and where he was to spend nearly half his life, he cherished as his second home, and as the homeland of his family and his dearest friends. Those among them who were members and fellow-founders of the Royal Society had a high opinion of the accuracy and objectivity of the illustrations he made for history and natural history books. But, it was only later generations who could fully appreciate the documentary value of Hollar's portrayals of the English countryside, cities and ancient abbeys, the precision of his maps of the world and its several regions, and above all the excellence of his views of London itself. (A complete edition of these was issued in 1922 with a comprehensive illustrated monograph by Arthur M. Hind of the British Museum, a perceptive admirer of Hollar's work.) Hollar's views provide in many cases unique testimony to the face of London and its dominant buildings which existed before the Great Fire. As Hollar himself wrote under his view of the original building of St Paul's, he had 'in this fashion preserved its memory'.

Again, it was left to modern English historians to discover the value of Hollar's figure-drawings and etchings in reliably documenting the actual appearance of various public personalities and the dramatic events of the seventeenth century. Thus Hollar repaid a debt of gratitude to his second home.

Through the vagaries of his life – ten years were also spent in Germany and eight in the Netherlands – as well as by his breadth of mind and artistic conviction, Wenceslaus Hollar became a European. But his achievements make him a citizen of the world.

What we have surveyed is only one portion of Hollar's output, his drawings. But it is these, perhaps *par excellence*, which reflect the whole of Hollar: the artist-creator and the humble servant of art, the tireless observer of life and devotee of sheer hard work. In his urban prospects he transformed the traditional straightforward stereotype into the illusion of great cities, naturally integrated into their surroundings. In his landscapes he caught the personality of a given patch of countryside in its particular siting at a given hour of day, expressing the mood of the moment in the delicate lyricism of his sketchbook. He preserved for posterity the life of his own times through his figure compositions and accurate portraits. He revealed beauty in the detail of homely objects and put his skill to the service of scientific knowledge with his textbook illustrations.

For all its multifarious aspects his work remains a consistent whole. It has a firm inner structure, classically clear and balanced, imbued with calm and certainty of aim, watching the world's reality through curious and loving eyes. Hollar's was a fine, clean art that still excites the specialist, tempts the collector and wins ever-new admirers. His art belongs to all art-lovers, affording them the joy of experiencing life's bounty to the brim.

PLATES

All the drawings reproduced here are in the print collection of the Prague National Gallery, indexed under K. In the list below the title of each drawing is followed by its date of execution, National Gallery index entry, Sprinzels's catalogue number, medium, and height times width in millimetres and inches.

Roman numerals refer to colour plates and Arabic ones to black and white plates.

I *View of Cannstadt on the Neckar*, 1628. K 31 195, S 97. Pen and bistre with watercolour, 114 × 277 mm ($4\frac{1}{4} \times 10\frac{3}{4}$ ins). The date is given on etching P 757, for which this was the final draft

II *View of Strasbourg*, 1629. K 31 222, S 114. Pen and bistre with watercolour, 88 × 177 mm ($3\frac{1}{2} \times$ 7 ins). Signed bottom left: *W H 1629*. Sketch for an etching

1 *View of Strasbourg*, 1629. K 31 222. Detail from colour plate II

2 *The Strasbourg Shooting-range*, 1629? K 31 238, S 113. Pen and bistre and wash, 98 × 240 mm ($3\frac{3}{4} \times 9\frac{1}{4}$ ins). Sketch for an etching

3 *The Strasbourg Shooting-range*, 1629? K 31 238, detail

III *View of Mühlheim on the Rhine*, 1630? K 31 221, S 115. Pen and bistre with watercolour, 86 × 176 mm ($3\frac{1}{4} \times$ 7 ins). Signed bottom left: *W H*

4 *View of Mainz*, 1632. K 31 239, S 144. Pen and bistre and wash, 211 × 370 mm ($8\frac{1}{4} \times 14\frac{1}{2}$ ins), 211 × 380 mm ($8\frac{1}{4} \times 14\frac{3}{4}$ ins), 211 × 363 mm ($8\frac{1}{4} \times 14\frac{1}{4}$ ins). Signed in the middle: *W. Hollar delin.* Date determined by the signed and dated sketch S 145 of one part. Final draft for an etching

5 *View of Mainz*, 1632. K 31 239. Detail

6 *View of Mainz*, detail

7 *View of Mainz*, detail

8 *View of Cologne and Deutz*, 1633–6. K 31 204, S 120. Pen and rust ink with grey wash, 75 × 146 mm (3 × $5\frac{1}{2}$ ins). Date-range determined by completion of fortification of Deutz, 1633, and Hollar's departure from Cologne in 1636. Sketch for an etching

9 *View of Cologne and Deutz*, detail

10 *View of Düren*, 1634. K 31 209, S 286. Pen and ink with watercolour, 740 × 381 mm (29 × $14\frac{3}{4}$ ins). Signed bottom left: *W H 1634*. Final draft for an etching

11 *View of Düren*, detail

12 *The Rhine near Bonn*, 1635. K 31 203, S 133. Pen and ink with watercolour, 77 × 176 mm (3 × $6\frac{3}{4}$ ins). Signed bottom left: *W H 1635*. Final draft for an etching

13 *Rhine scene near Rolandseck Castle*, 1636. K 31 226, S 181. Pen and ink with watercolour, 122 × 291 mm ($4\frac{3}{4} \times 11\frac{1}{4}$ ins). Signed left: *W Hollar f. 9 Maij 1636*. The date of this and twenty-four other drawings follows from their association with the 1636 Arundel mission. Final draft for an etching

14 *Rhine scene near Rolandseck Castle*, detail

15 *View of Ober-Winter-on-Rhine*, 1636. K 31 212, S 209. Pen and ink with watercolour, 58 × 185 mm ($2\frac{1}{4} \times 7\frac{1}{4}$ ins). Magnification reveals the signature, bottom left: *W H 9 Maij 1636* (read by Sprinzels as *6 Maij*). The date May 9 corresponds to the record of the journey. Final draft for an etching

16 *View of Ober-Winter-on-Rhine*, detail

17 *View of Rheinmagen* (modern Remagen), 1636. K 31 225, S 186. Pen and ink with watercolour, 122 × 290 mm ($4\frac{3}{4} \times 11\frac{1}{4}$ ins). Signed bottom left: *9 Maij 1636*. Final draft for an etching

18 *View of Rheinmagen*, detail

19 *View of Linz-on-Rhein*, 1636. K 31 199, S 183. Pen and bistre with rust ink and watercolour, 106 × 275 mm (4 × $10\frac{3}{4}$ ins). Signed bottom left: *9 Maij 1636*. Final draft for an etching

20 *View of Linz-on-Rhein*, detail

21 *View of Lahneck-Lahnstein*, 1636. K 31 208, S 195. Pen and ink and bistre, wash, 131 × 309 mm (5 × 11 ins). Signed bottom left: 1636. Sketch for final draft K 31 224, no. 23 below

22 *View of Lahneck-Lahnstein*, detail

23 *View of Lahneck-Lahnstein*, 1636. K 31 224, S 194. Pen and ink with watercolour, 107 × 278 mm (4 × $10\frac{3}{4}$ ins). Signed bottom right: *10 Maij 1636*. Final draft for an etching

24 *View of Lahneck-Lahnstein*, detail

25 *View of Boppard*, 1636. K 31 214, S 196. Pen and ink and bistre, wash, 131 × 311 mm (5 × 12 ins). Sketch for an etching

26 *View of Boppard*, detail
27 *View of Bingen*, 1636. K 31 197, S 207. Pen and ink and bistre, wash, 130 × 309 mm (5 × 11¾ ins). Sketch for an etching
28 *View of Bingen*, detail
29 *View of Rüdesheim*, 1636. K 31 234, S 205. Pen and ink and bistre, wash, 131 × 313 mm (5 × 12 ins). Sketch for final draft K 31 223 no. 31 below
30 *View of Rüdesheim*, detail
31 *View of Rüdesheim*, 1636. K 31 223, S 206. Pen and ink with watercolour, 106 × 217 mm (4 × 8¼ ins). Signed bottom right: *12 Maij 1636*. Final draft for an etching
32 *View of Rüdesheim*, detail
IV *View of Geldersbach near Hoechst*, 1636. k 31 227, S 210. Pen and ink with watercolour, 93 × 192 mm (3½ × 7½ ins). Signed bottom right: *W H 2/12 Maij 1636*. Final draft for an etching
33 *View of Geldersbach near Hoechst*, 1636. K 31 227. Detail of colour plate IV
34 *View of Hoechst*, 1636. K 31 202, S 212. Pen and ink with watercolour, 108 × 270 mm (4 × 10½ ins). Signed bottom right: *2/12 Maij 1636*. Final draft for an etching
35 *View of Hoechst*, detail
36 *View of Würzburg*, 1636. K 31 228, S 220. Pen and ink with watercolour, 102 × 268 mm (4 × 10½ ins). Final draft for an etching
37 *View of Würzburg*, detail
38 *View of Donaustauf*, 1636. K 31 230, S 229. Pen and ink with wash, 118 × 235 mm (4½ × 9 ins). Final draft for an etching
39 *View of Donaustauf*, detail of colour plate VI
40 *View of Deggendorf on the Danube*, 1636. K 31 231, S 233. Pen and bistre with watercolour. 105 × 271 mm (4 × 10½ ins). Final draft for an etching
41 *View of Deggendorf on the Danube*, detail
V *View of Wintzen* (modern Wüntzen), 1636. K 31 201, S 235. Pen and bistre with watercolour, 113 × 257 mm (4¼ × 10 ins). Final draft for an etching
42 *View of Wintzen* 1636. K 31 201. Detail of colour plate V
43 *View of Wilshofen*, 1636. K 31 217, S 239. Pen and bistre with watercolour, 131 × 312 mm (5 × 12 ins)
44 *View of Wilshofen*, detail of colour plate VIII
45 *View of Neuhaus*, 1636. K 31 232, S 250. Pen and bistre with watercolour, 123 × 254 mm (4¾ × 10 ins). Final draft for an etching
46 *View of Neuhaus*, detail
47 *View of Grein*, 1636. K 31 233, S 262. Pen and ink and bistre, wash, 130 × 311 mm (5 × 12 ins). Sketch for final draft K 31 200, no. 49 below
48 *View of Grein*, detail
49 *View of Grein*, 1636. Grein was formally called Crain – hence the inscription on this work. K 31 200, S 261. Pen and ink with watercolour, 88 × 177 mm (3½ × 7 ins). Signed bottom left: *W H 1629*. Sketch for an etching
50 *View of Püssingen*, 1636. K 31 194, S 282. Pen and ink and bistre, with watercolour, 131 × 311 mm (5 × 12 ins). Sketch for final draft K 31 229
51 *View of Püssingen-Dillingen*, 1636. K 31 229, S 281. Pen and ink and bistre, with watercolour, 114 × 228 mm (4½ × 9 ins). Final draft for an etching
52 *View of Püssingen-Dillingen*, detail
53 *Danube landscape*, 1636. K 31 207, S 253. Pen and bistre with watercolour, 106 × 260 mm (4 × 10 ins). Final draft for an etching
VI *View of Znojmo*, 1636. K 31 213, S 272. Pen and bistre with watercolour, 131 × 312 mm (5 × 12 ins). Final draft for an etching
54 *General view of Prague from the Petřín slope*, 1636. K 33 360, S 273. Pen and ink with watercolour, 120 × 279 mm (4½ × 11¼ ins), 121 × 281 mm (4½ × 11¼ ins). Signed below, left of centre: *W. Hollar delin in Augusto 1636*
55 *General view of Prague from the Petřín slope*, detail
56 *General view of Prague from the Petřín slope*, detail
57 *General view of Prague from the Petřín slope*, detail
VII *General view of Prague from the Petřín slope*, 1636. K 33 360. Detail of black and white plate no.54 above
58 *View of a fortified city*, K 31 196, S 121. Pen and watercolour, 80 × 162 mm (3 × 6¼ ins)
59 *View of Deventer*, 1650. K 31 198, S 349. Pen and ink with watercolour, 100 × 393 mm (4 × 15½ ins)
60 *View of Deventer*, detail

61 *View of Deal Castle fortress*, after 1660? K 31 220, S 372. Pen and ink with watercolour, 85 × 225 mm ($3\frac{1}{4}$ × $8\frac{1}{2}$ ins). Sketch for an etching

62 *View of Algiers*, 1669. K 31 215, S 393. Pen and ink wash, 100 × 265 mm (4 × 10 ins). Done on the journey to Tangier

63 *View of Algiers*, detail

64 *Christ attended by angels*, before 1643? K 31 235, S 49, Pen and bistre, wash, 125 × 219 mm ($4\frac{1}{2}$ × $8\frac{1}{2}$ ins). Copy of a work by Adam Elsheimer, probably in the Arundel collection, now lost. Preparatory draft for an etching

65 *Hull of a ship*, 1634? K 31 236, S 90. Pen and watercolour, 72 × 134 mm ($2\frac{3}{4}$ × $5\frac{1}{4}$ ins). Additional drawing for etching P 1264, whose final draft S 91a is signed and dated 1634

66 *Hull of a ship*, detail

VIII *Three-master*, K 31 210, S 84. Pen and bistre with watercolour, 210 × 281 mm (8 × $10\frac{3}{4}$ ins)

67 *Portrait of the goldsmith Hans von Zürs*, before 1647. K 22 384, S 1. Pen and bistre, 205 × 171 mm (8 × $6\frac{1}{2}$ ins). Drawing after an original by Hans Holbein in the Arundel collection, subsequently lost. Final draft for an etching

68 *Girl's head in profile*, 1637–44. K 31 237, S 9. Pen and bistre, 51 × 47 mm (2 × $1\frac{3}{4}$ ins). Original size

69 *Girl's head in profile*

70 *Reclining female nude*, K 31 216, S 12. Pen and sepia with watercolour, 109 × 171 mm ($4\frac{1}{4}$ × $6\frac{1}{2}$ ins). An attached slip bears a dedication dated 31 July 1633, Cologne

71 *Costume study*, K 31 219, S 22. Gouache, 218 × 118 mm (8.5 × $4\frac{1}{2}$ ins). Traditionally ascribed to Hollar

PLATES

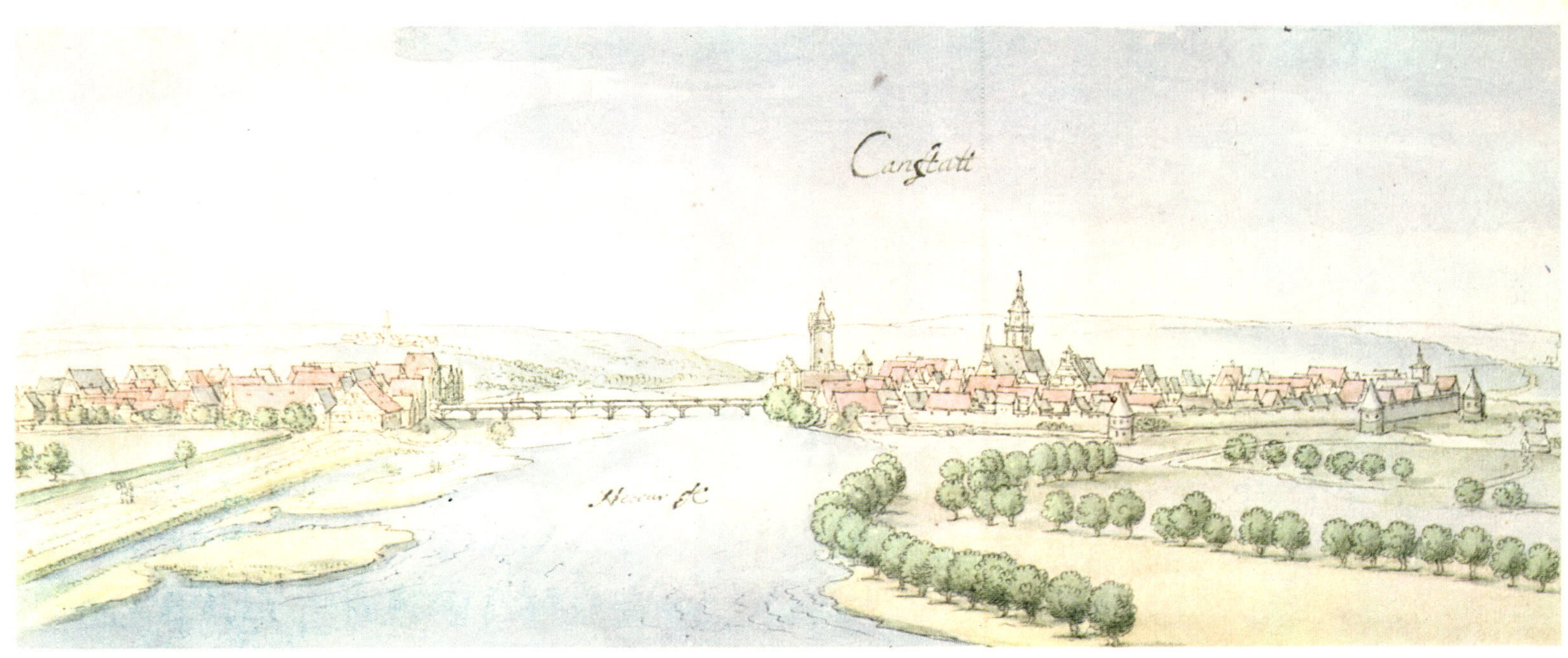
Canstatt

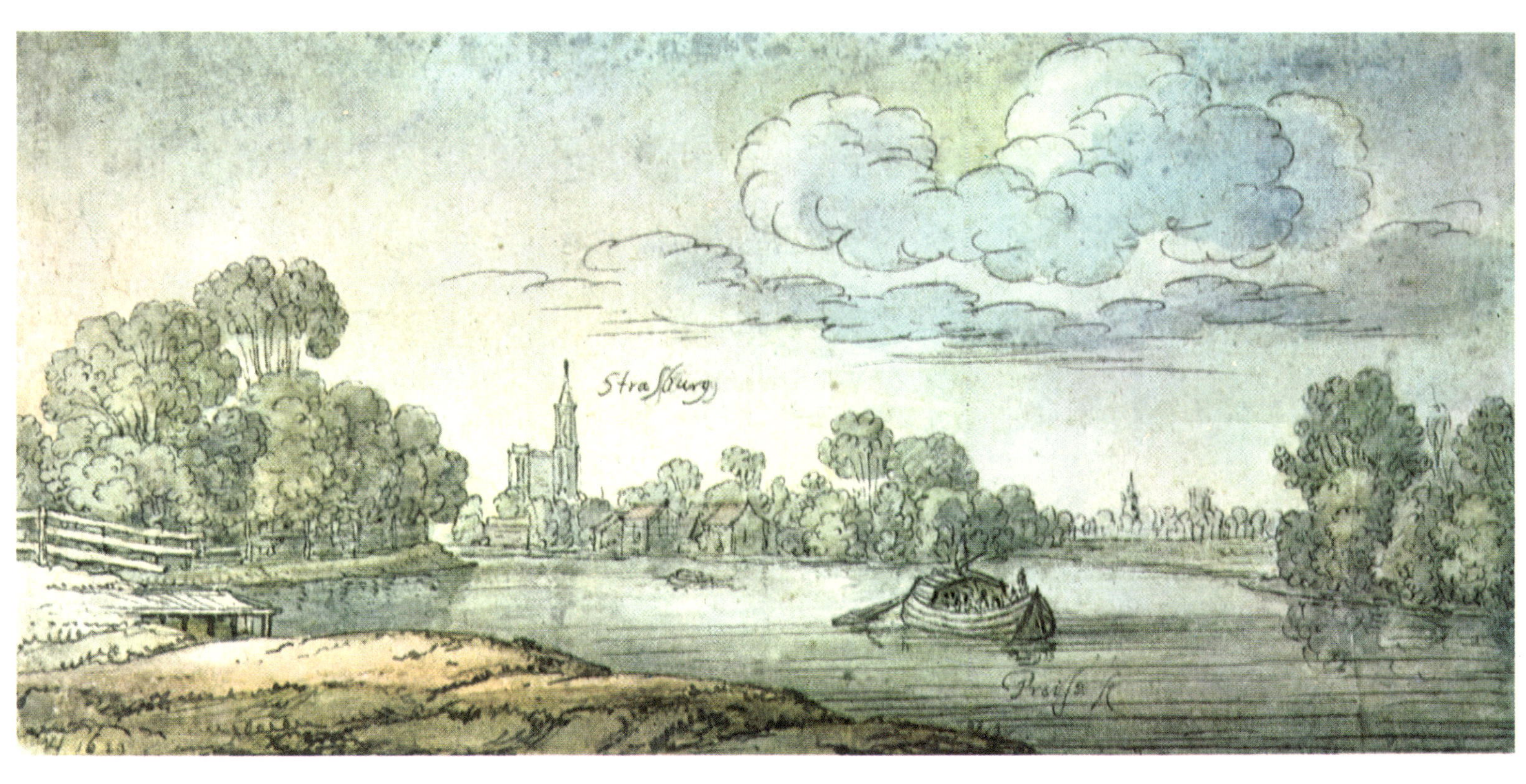
Strassburg

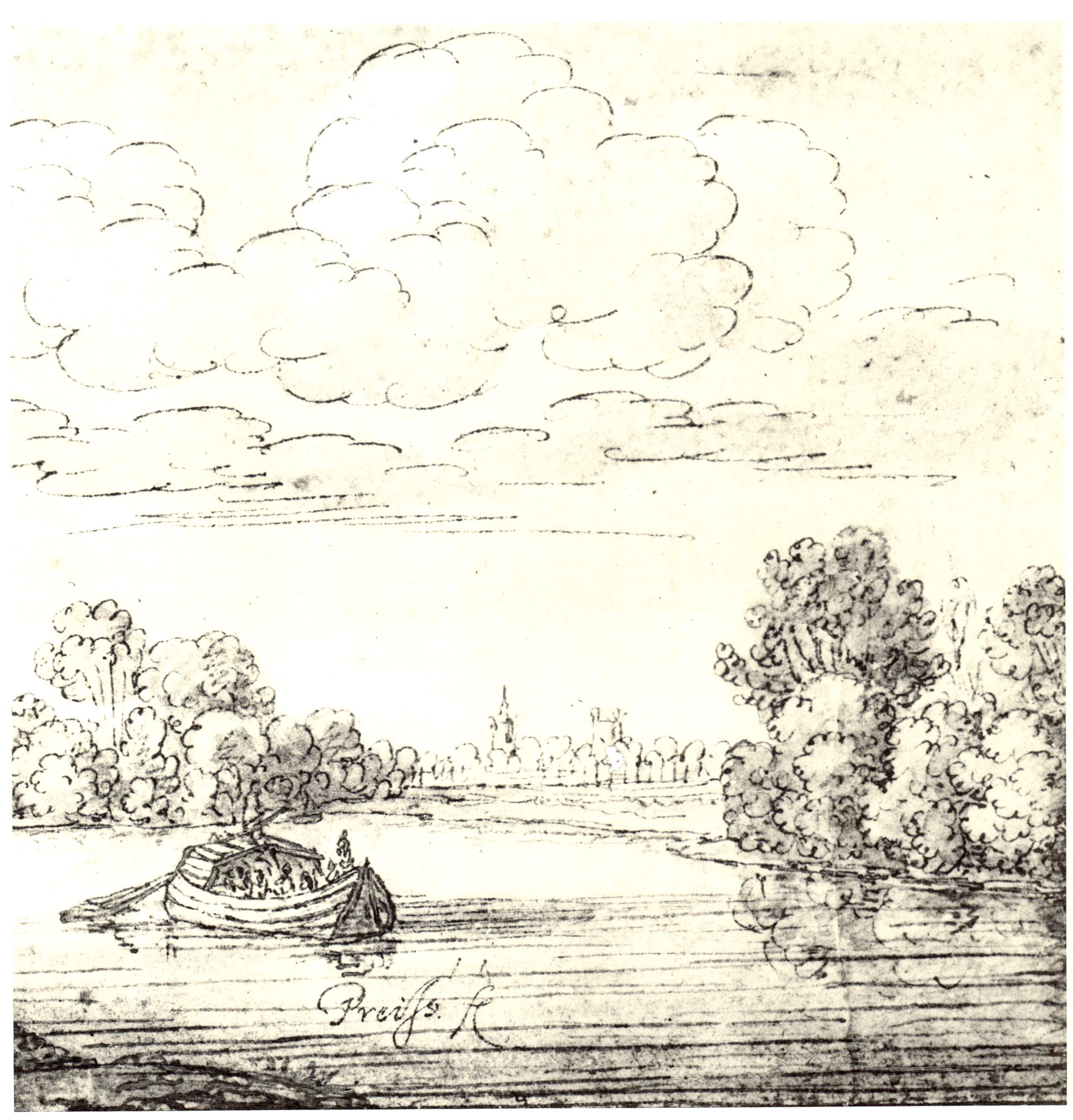

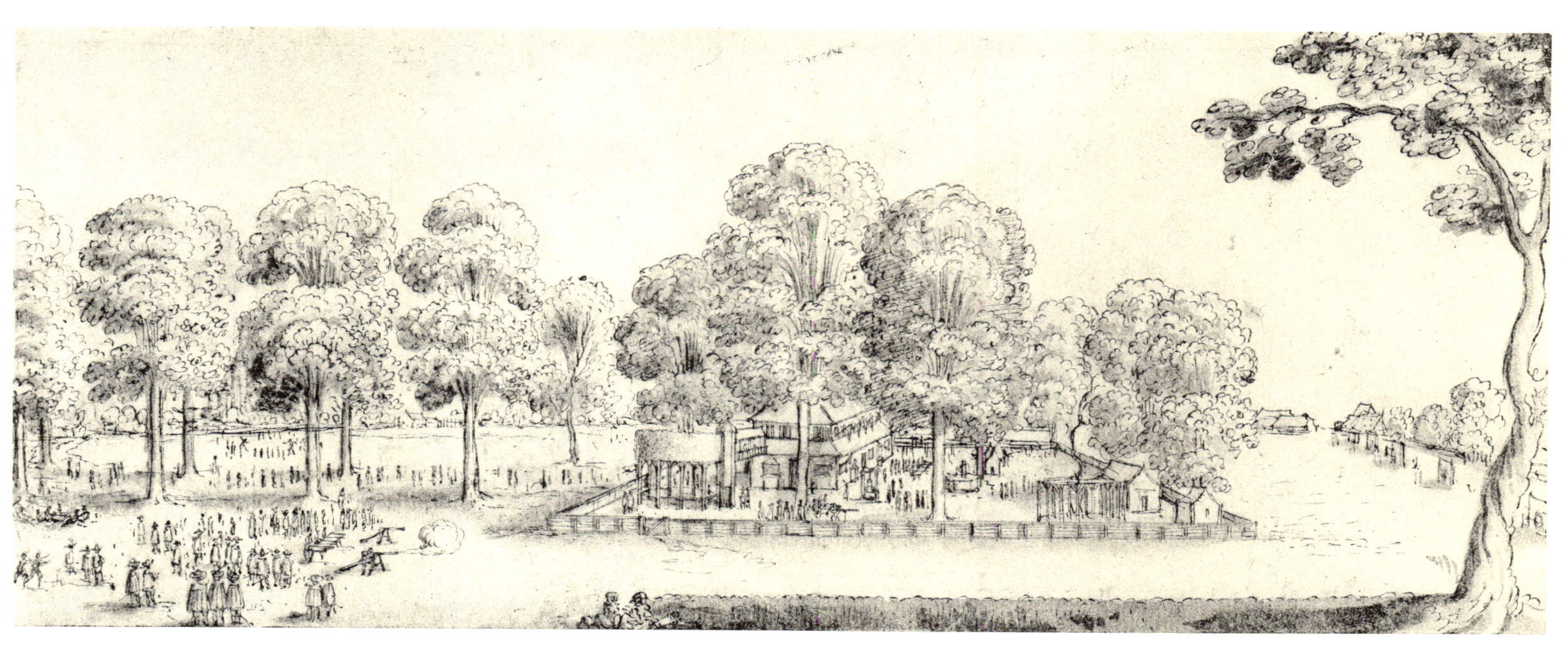

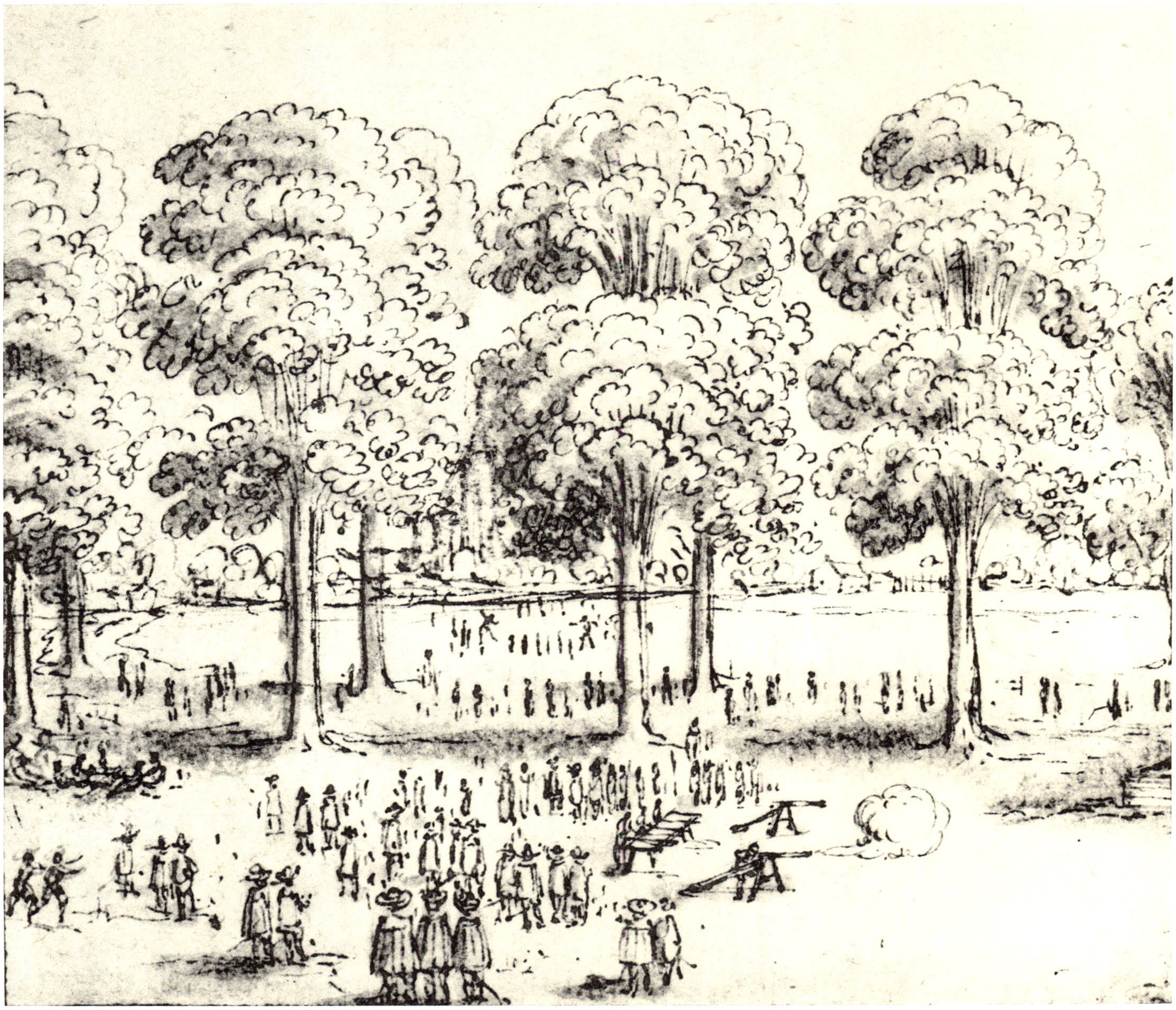

2/3

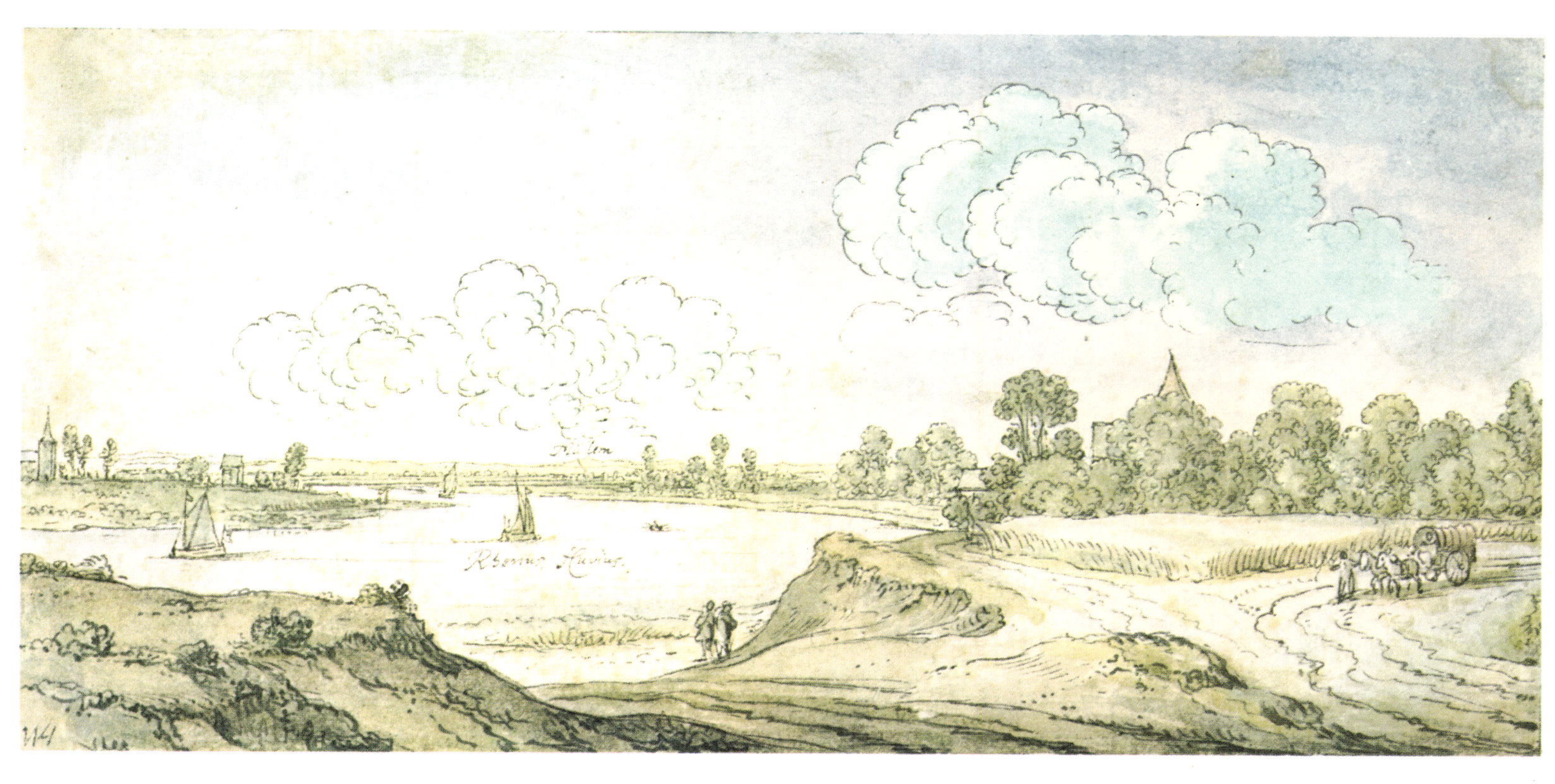
Rhenus fluvius

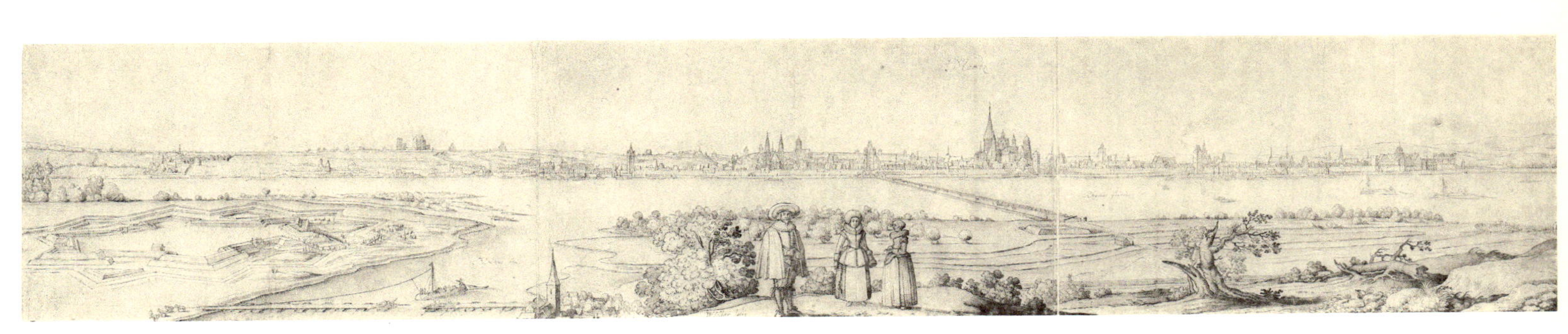

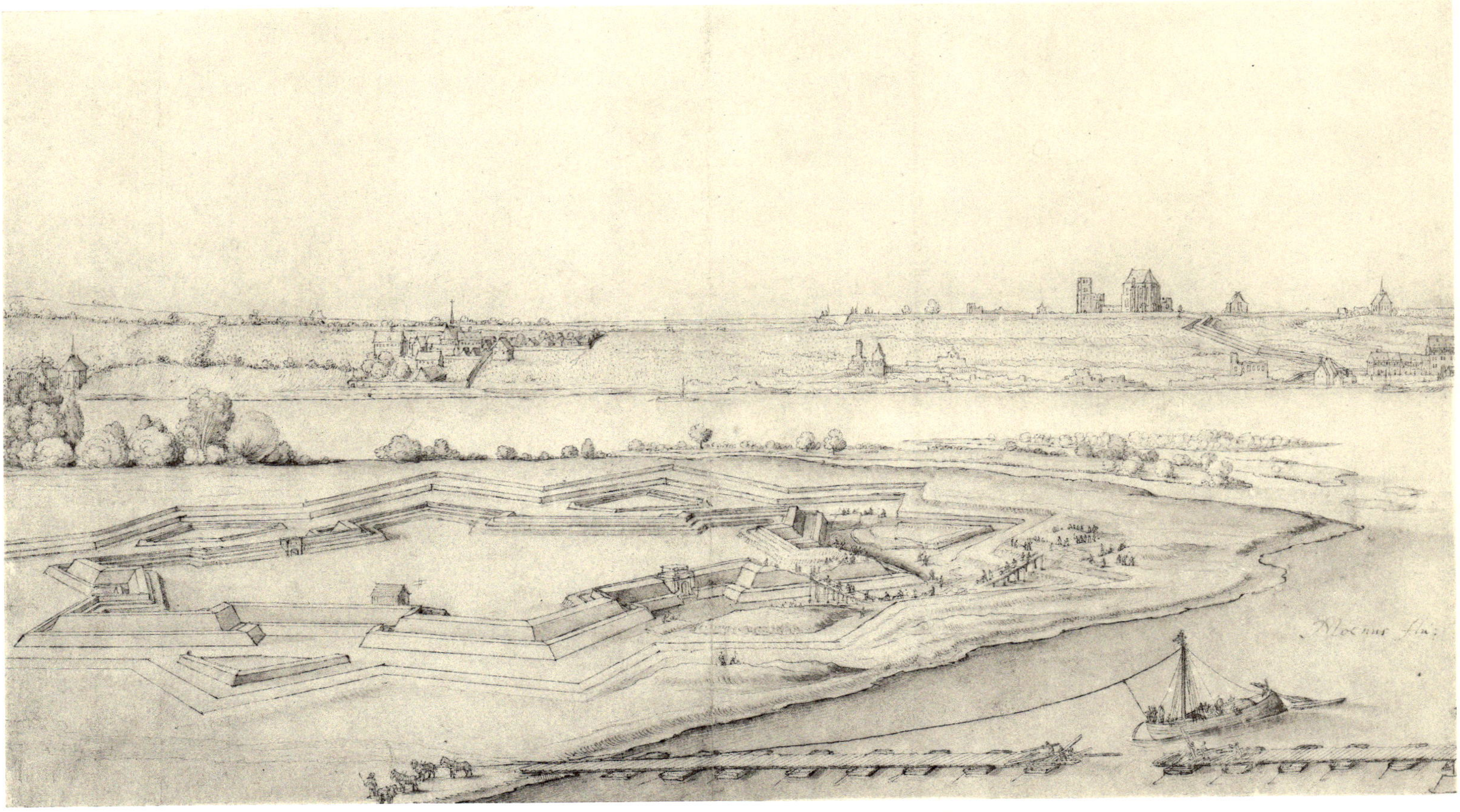

4/5

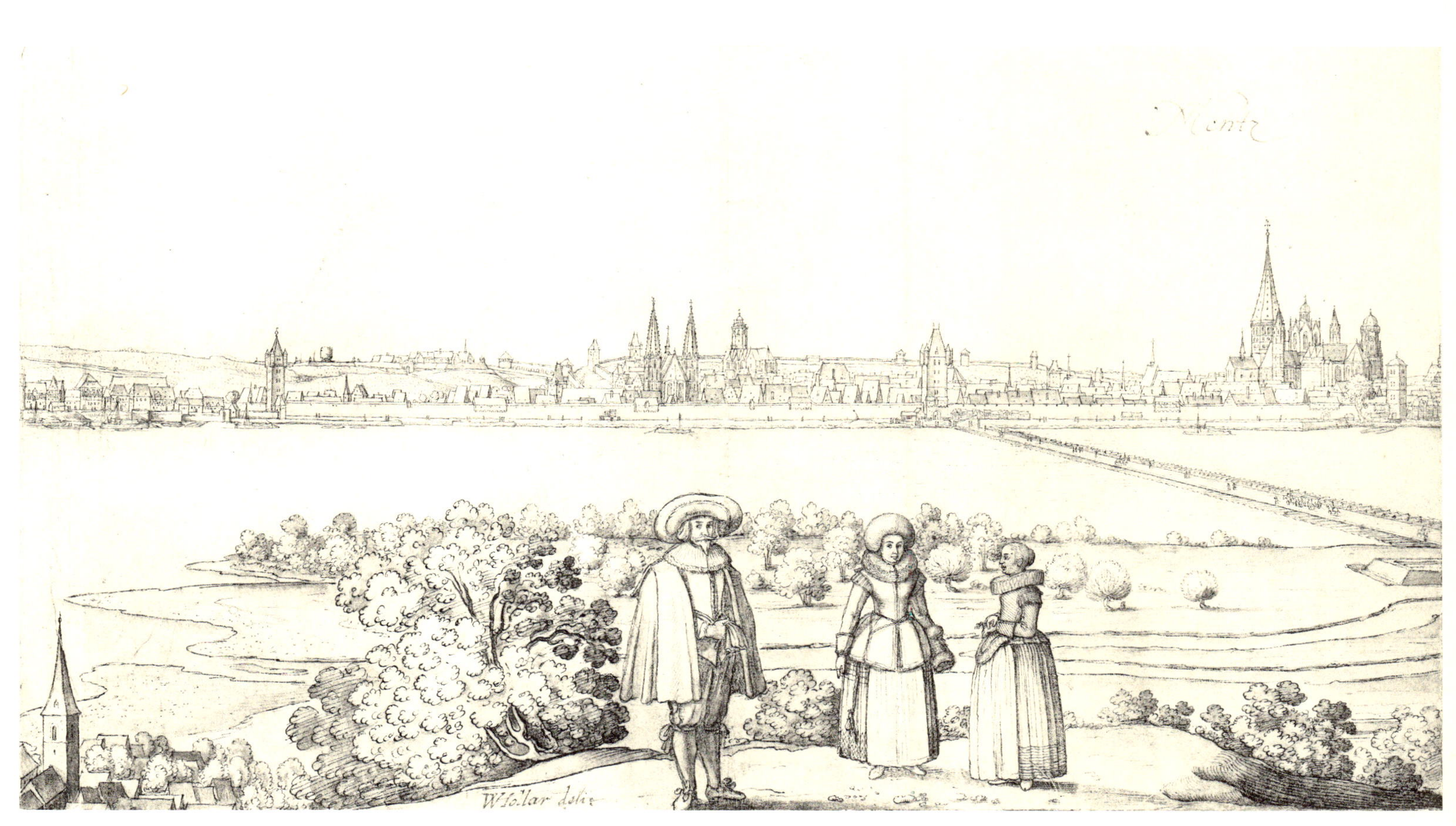
Mentz
WHollar delin

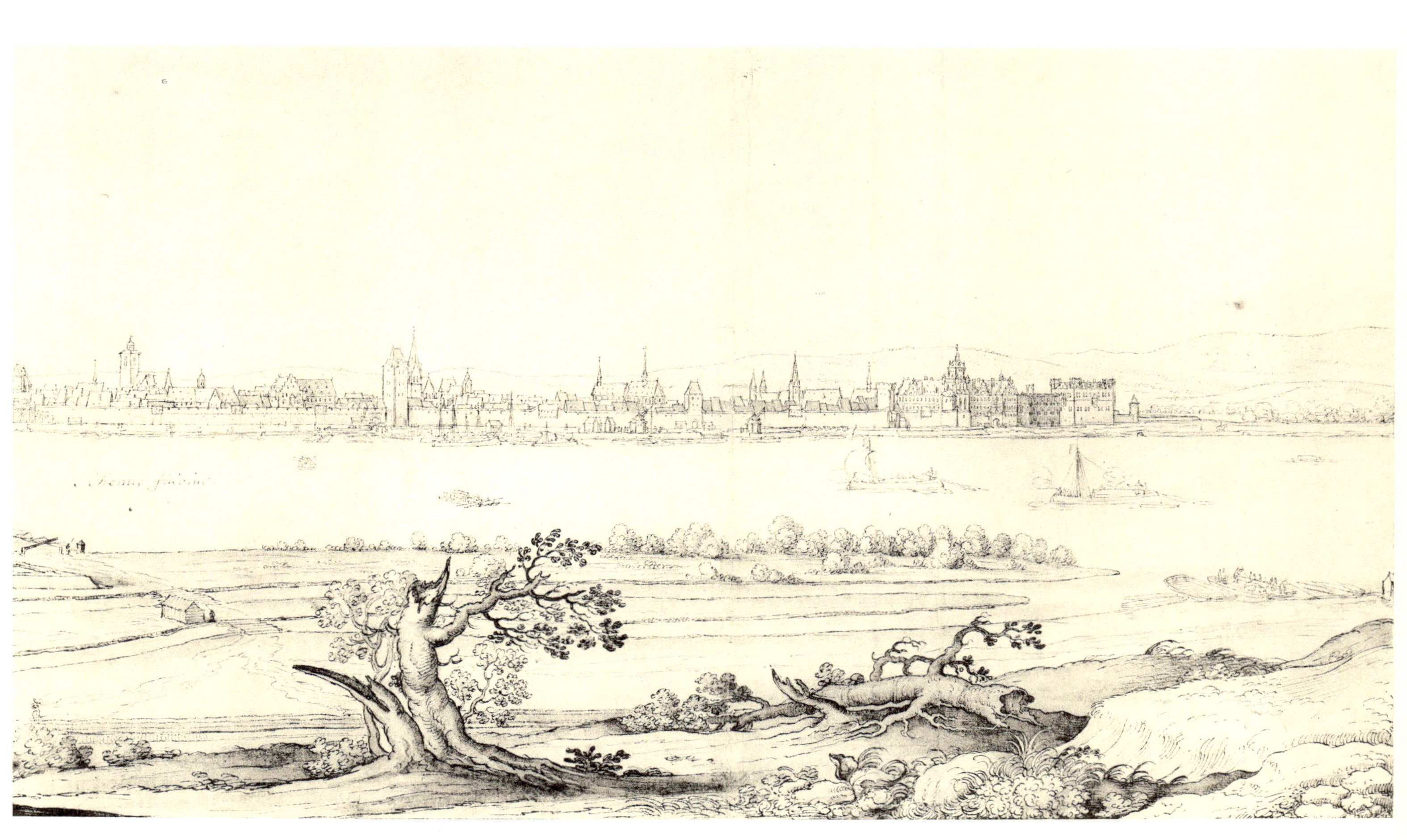

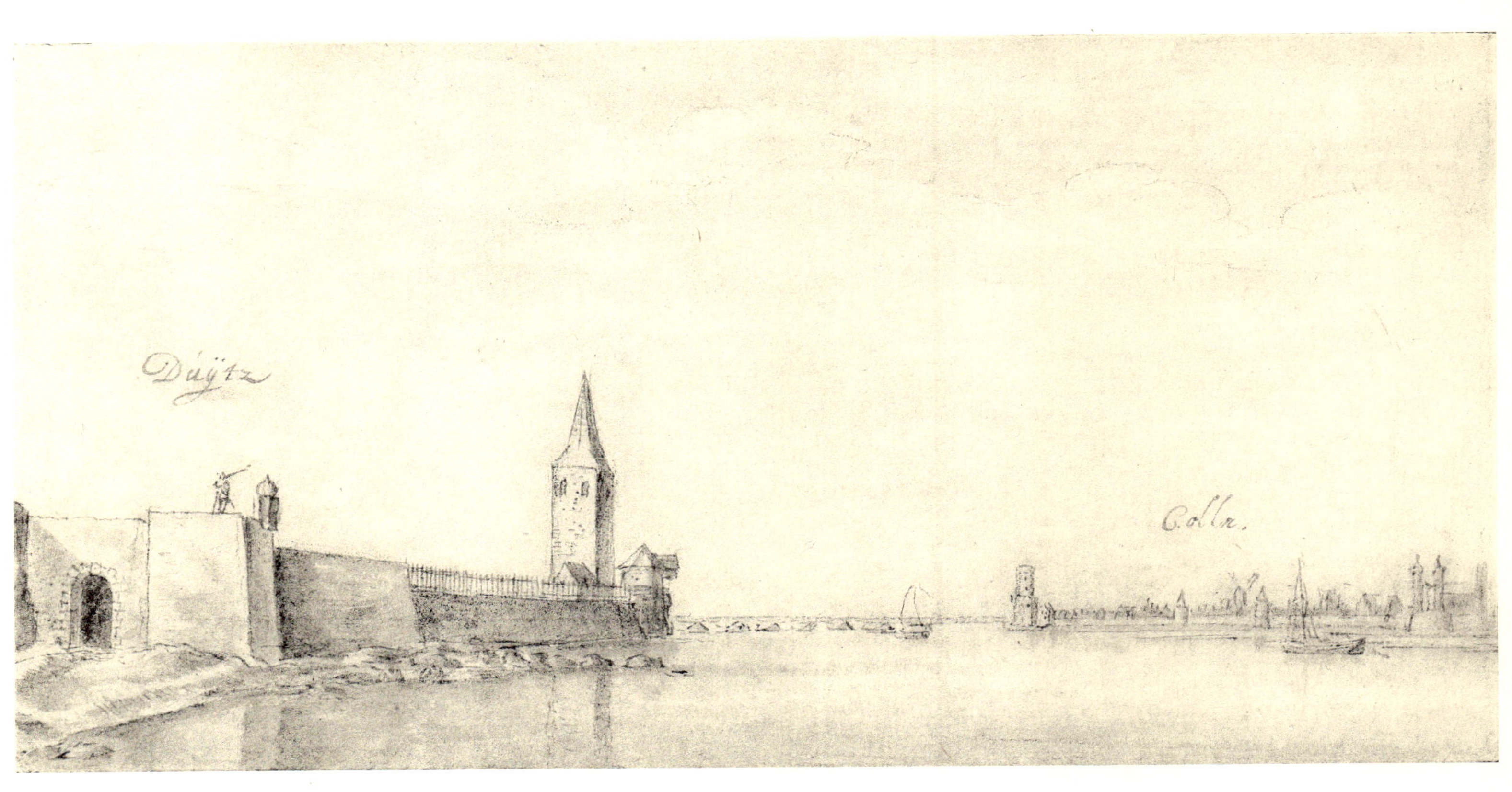

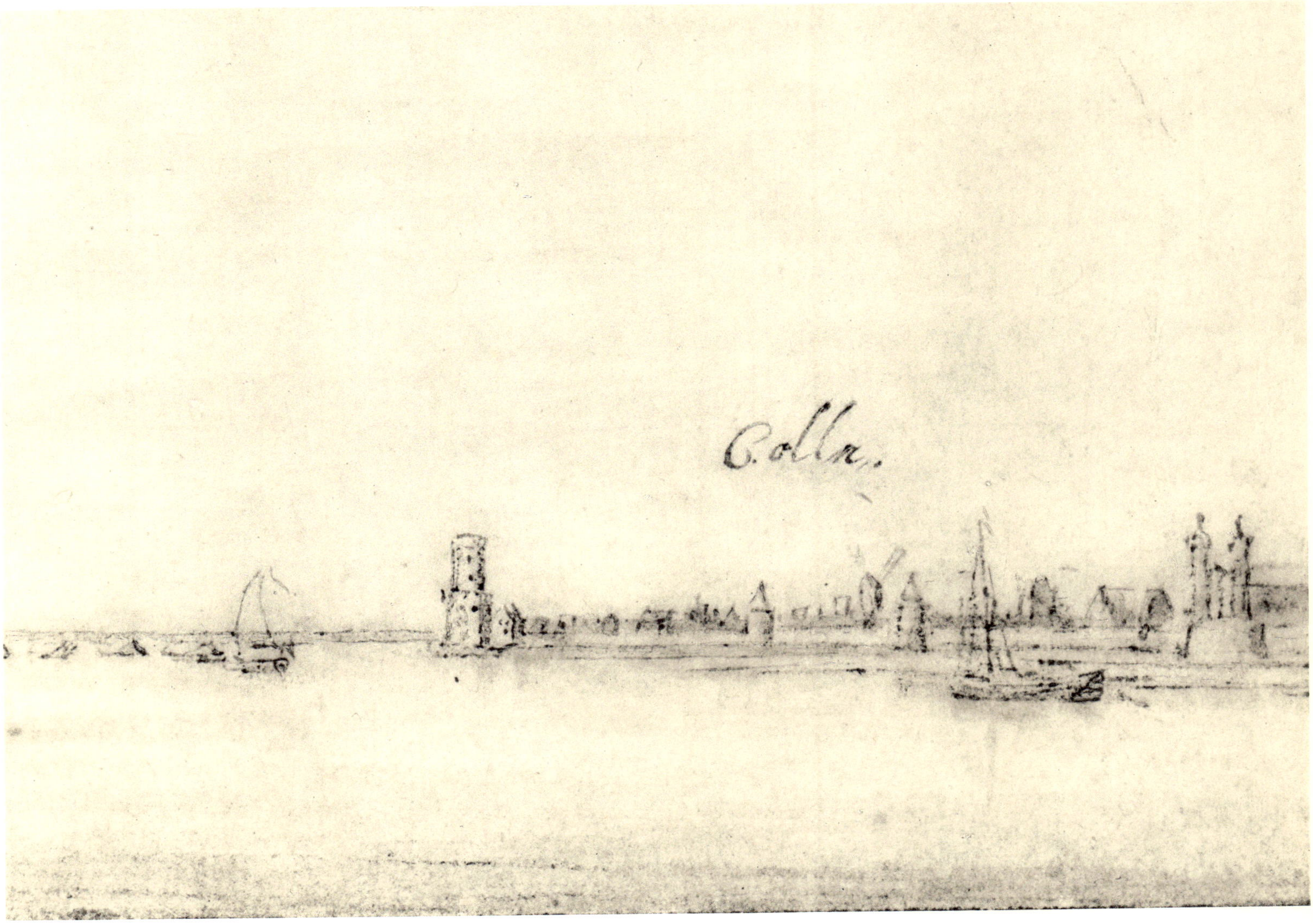

8/9

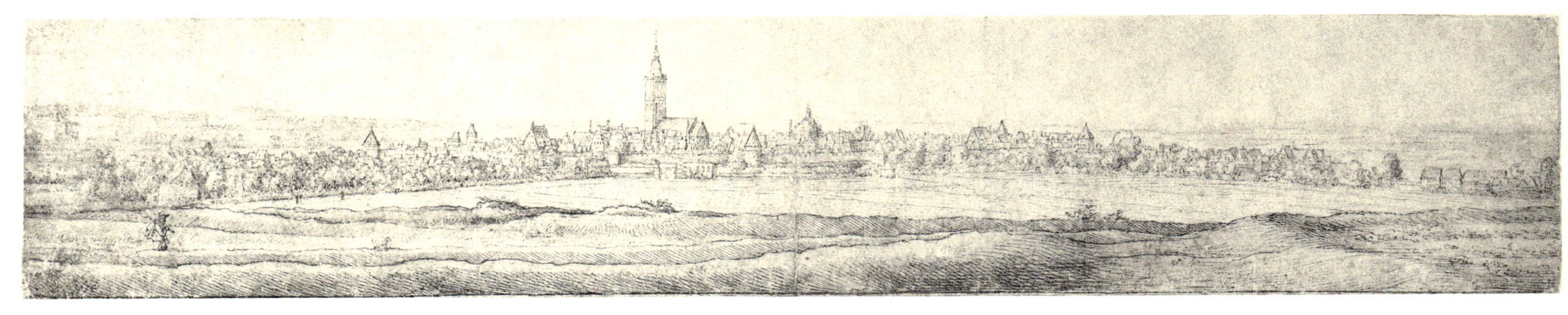

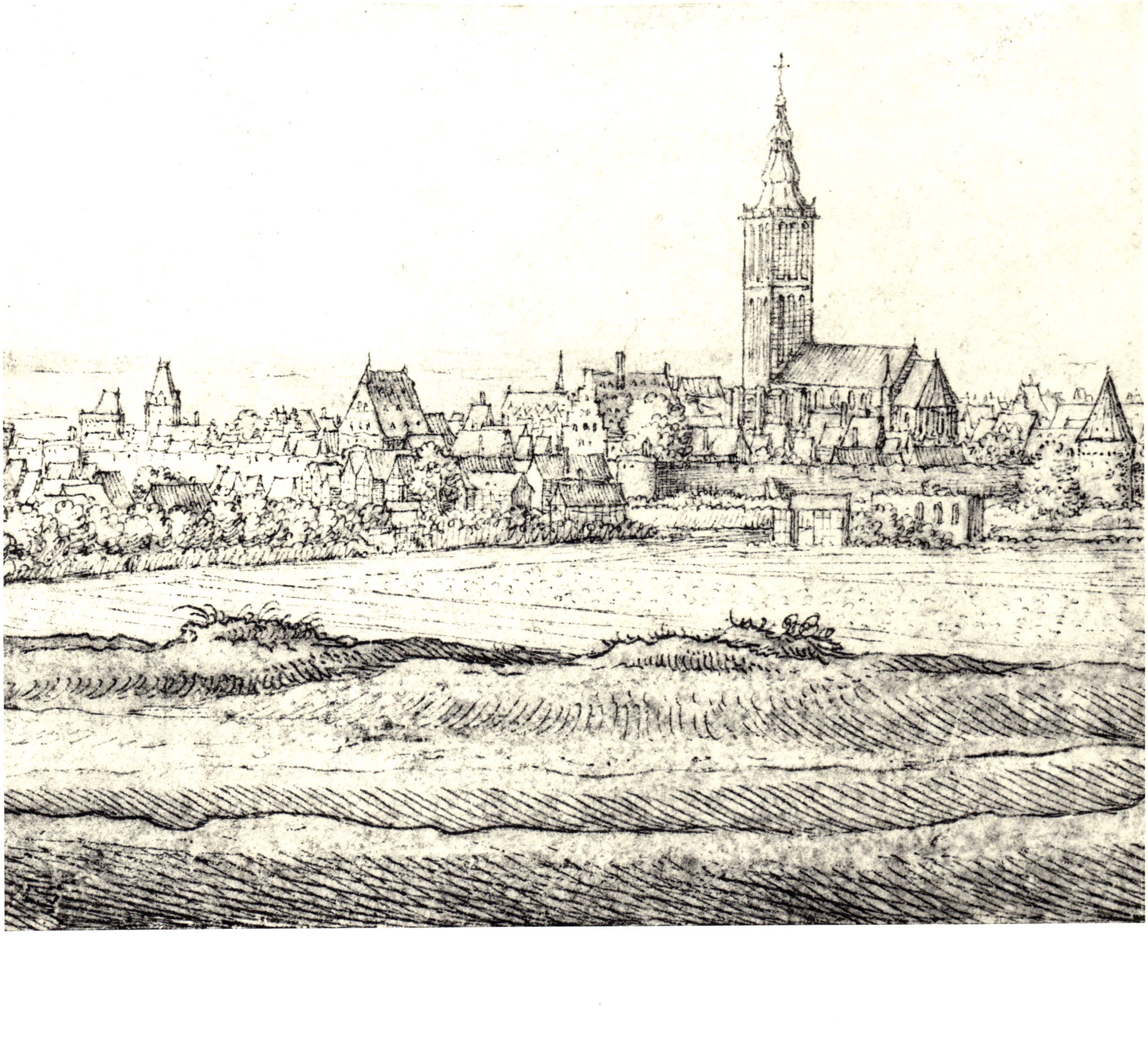

10/11

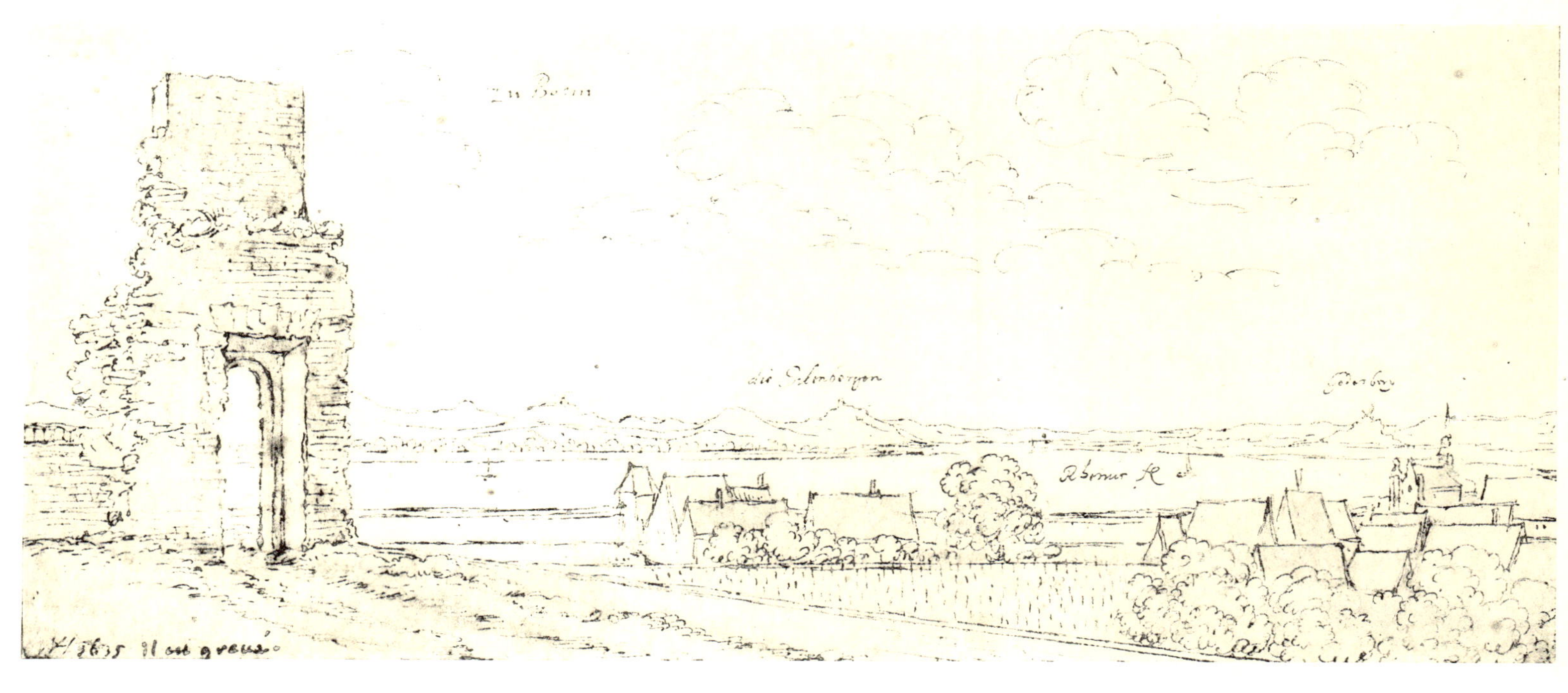

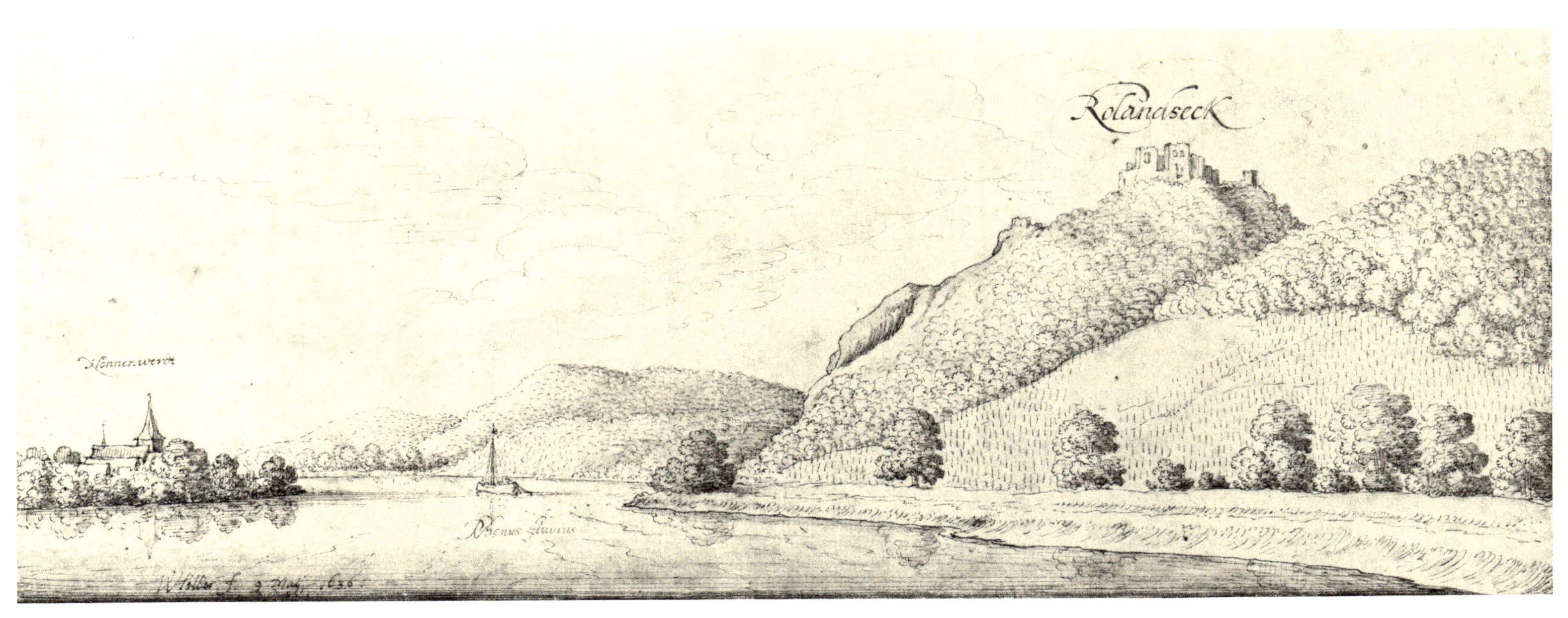

13/14

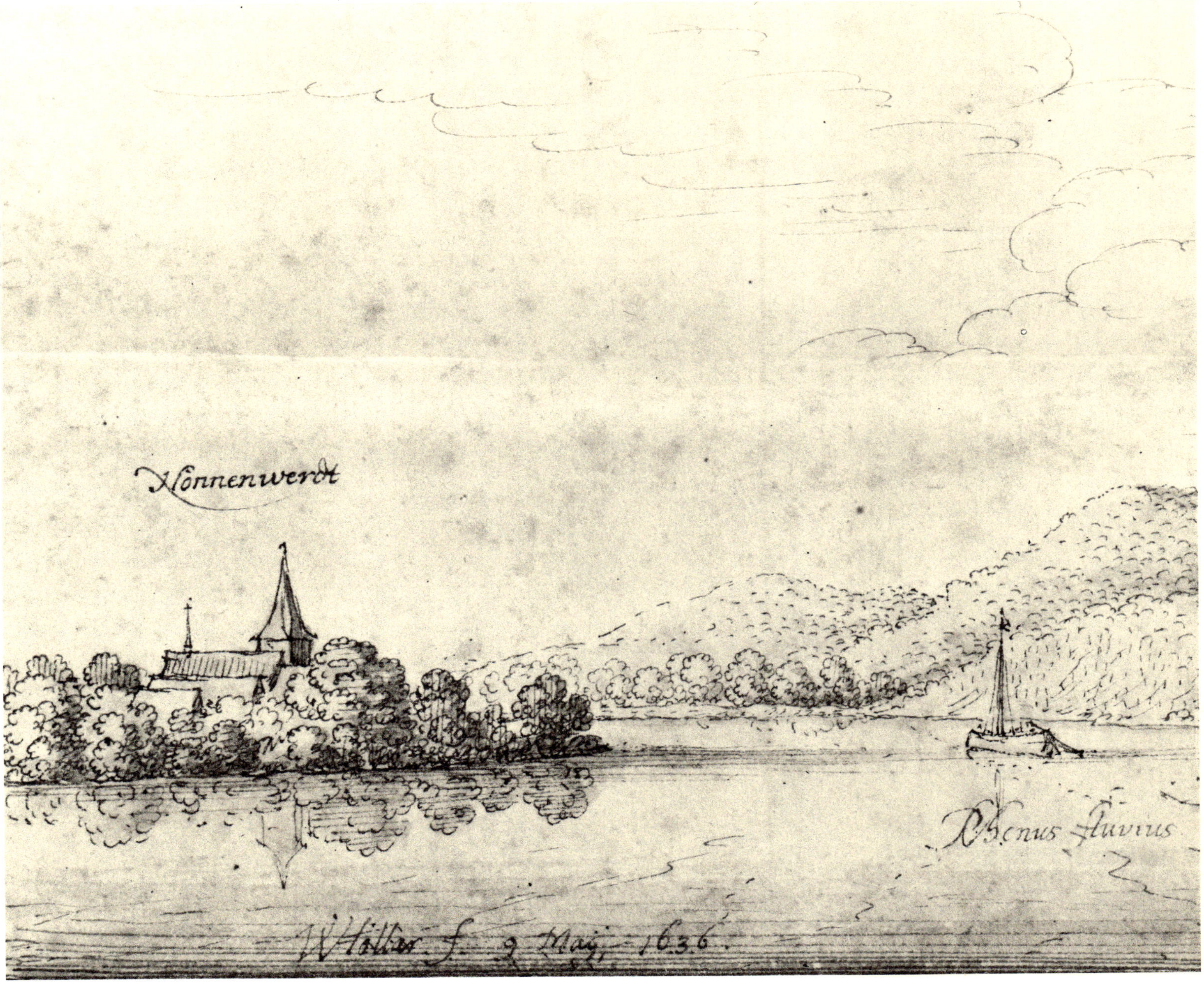

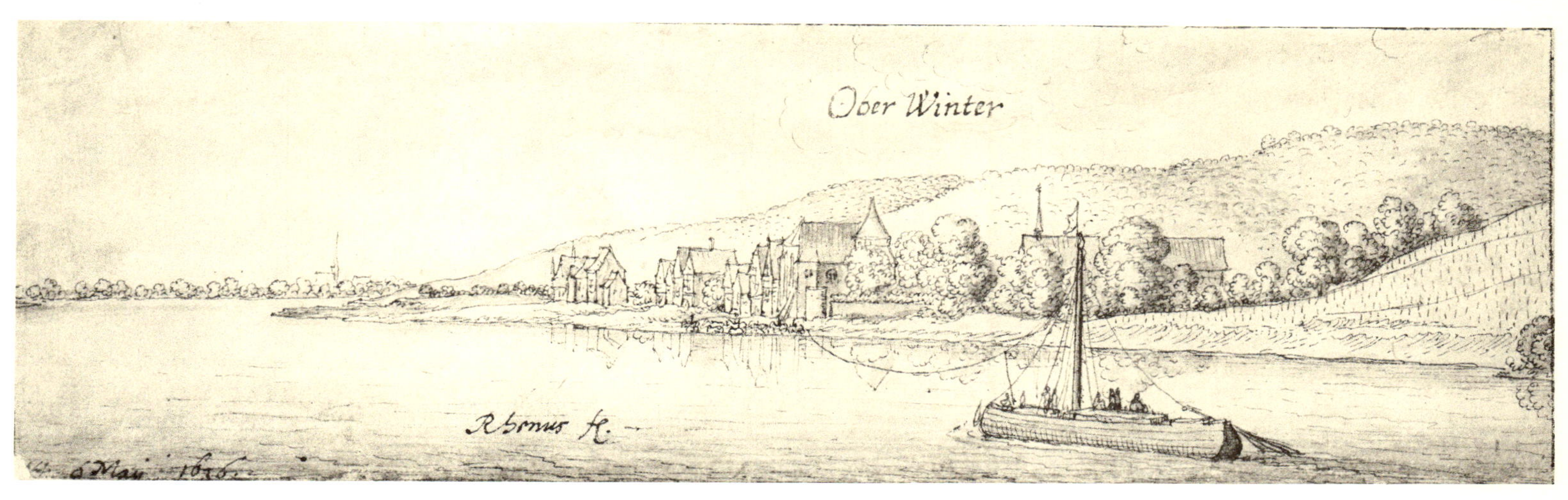

15/16

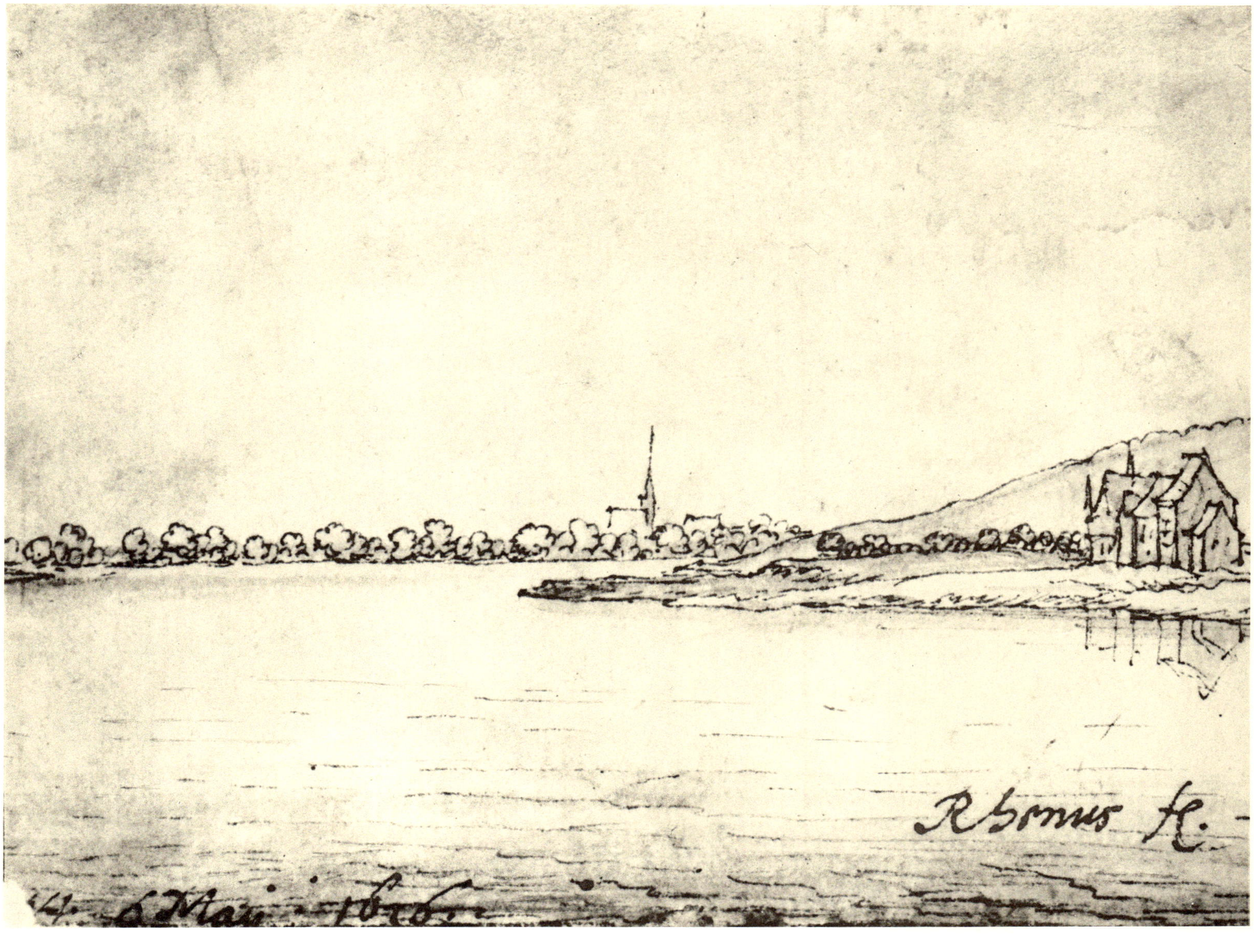

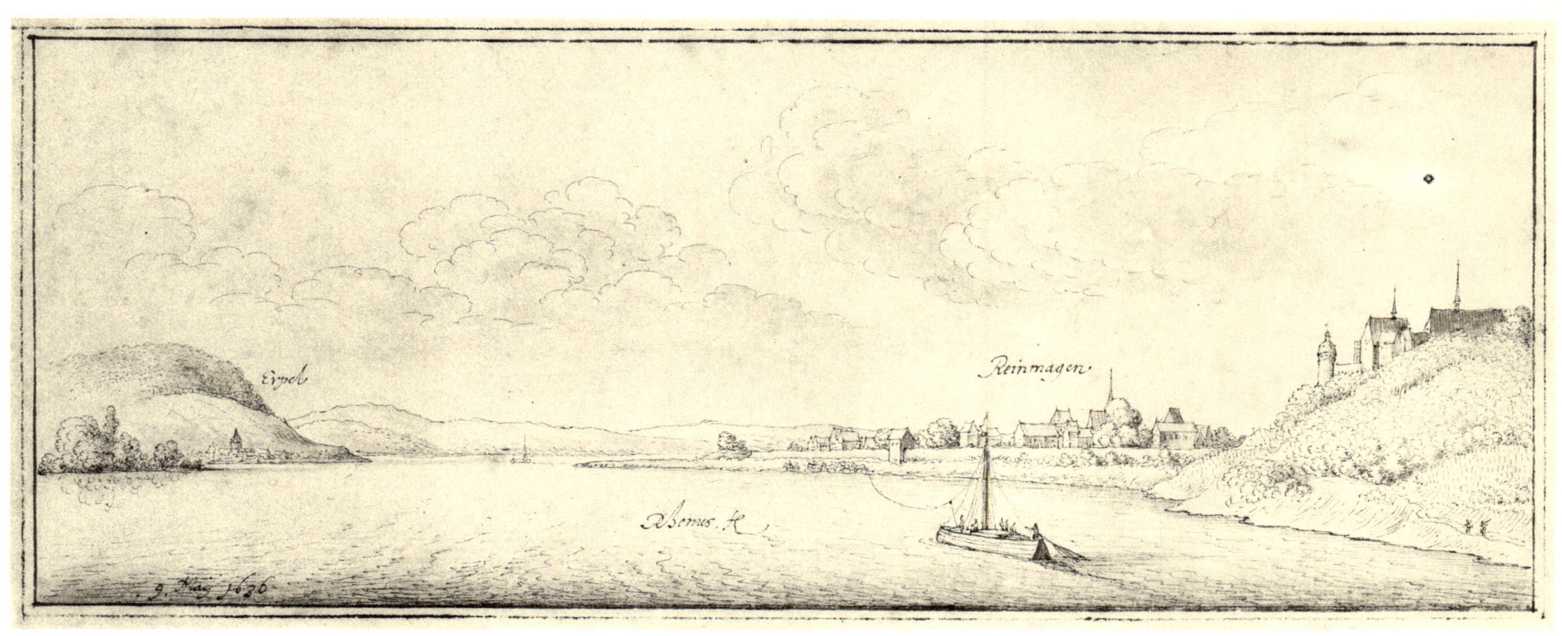
Erpel
Reinmagen

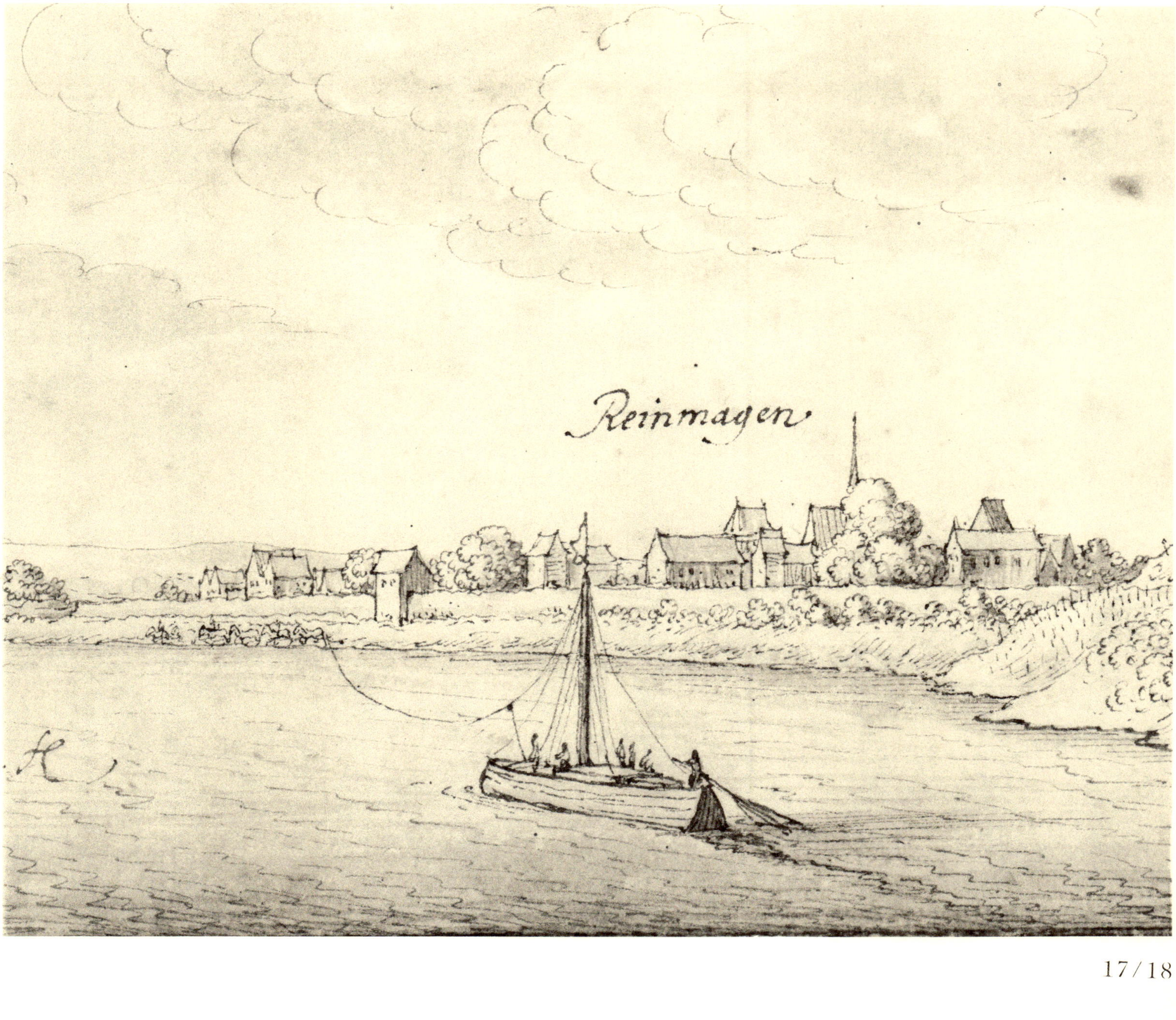

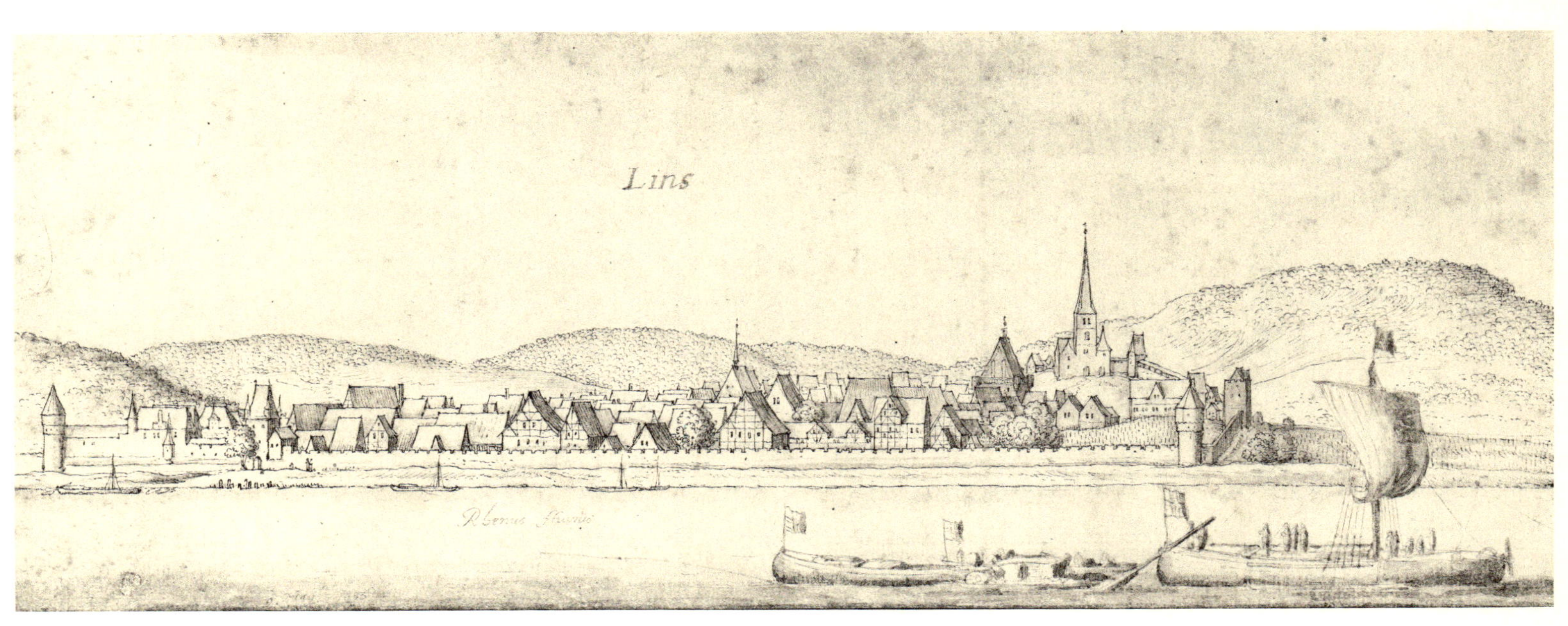

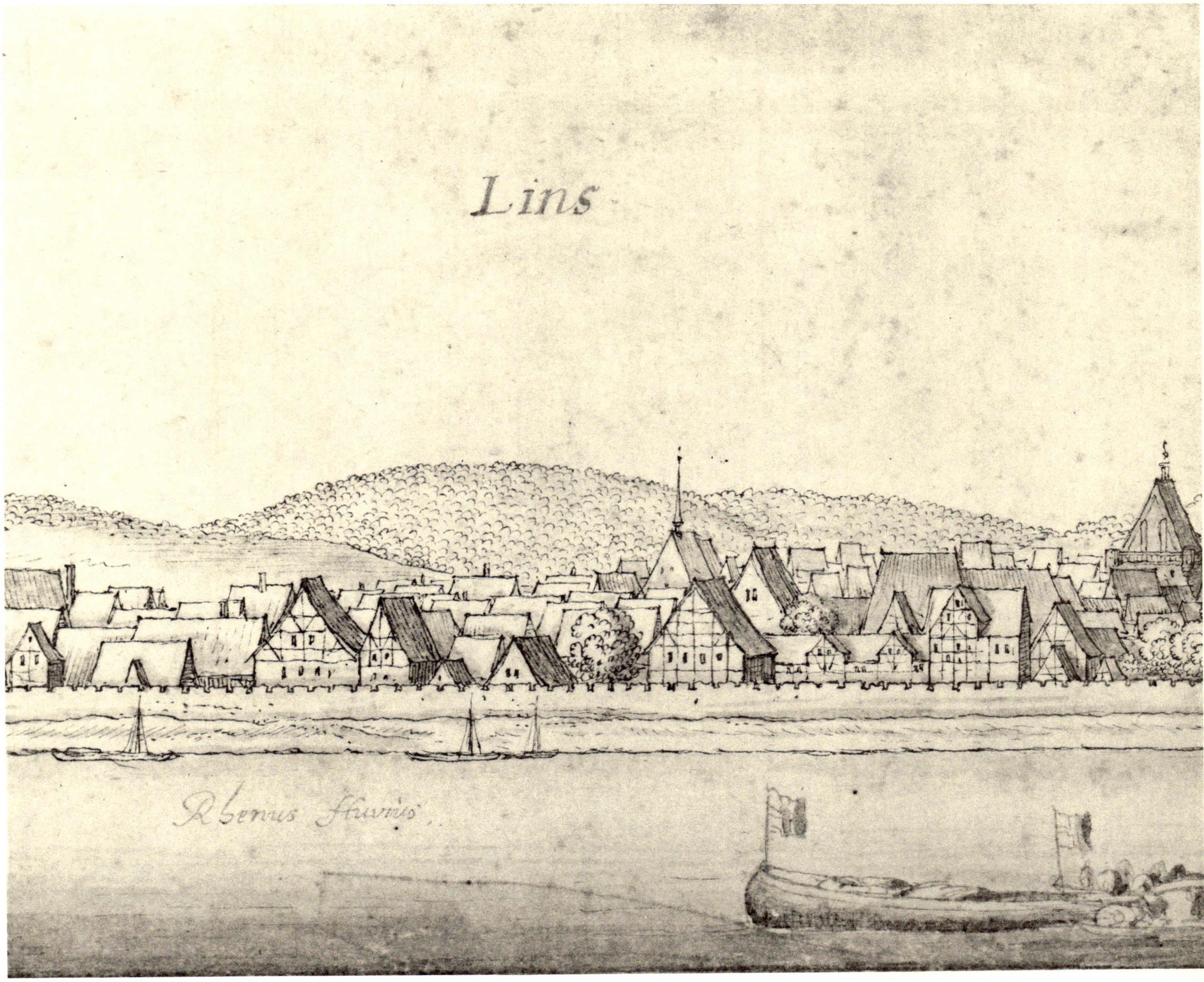

Lins

Rhenus fluvius

19/20

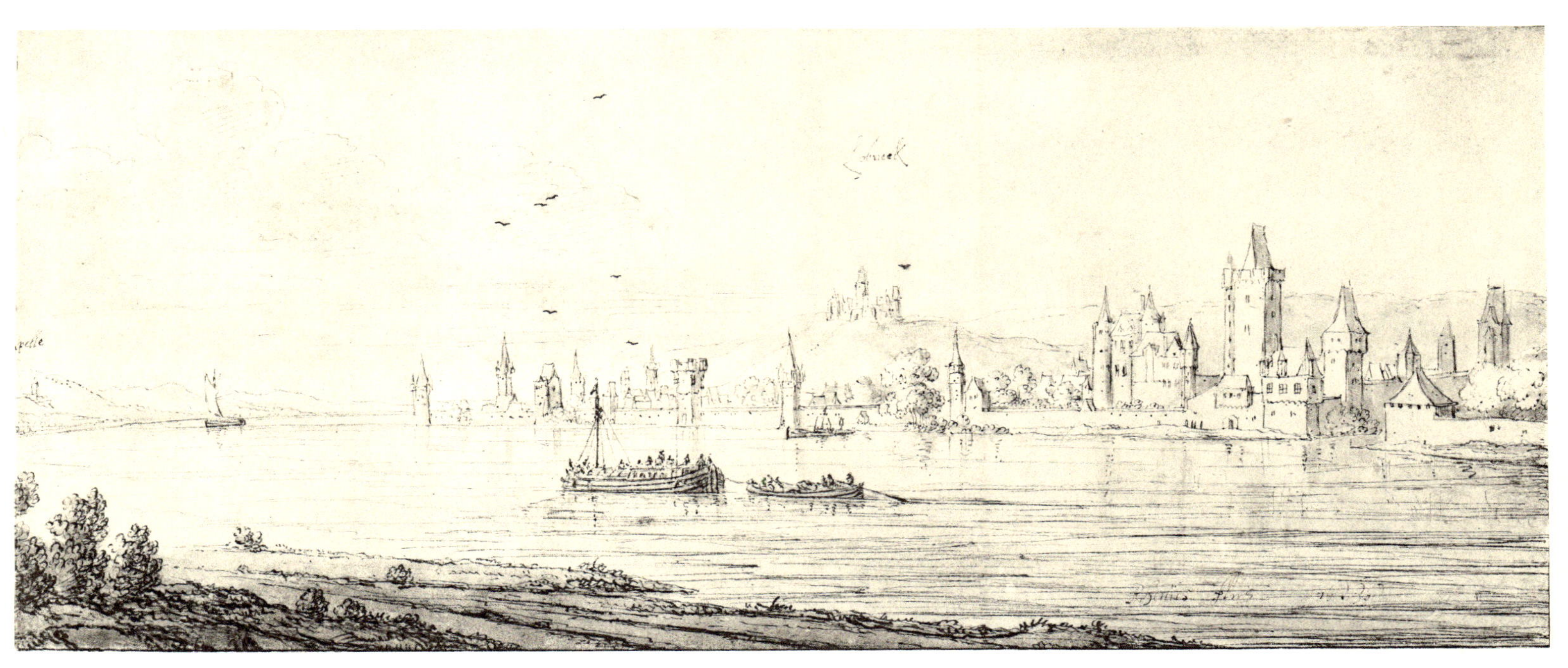

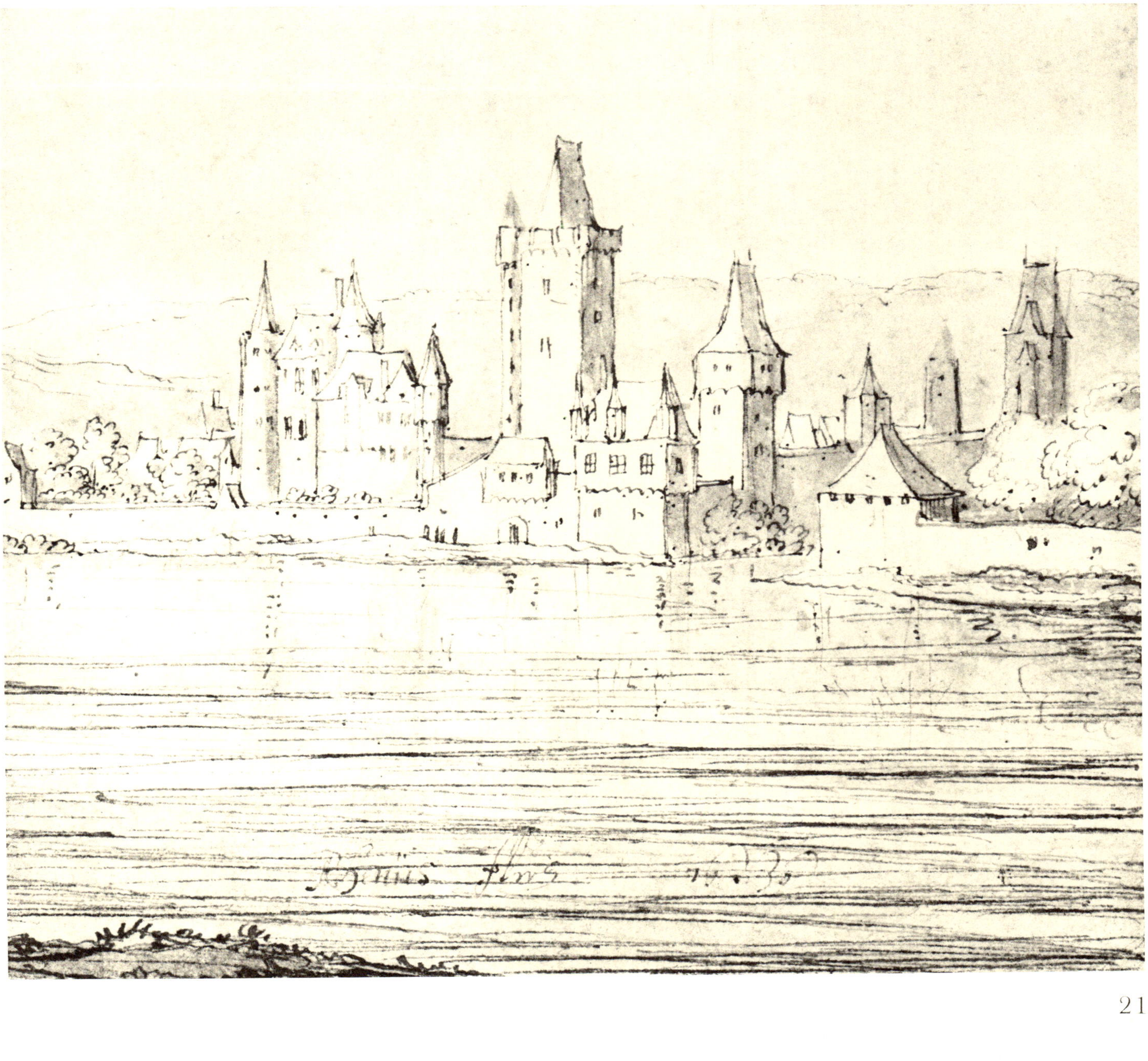

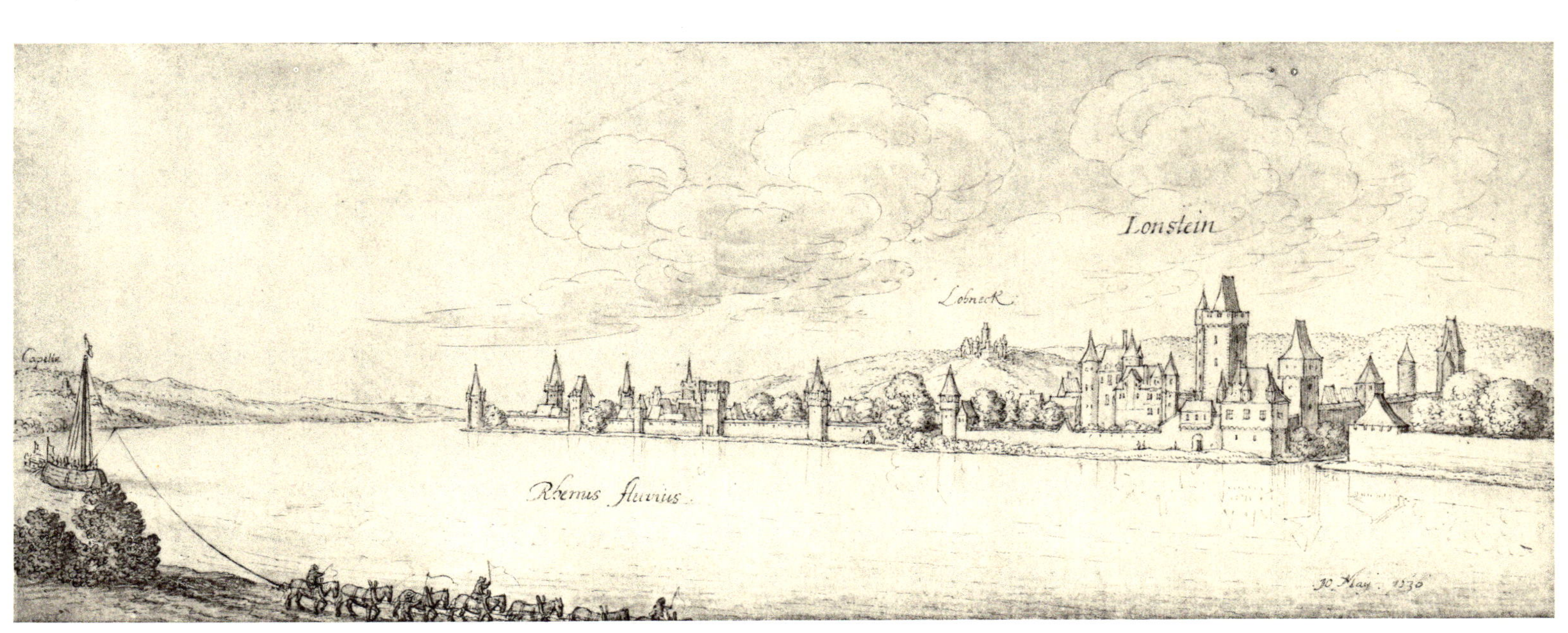

23/24

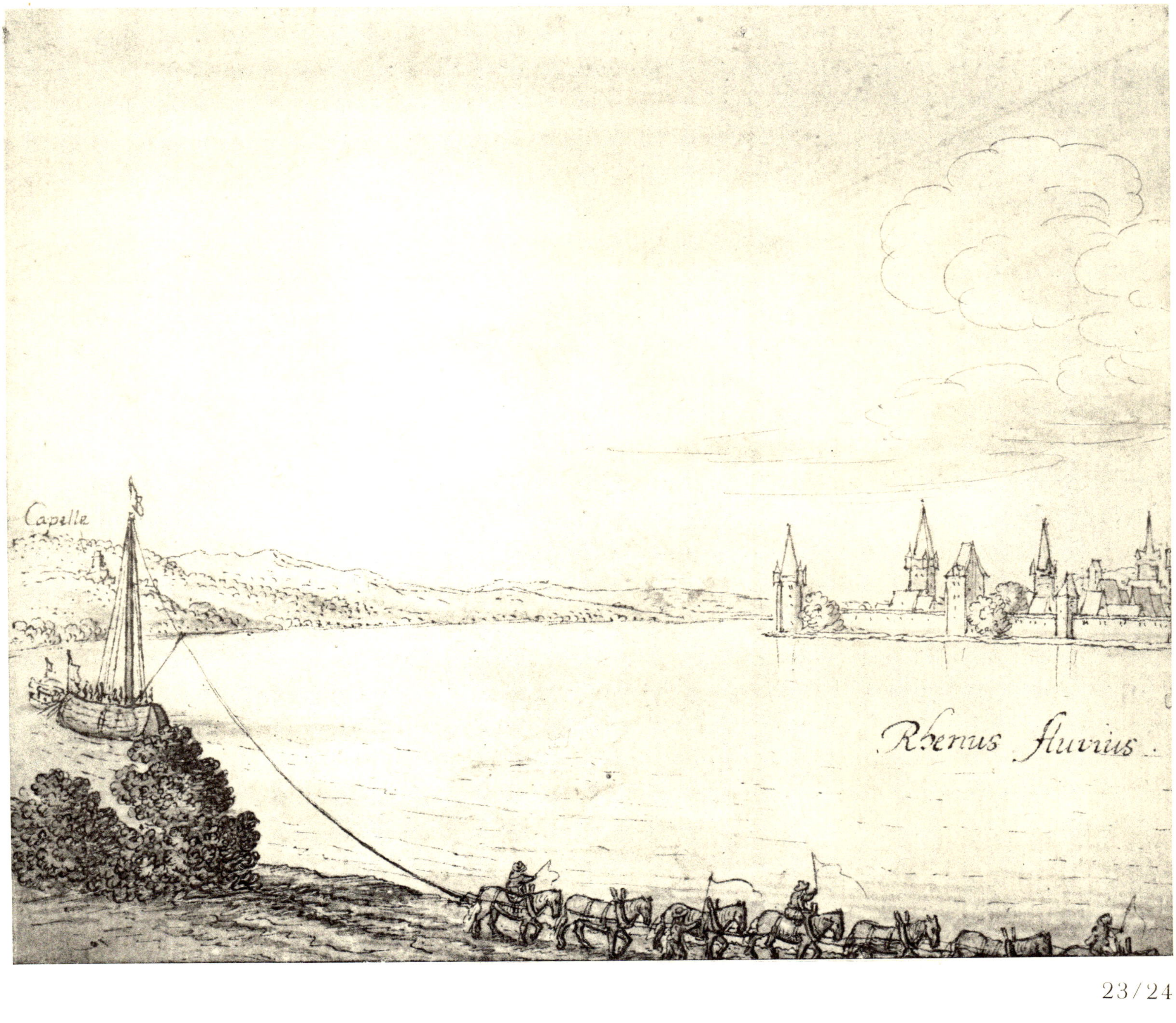

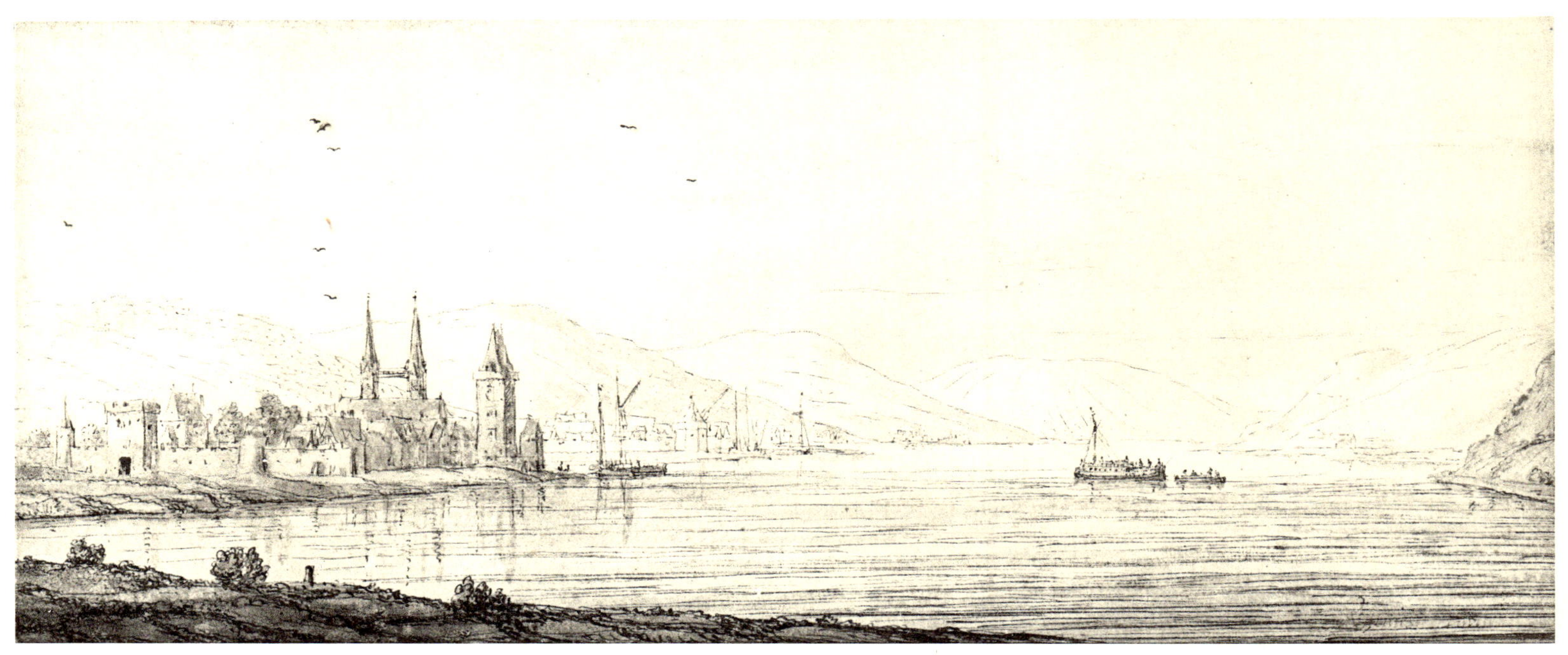

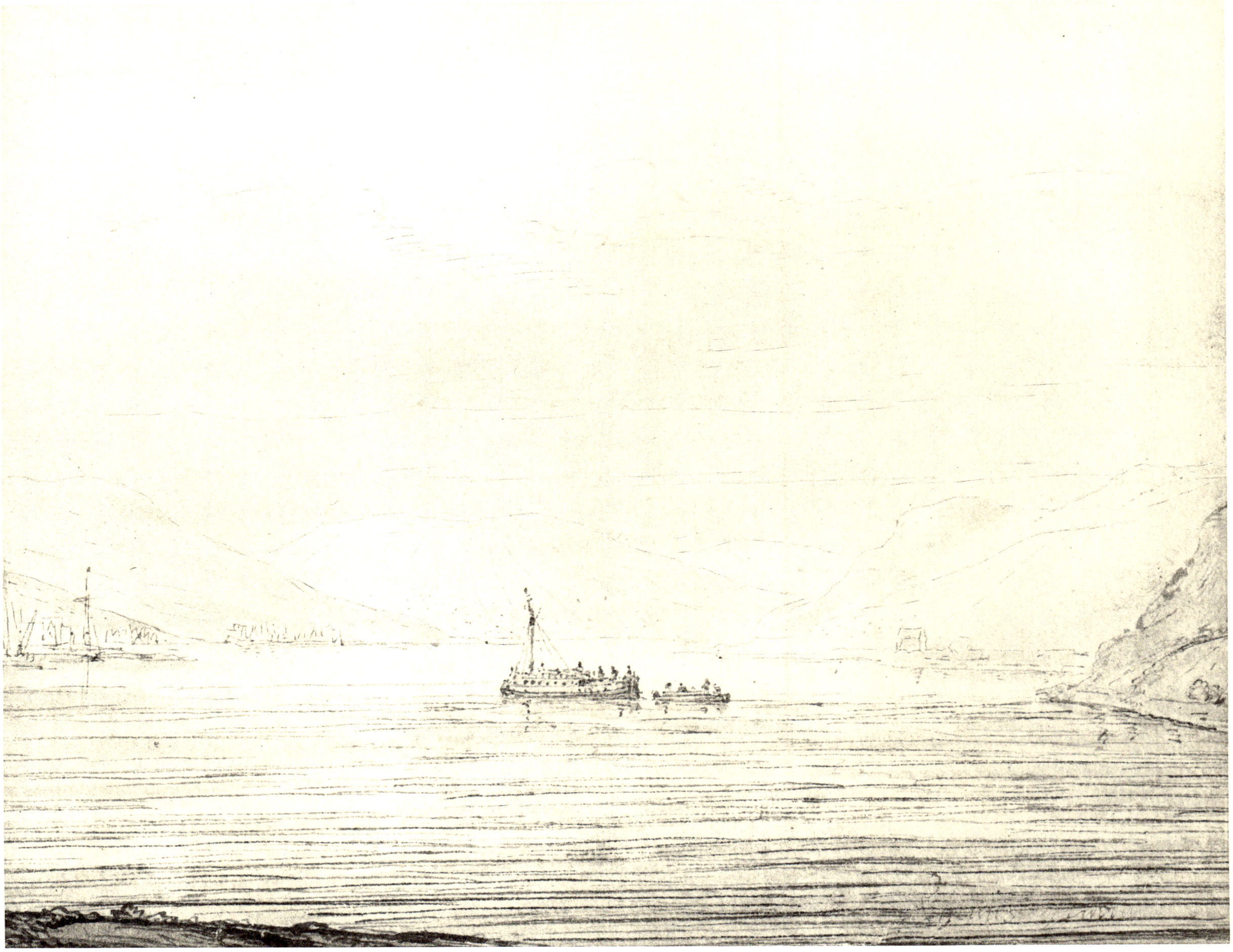

25/26

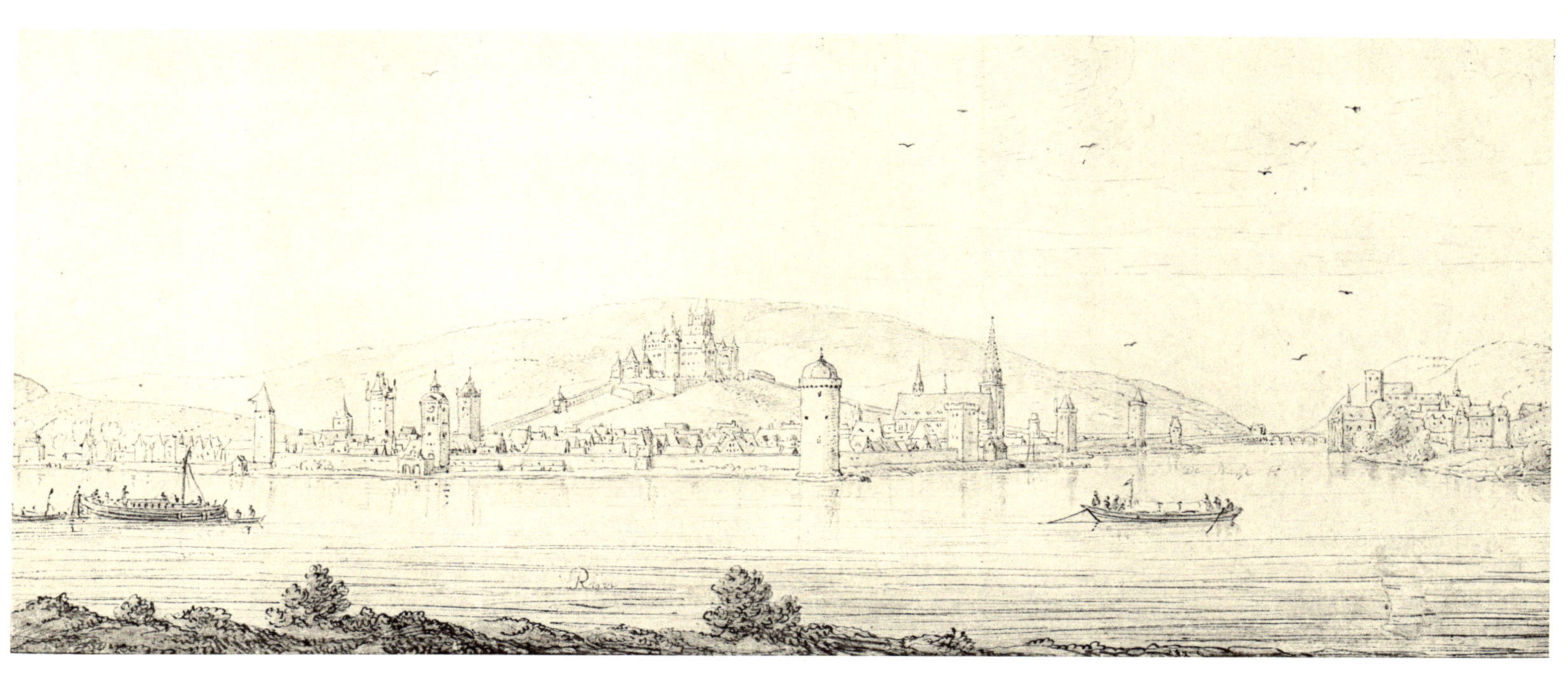

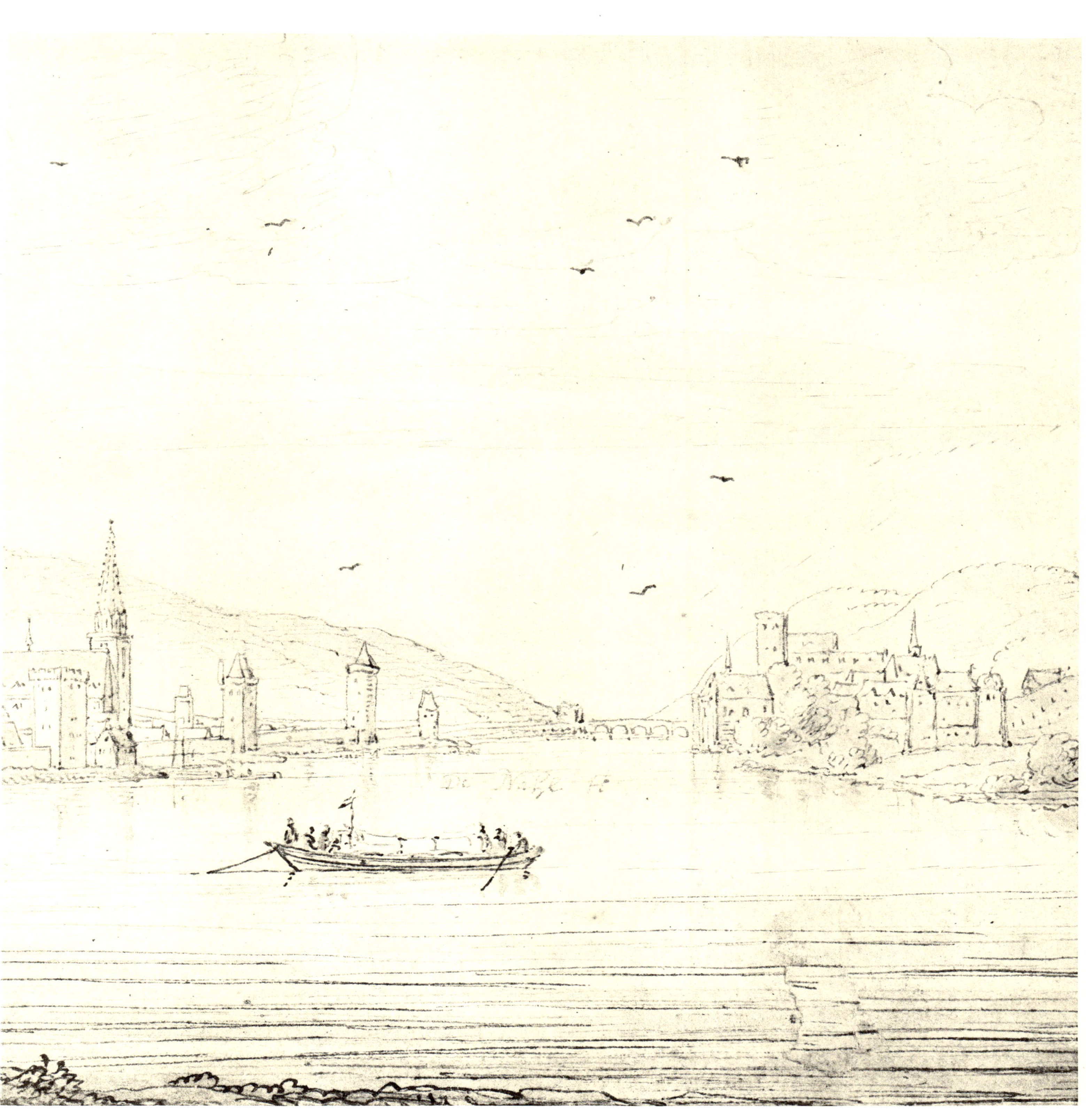

28

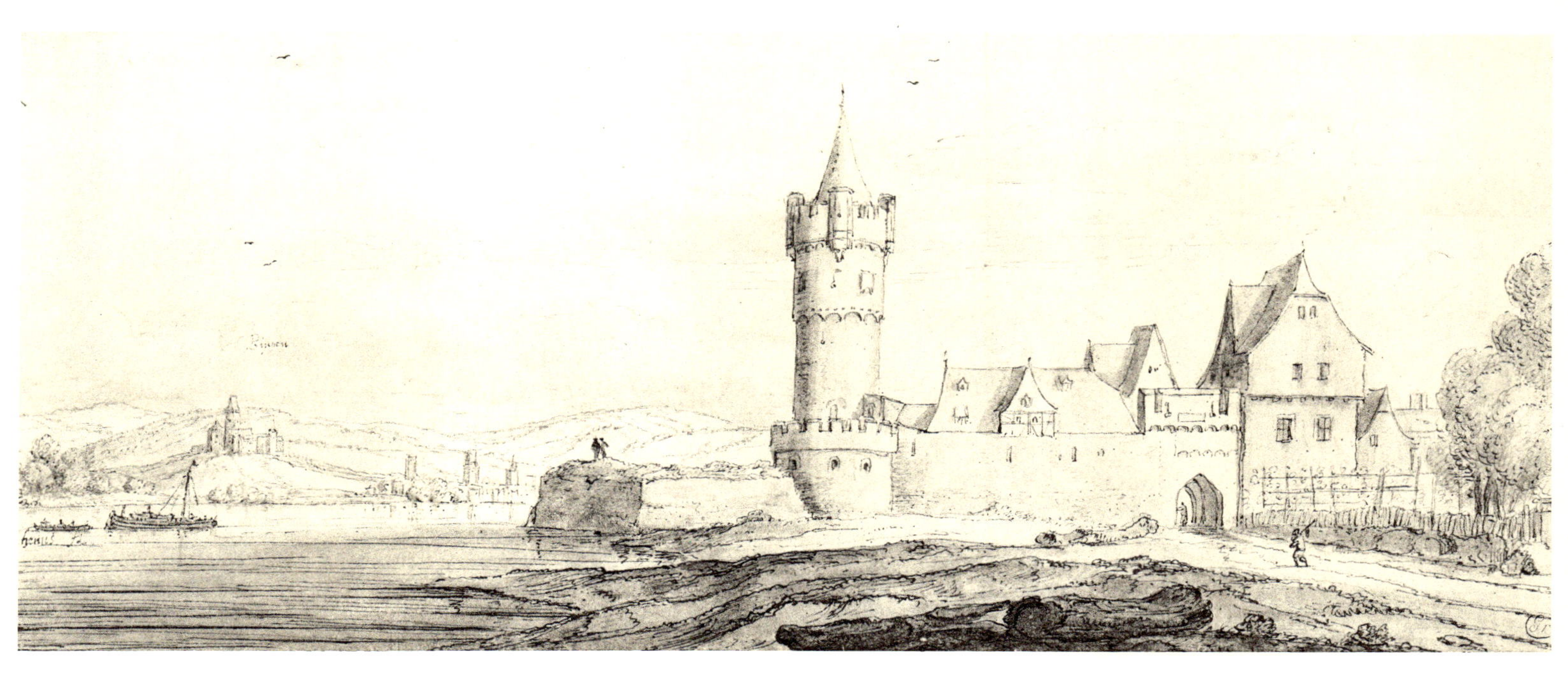

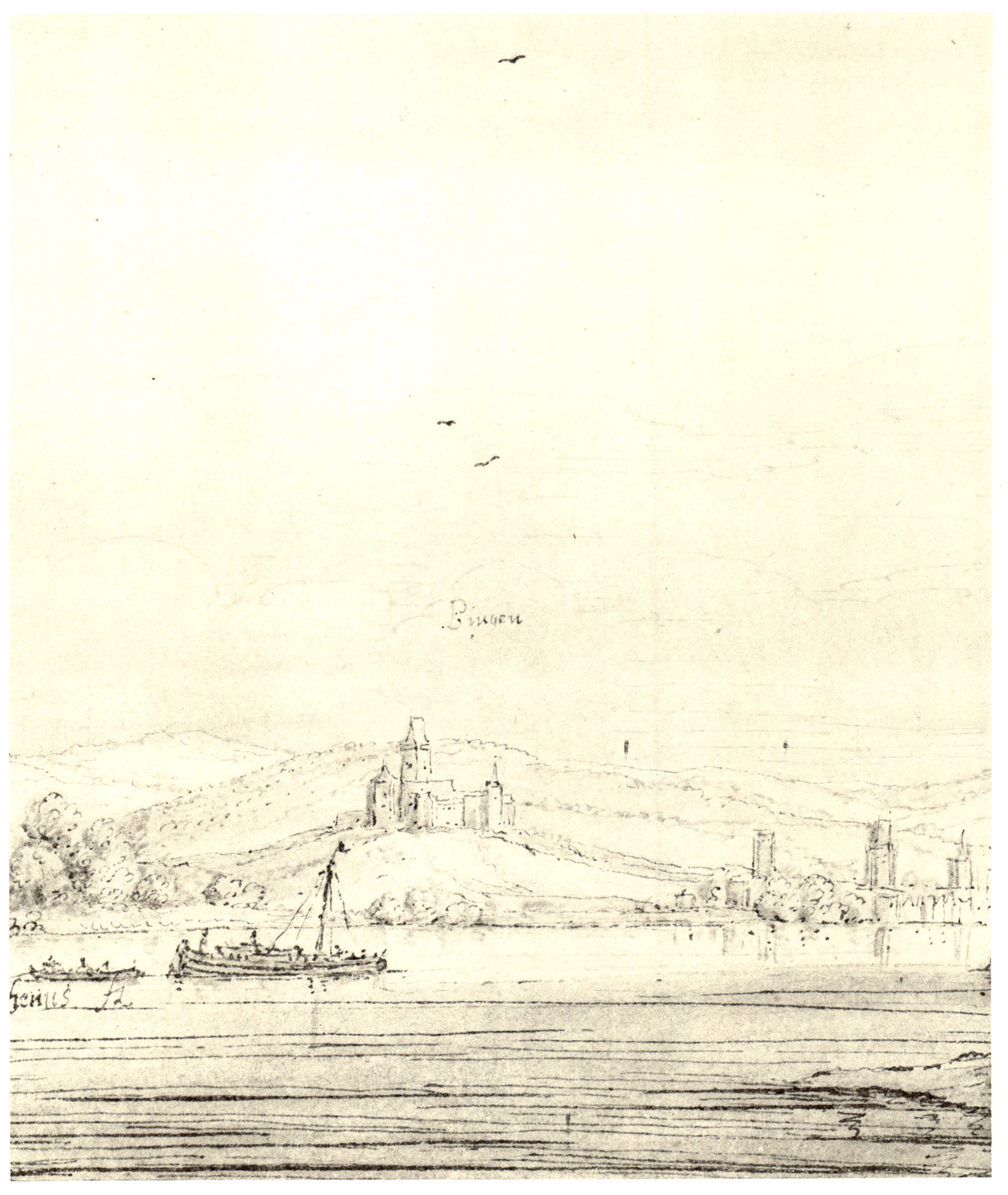
Bingen

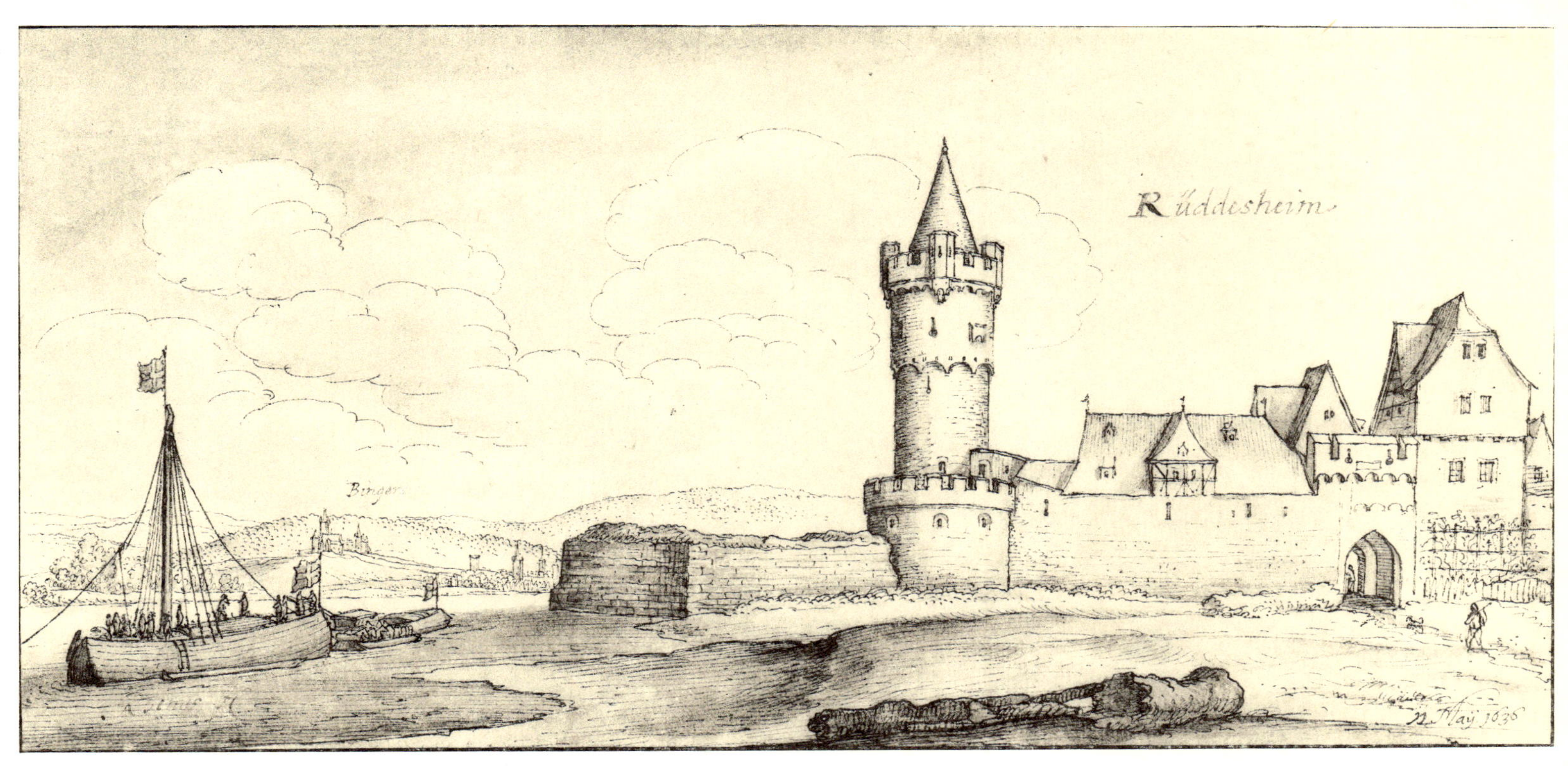
Rüddesheim
Bingen
12 Maij 1636

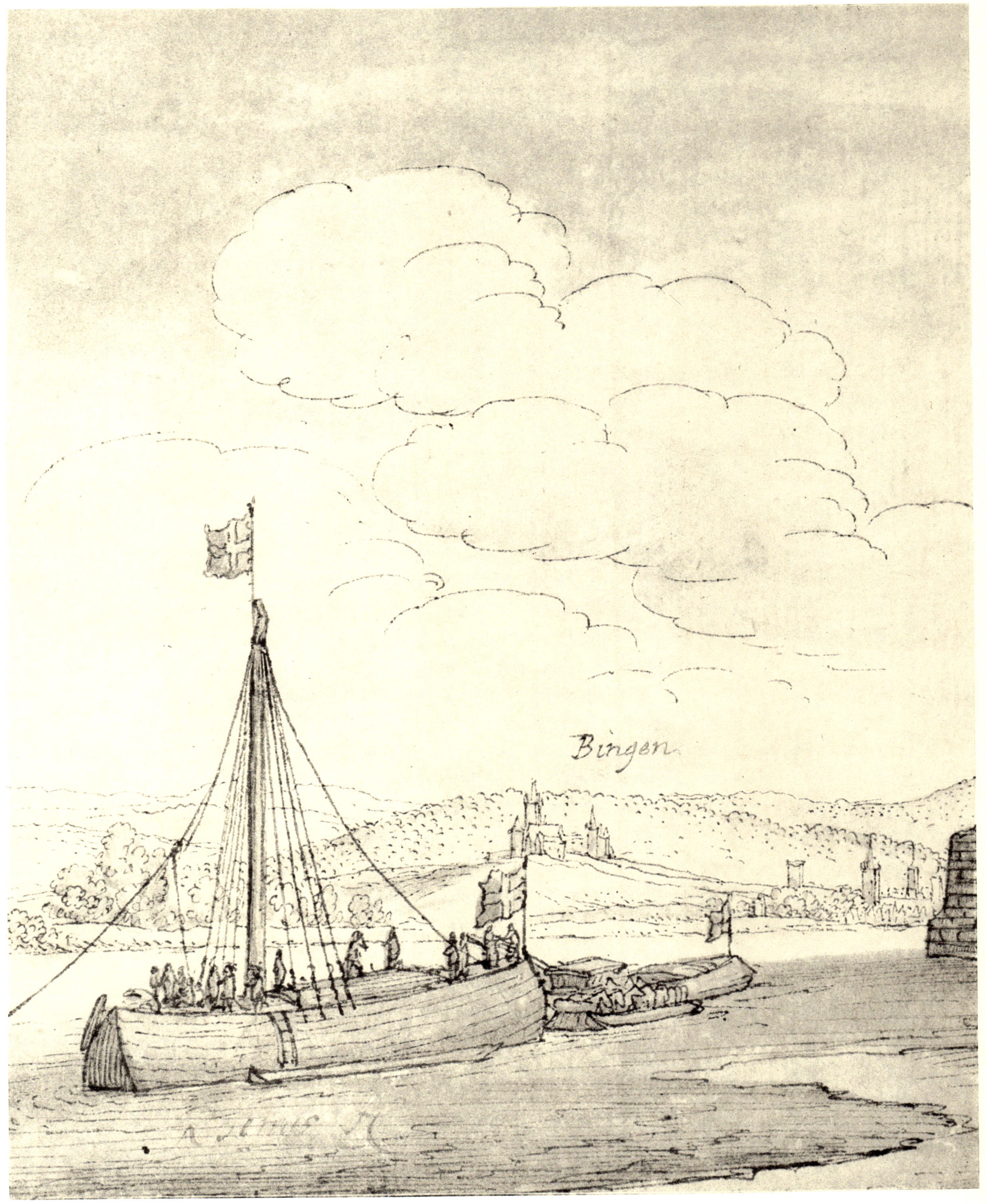
Bingen

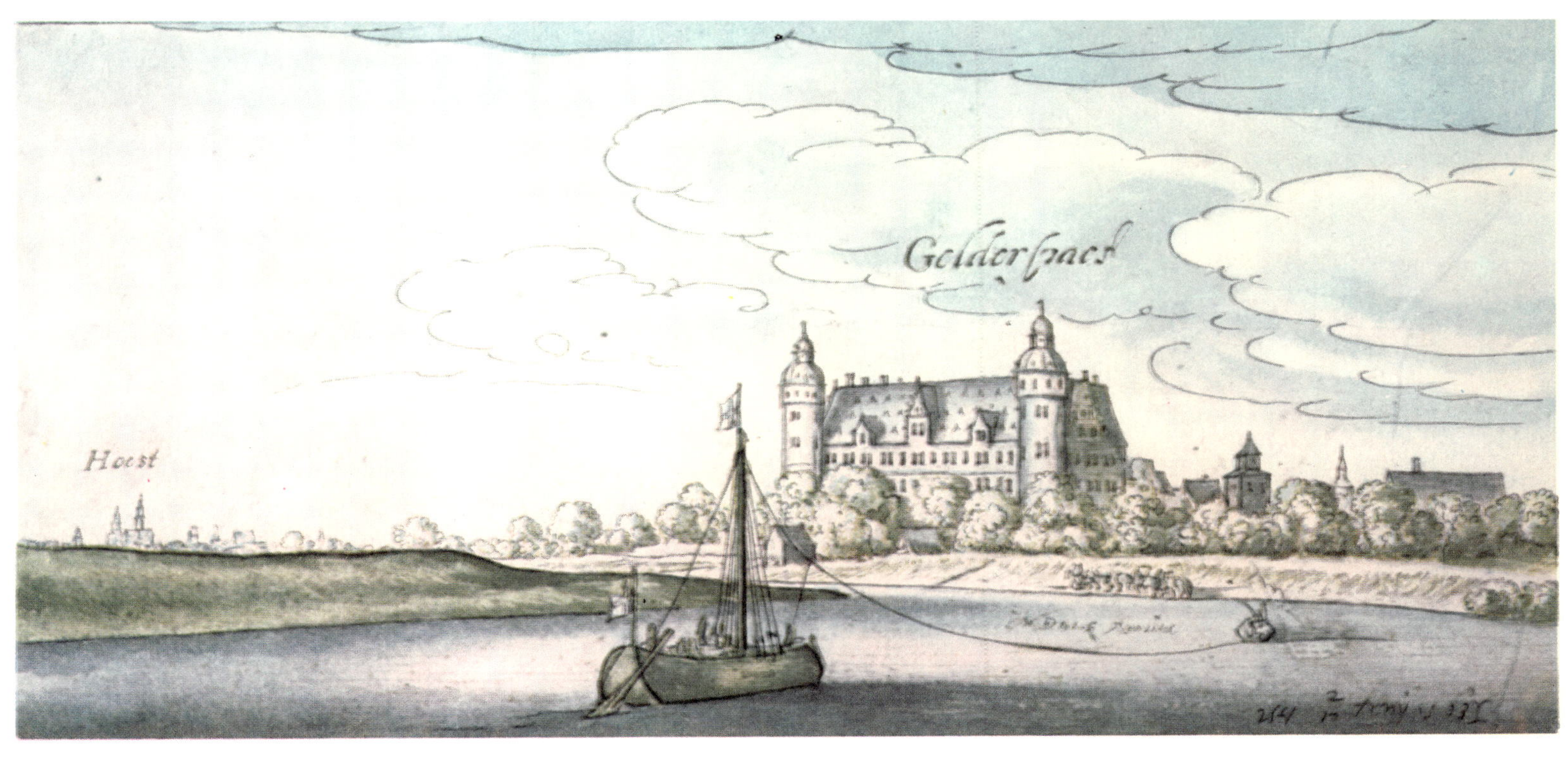
Hoest

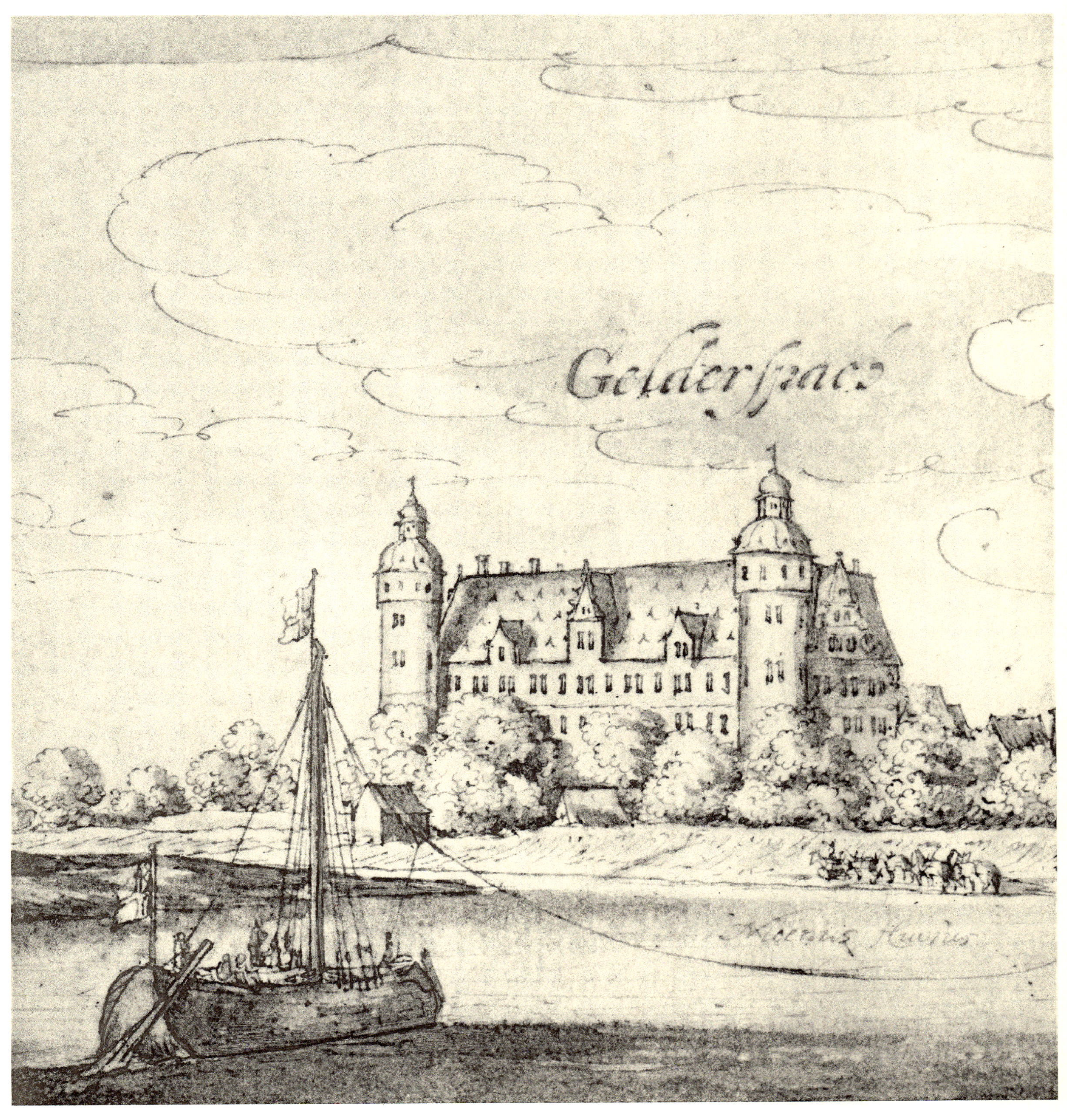

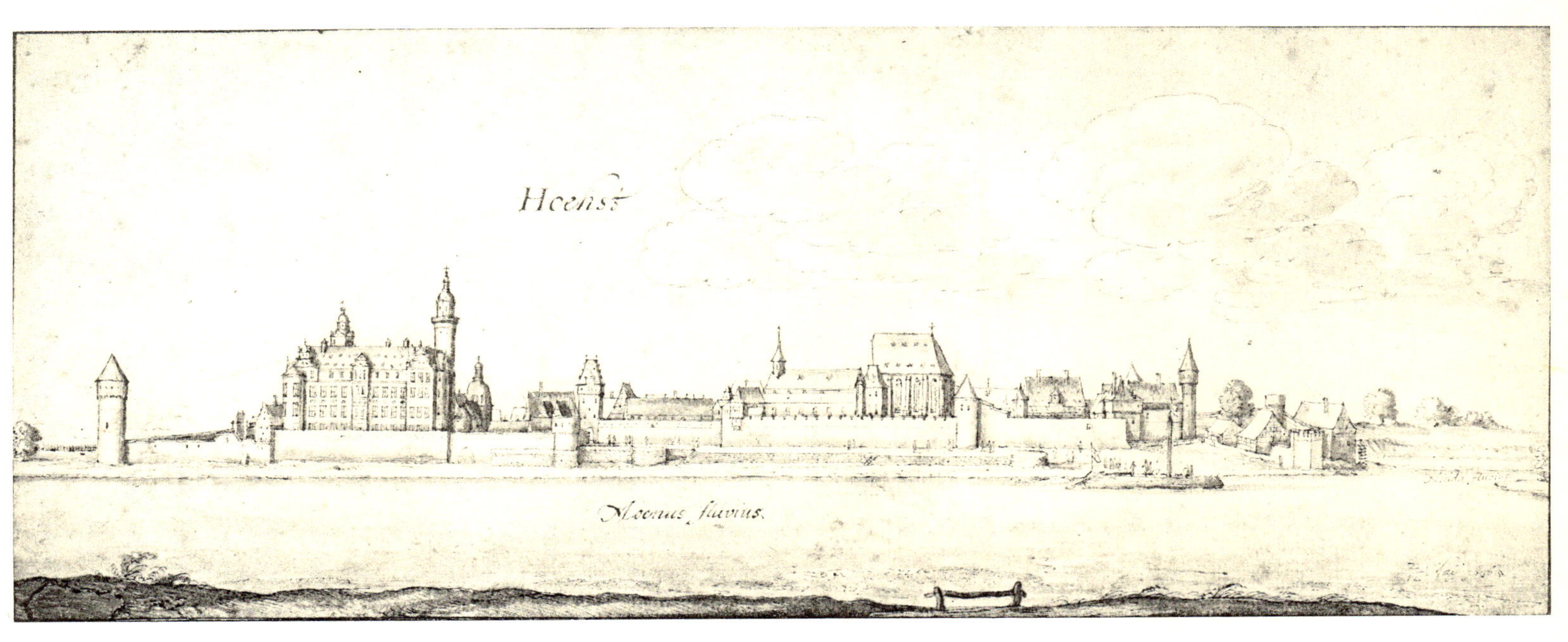

Hoenst
Moenus fluvius

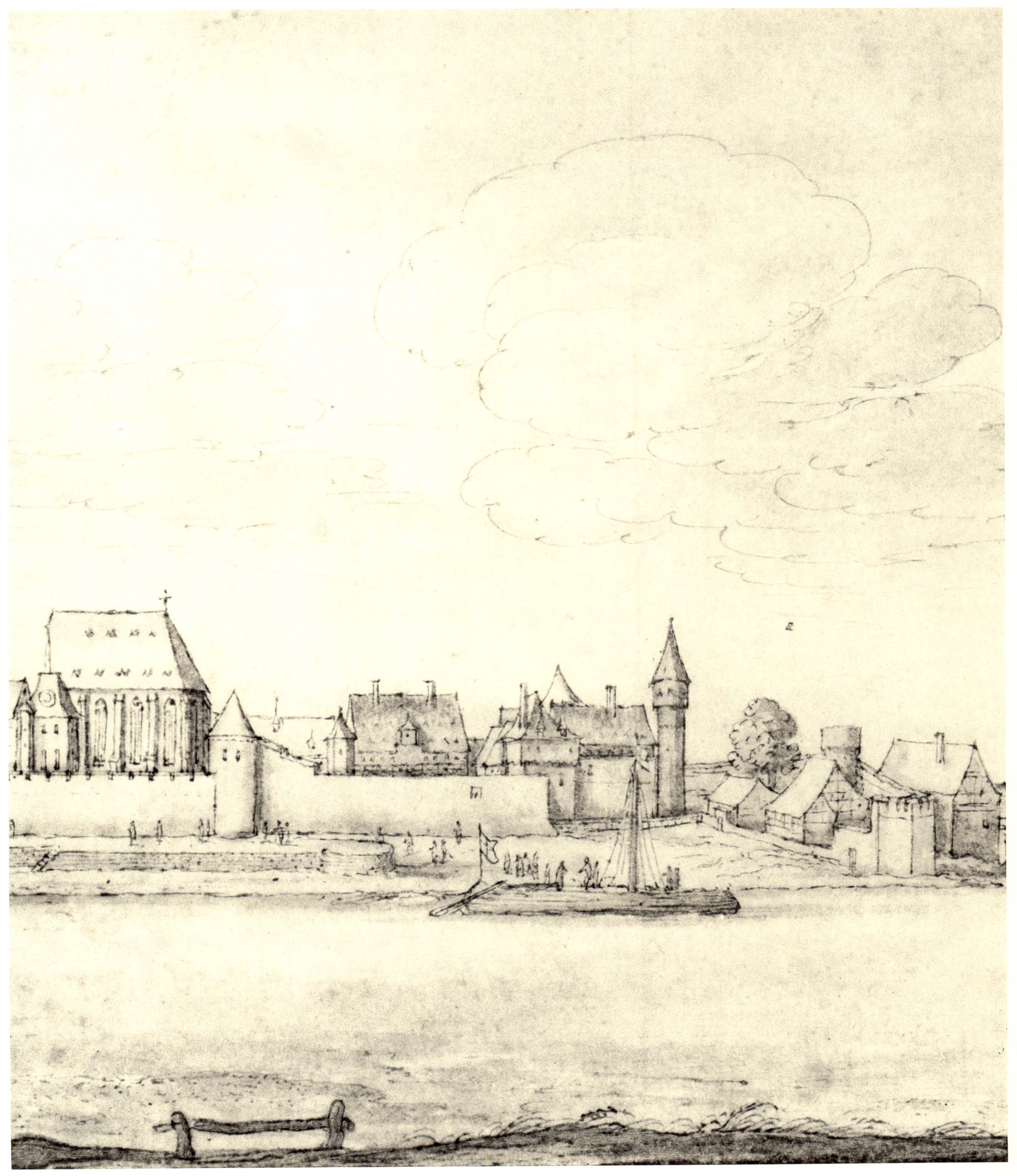

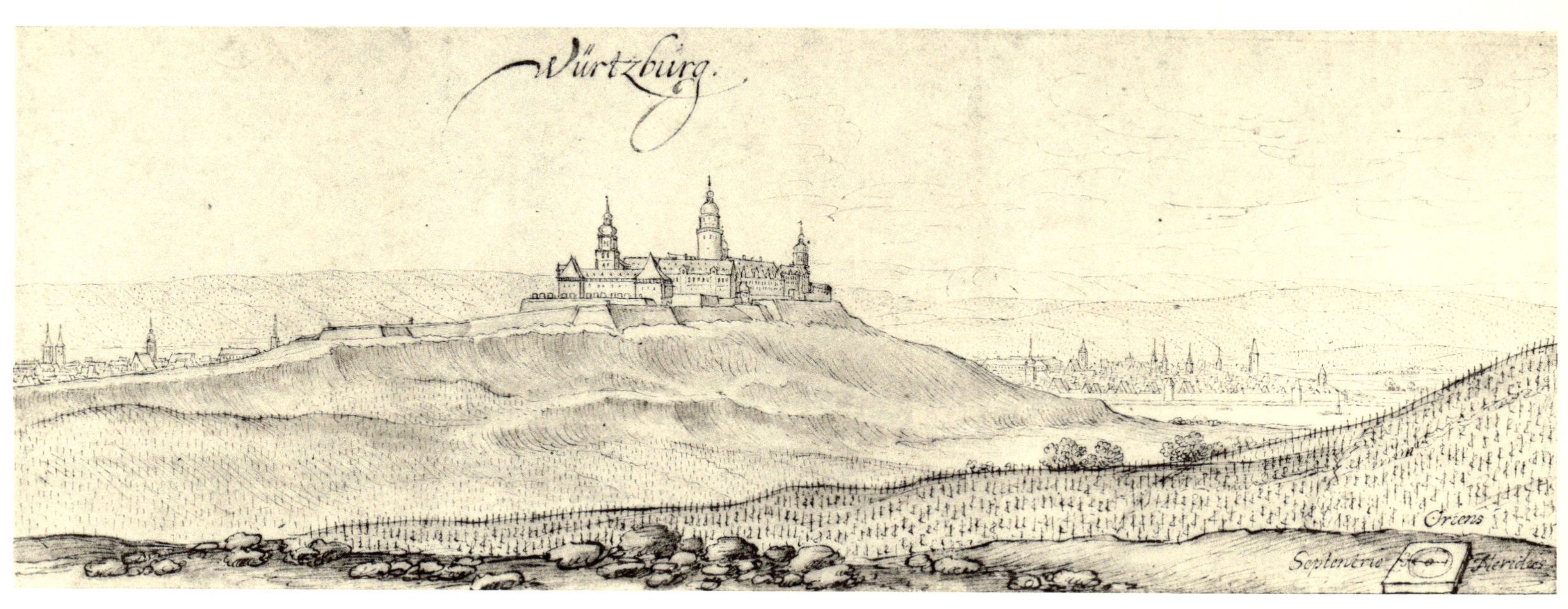
Würtzburg.
Oriens
Septentrio
Meridies

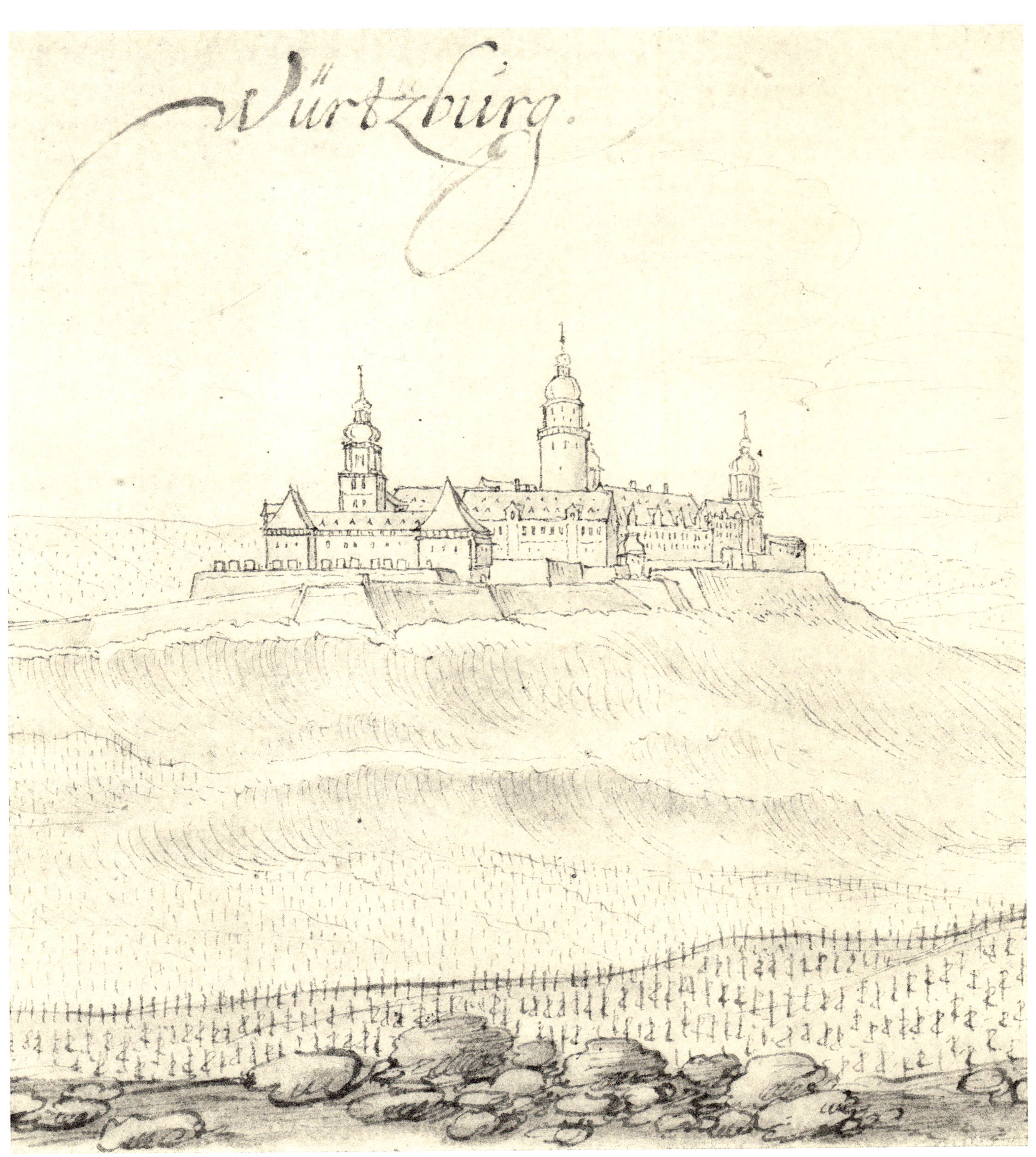
Würtzburg

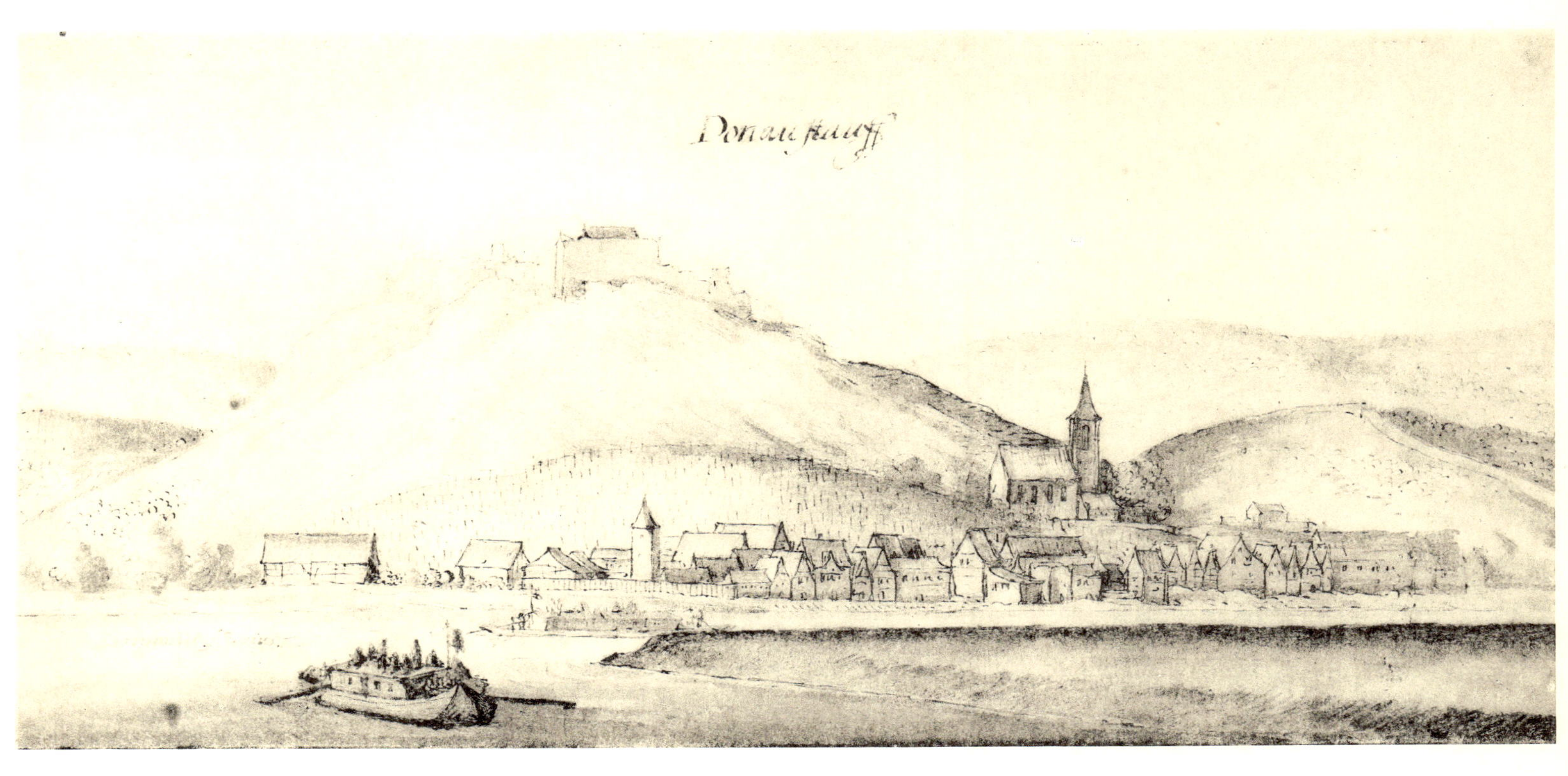
Donaustauff

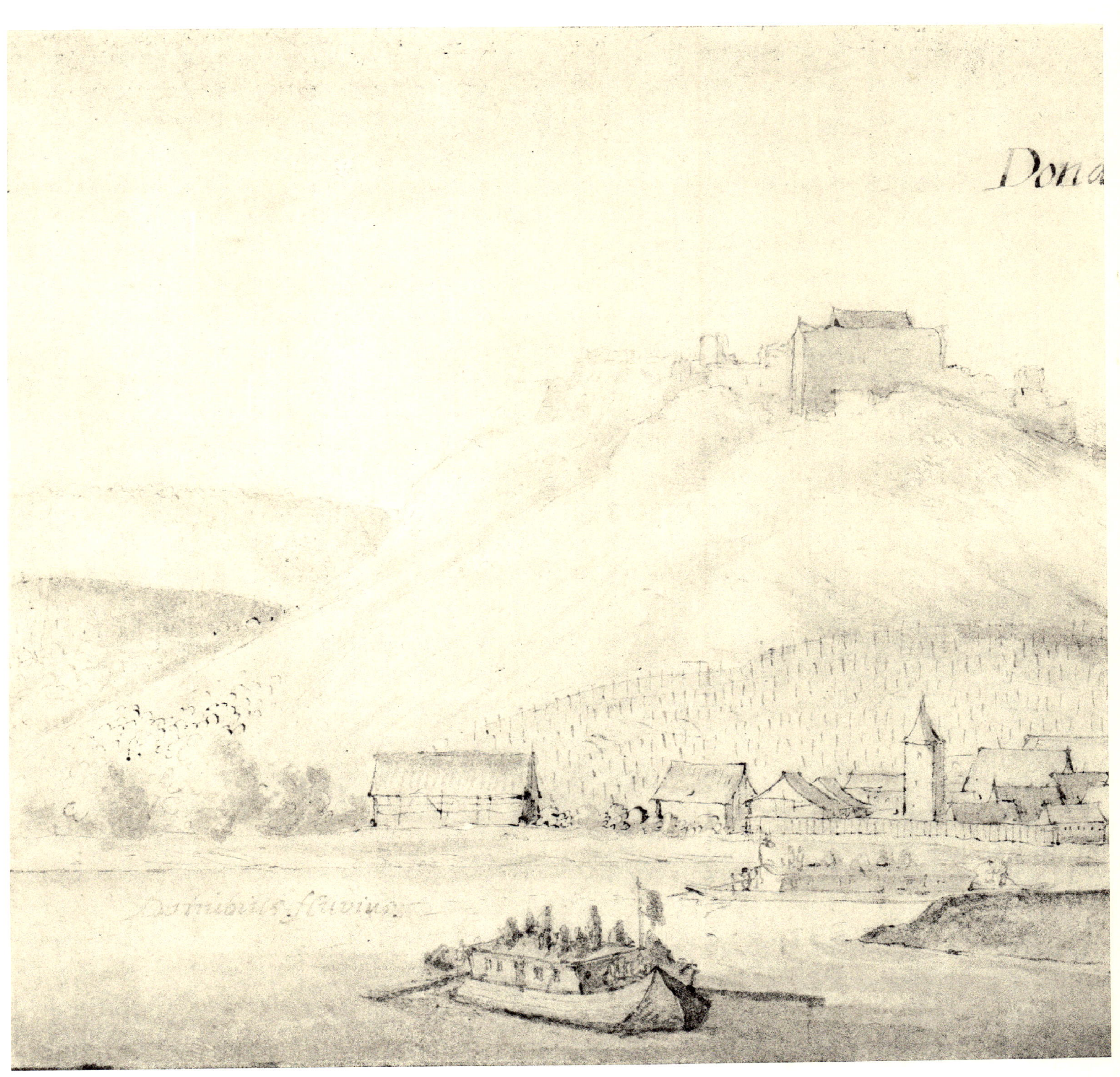
Dona
Danubius fluvius

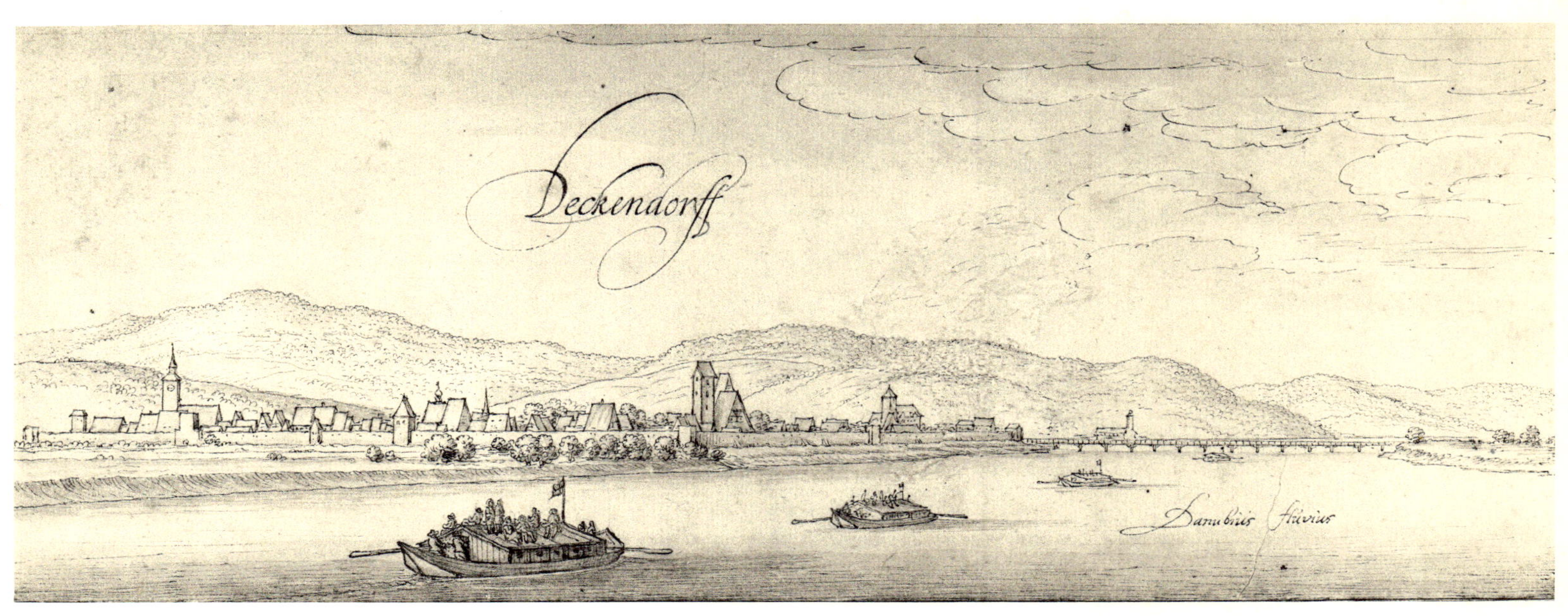
Deckendorff
Danubius fluvius

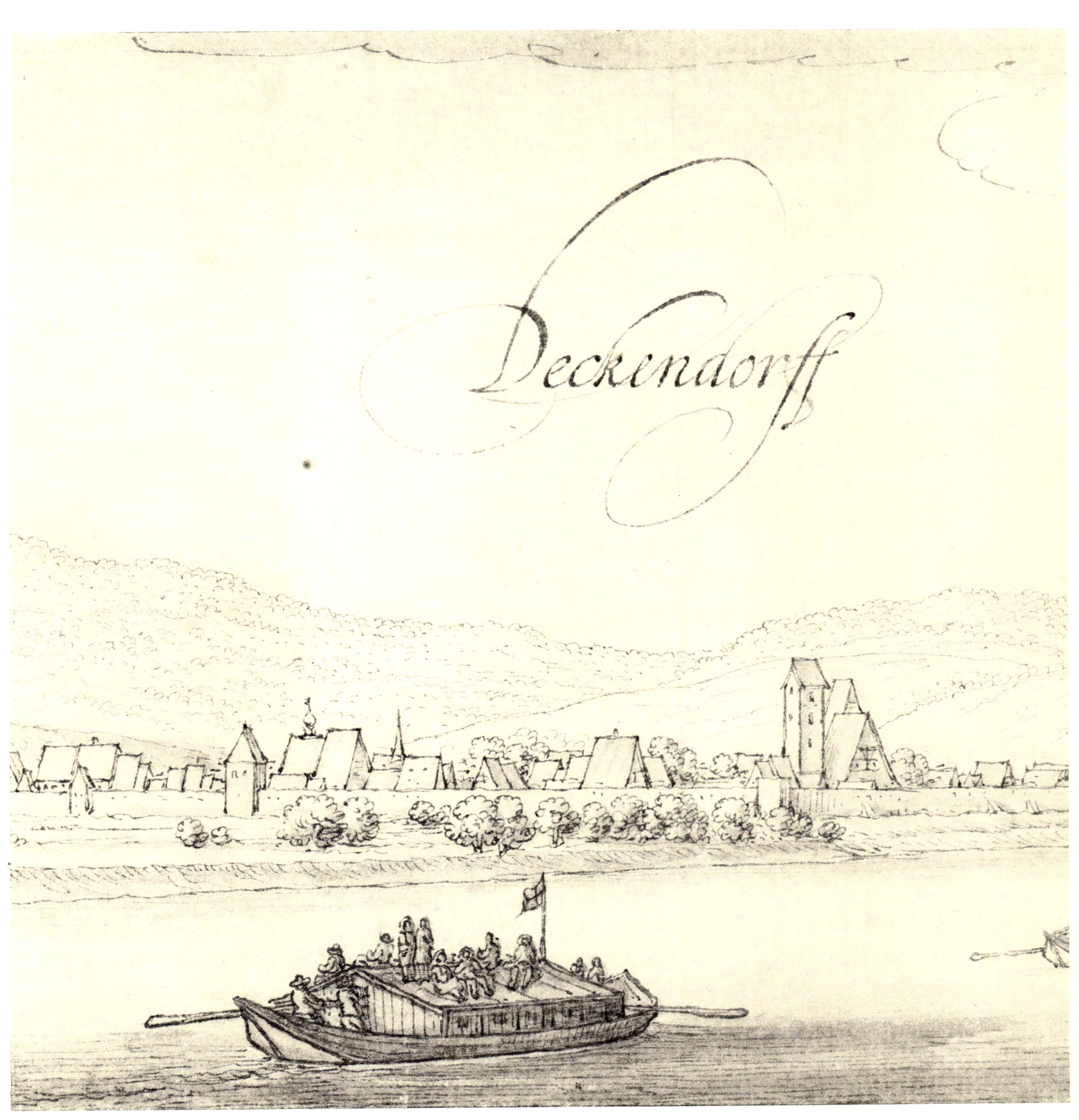
Deckendorff

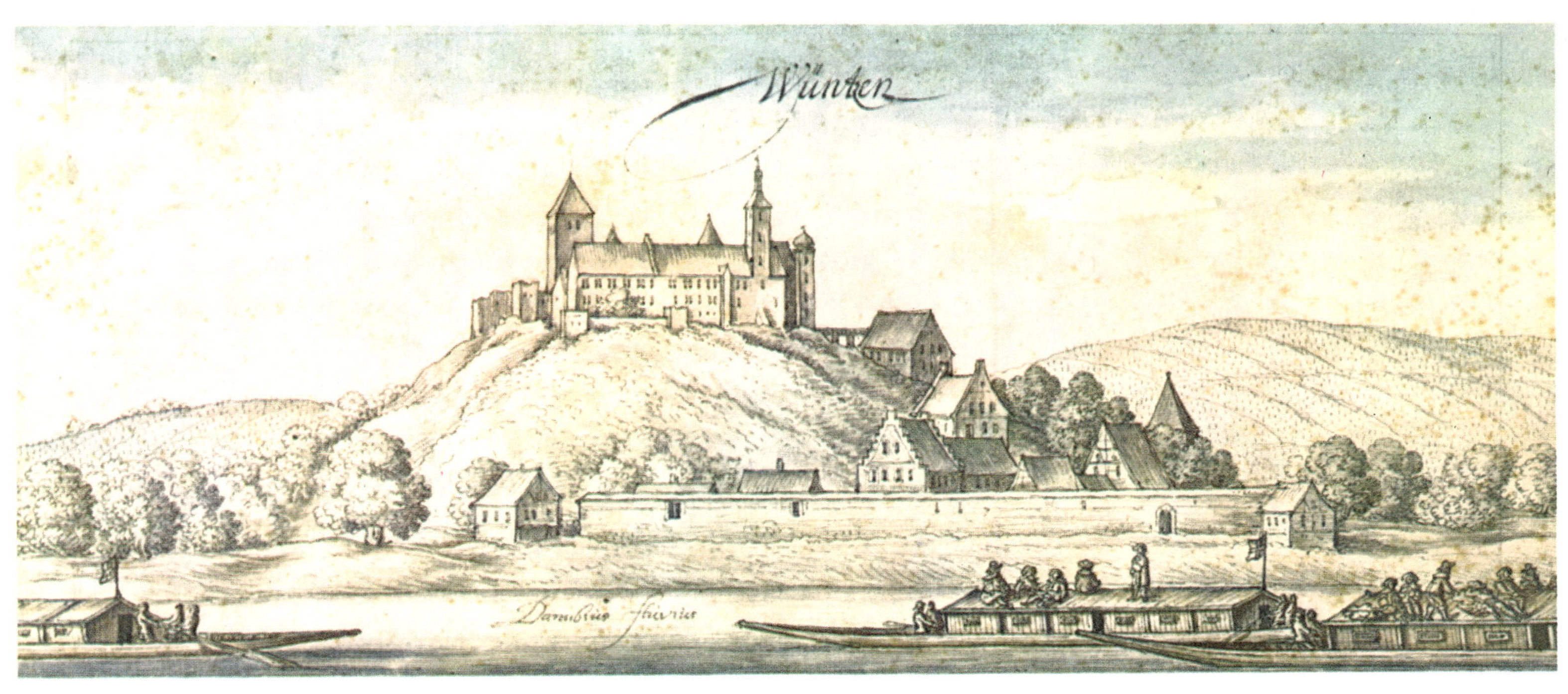

V

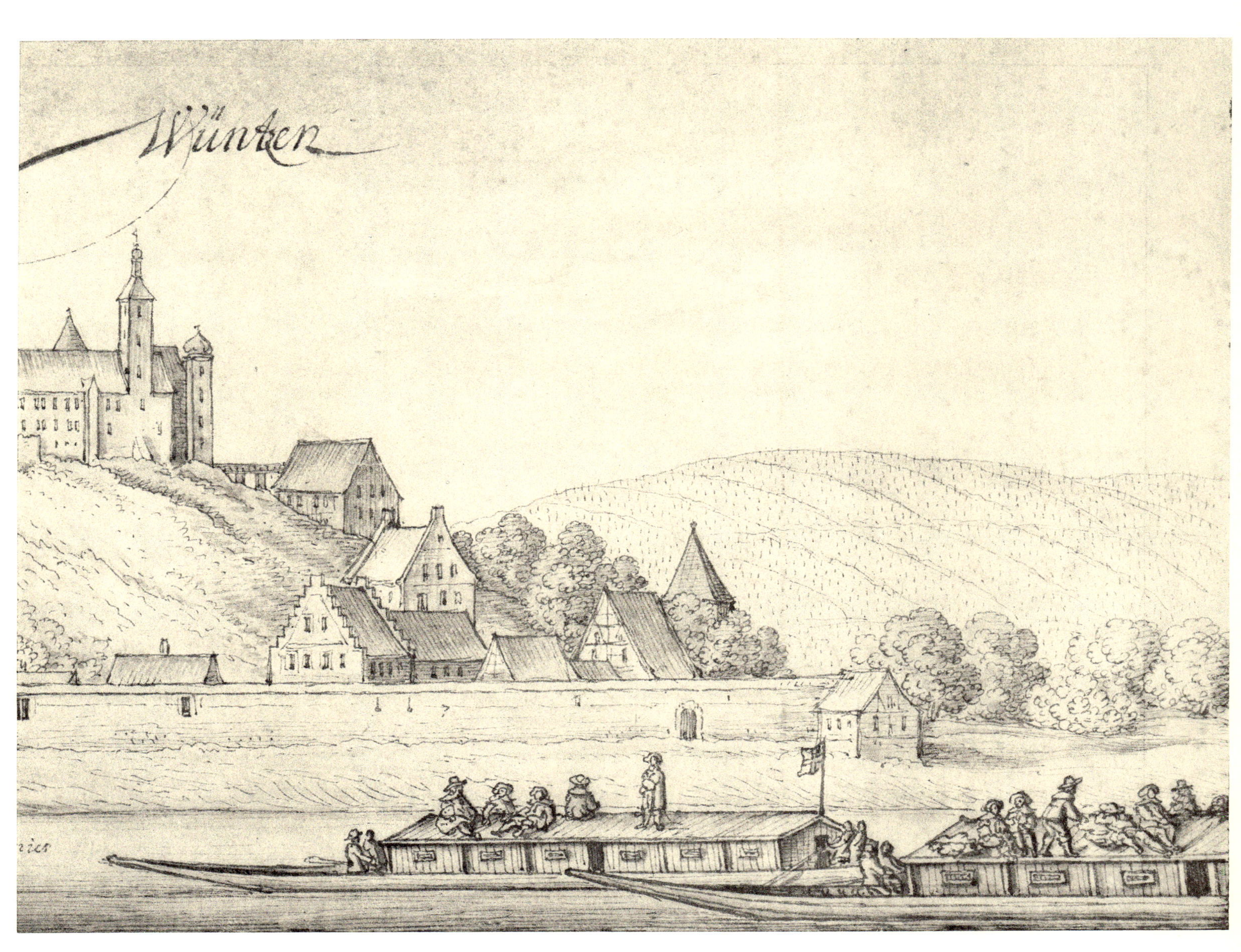

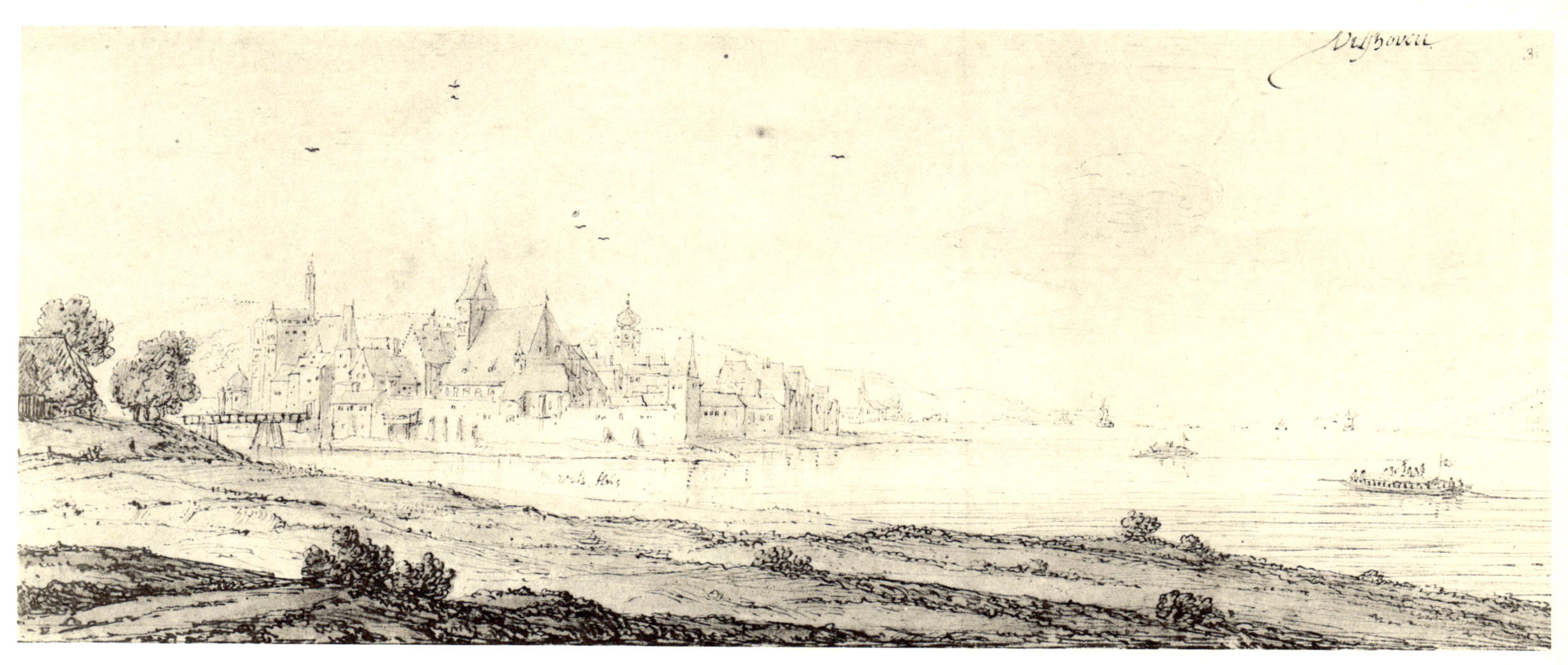

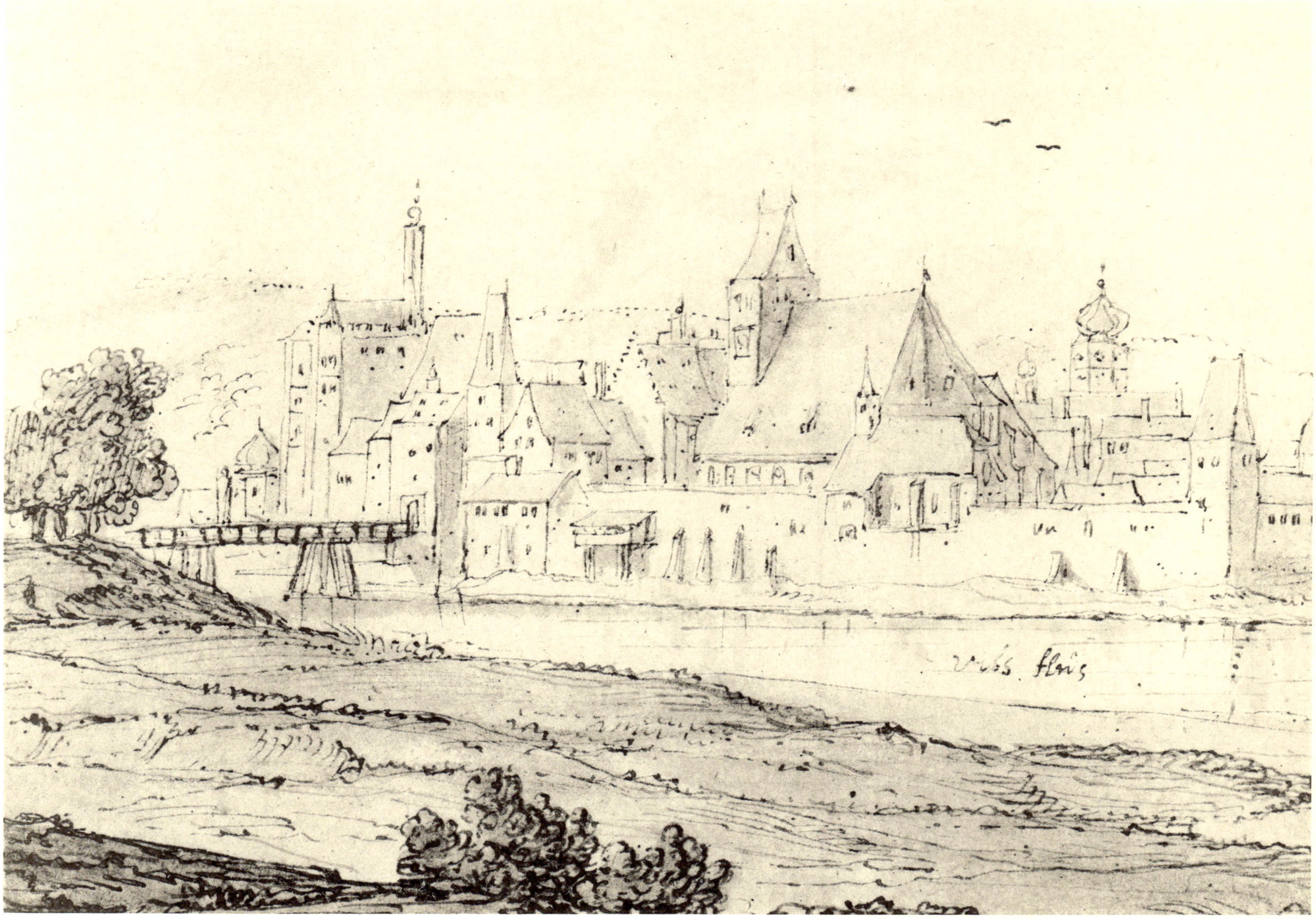

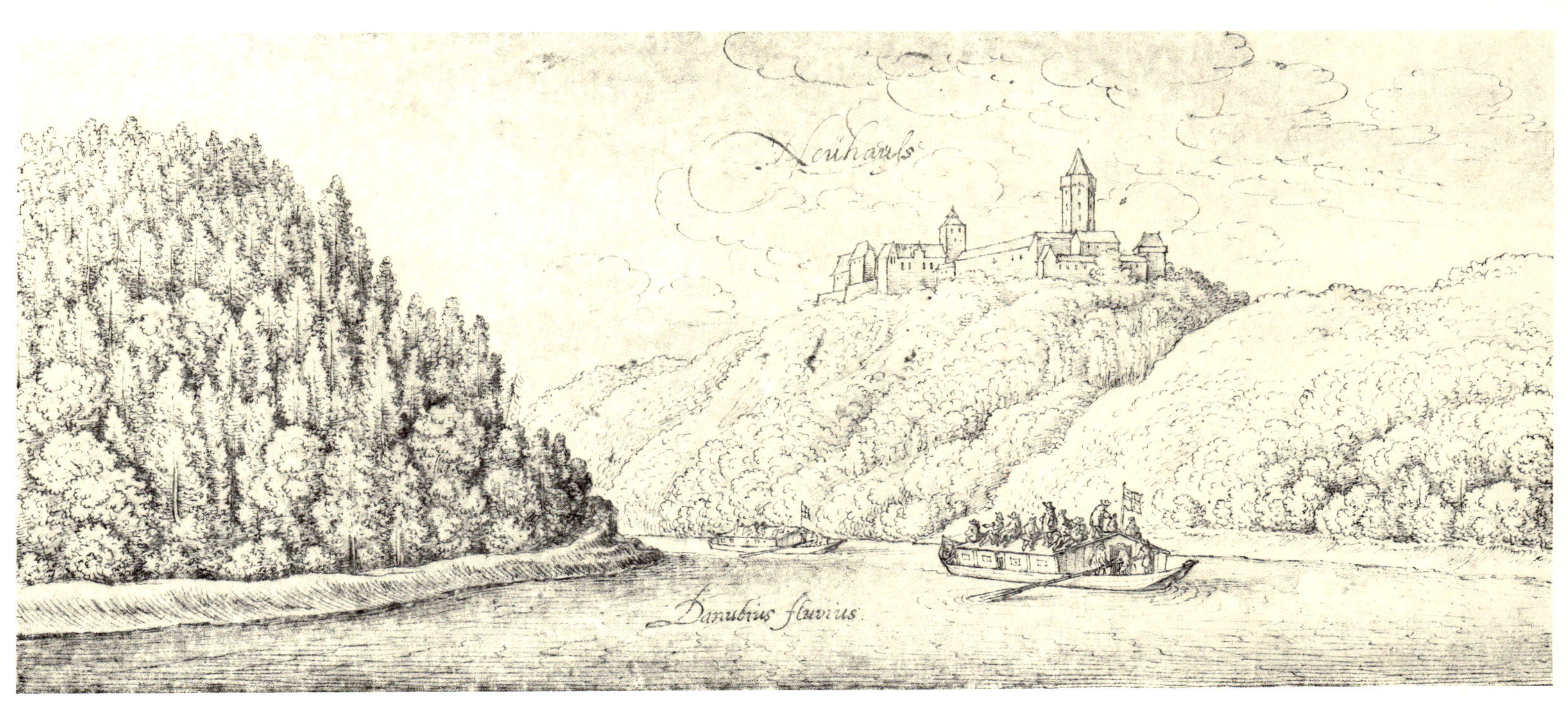
Danubius fluvius

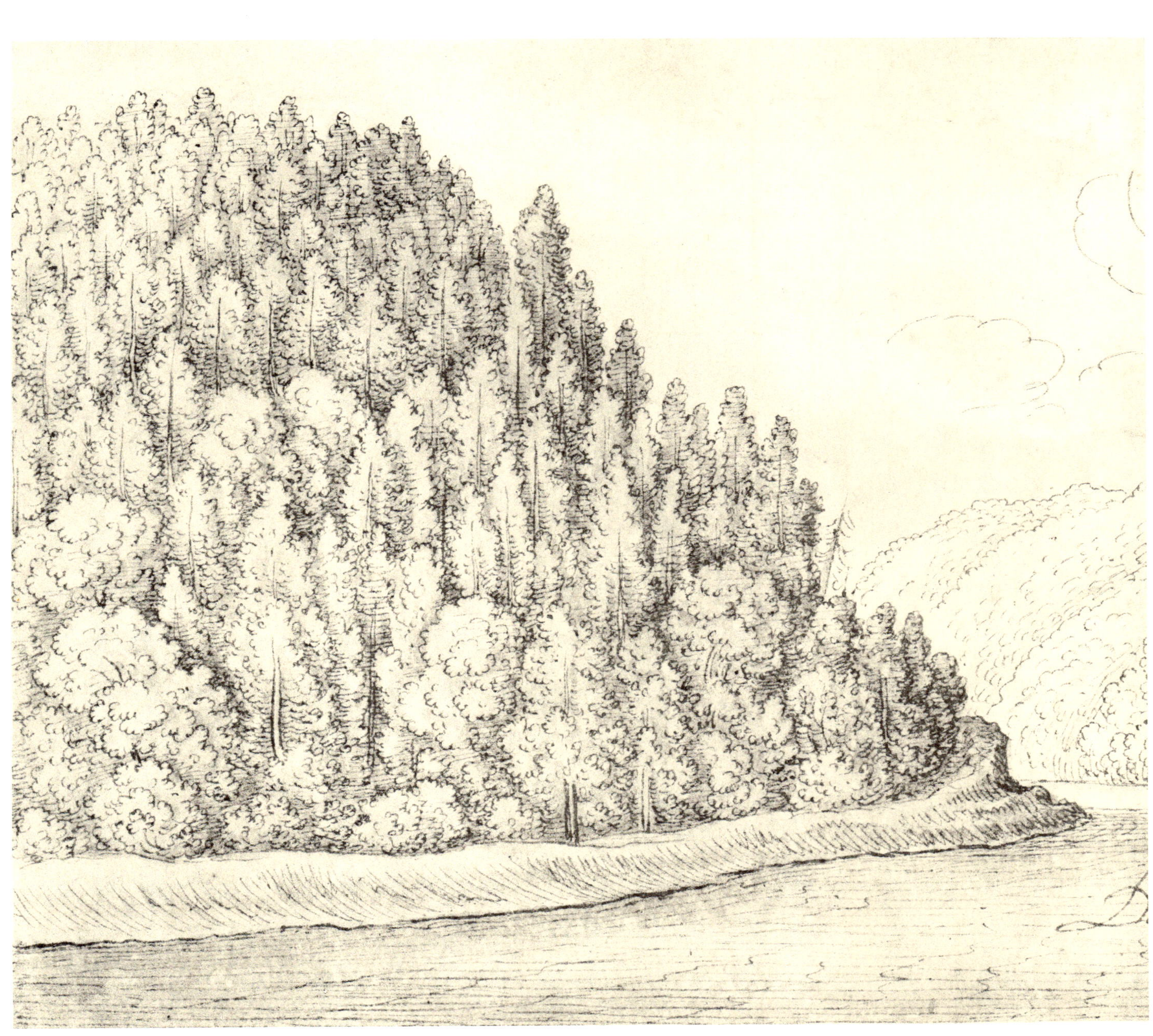

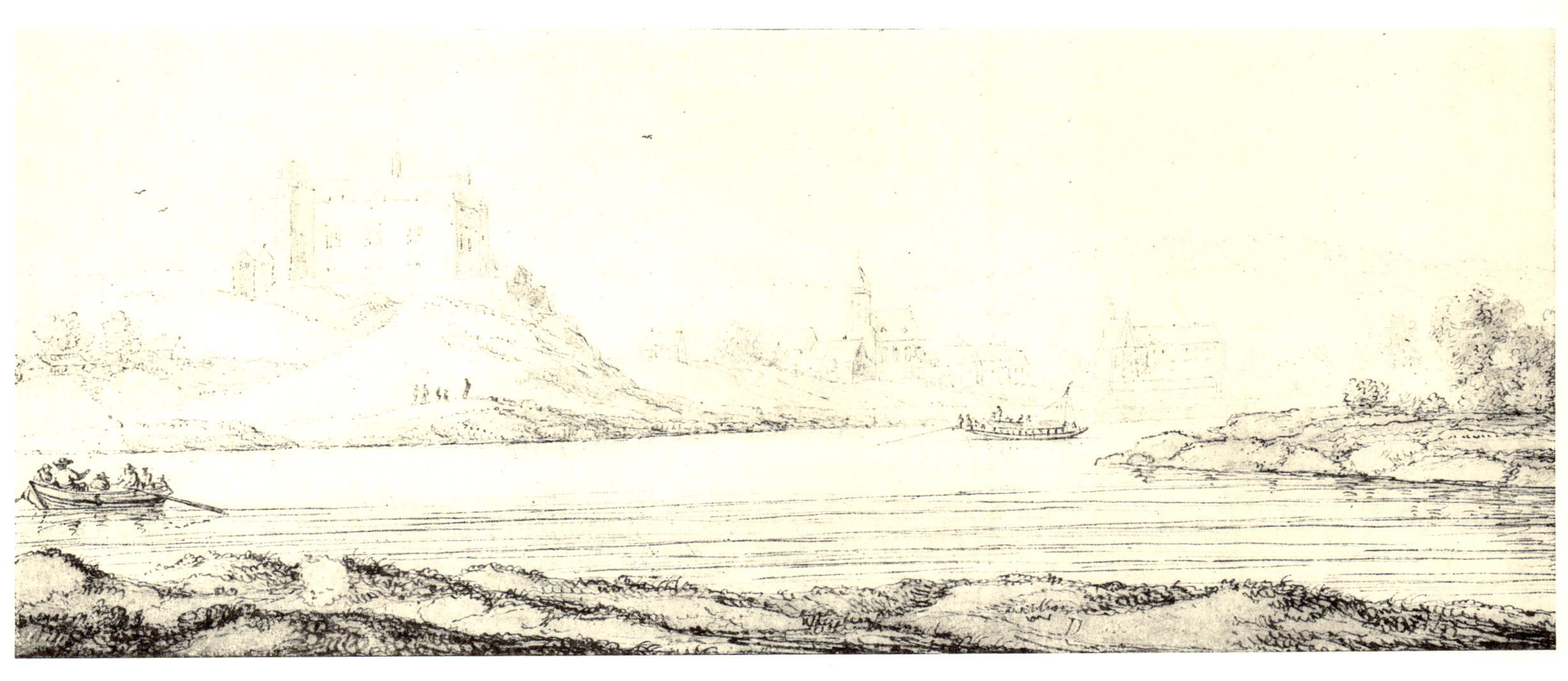

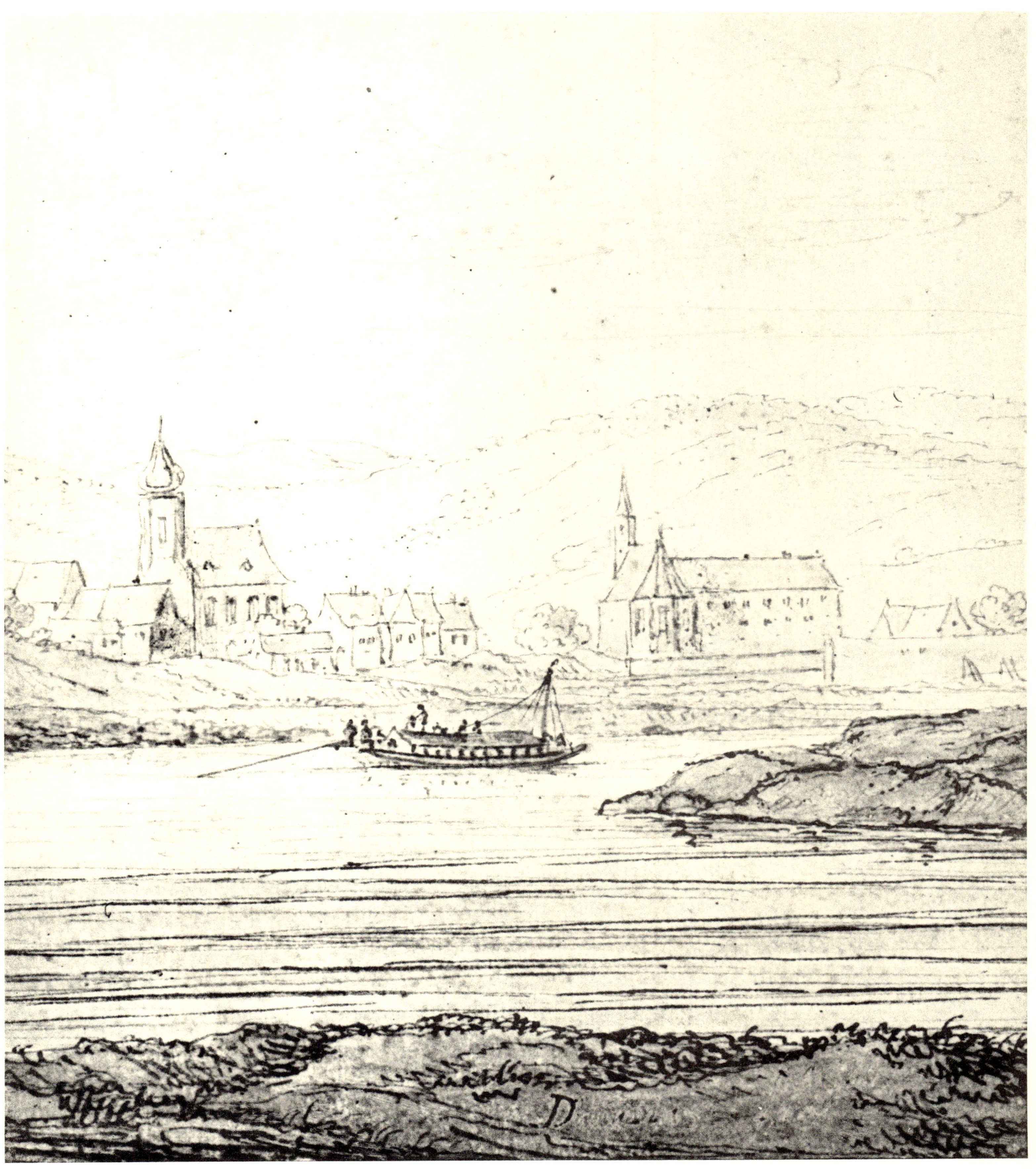

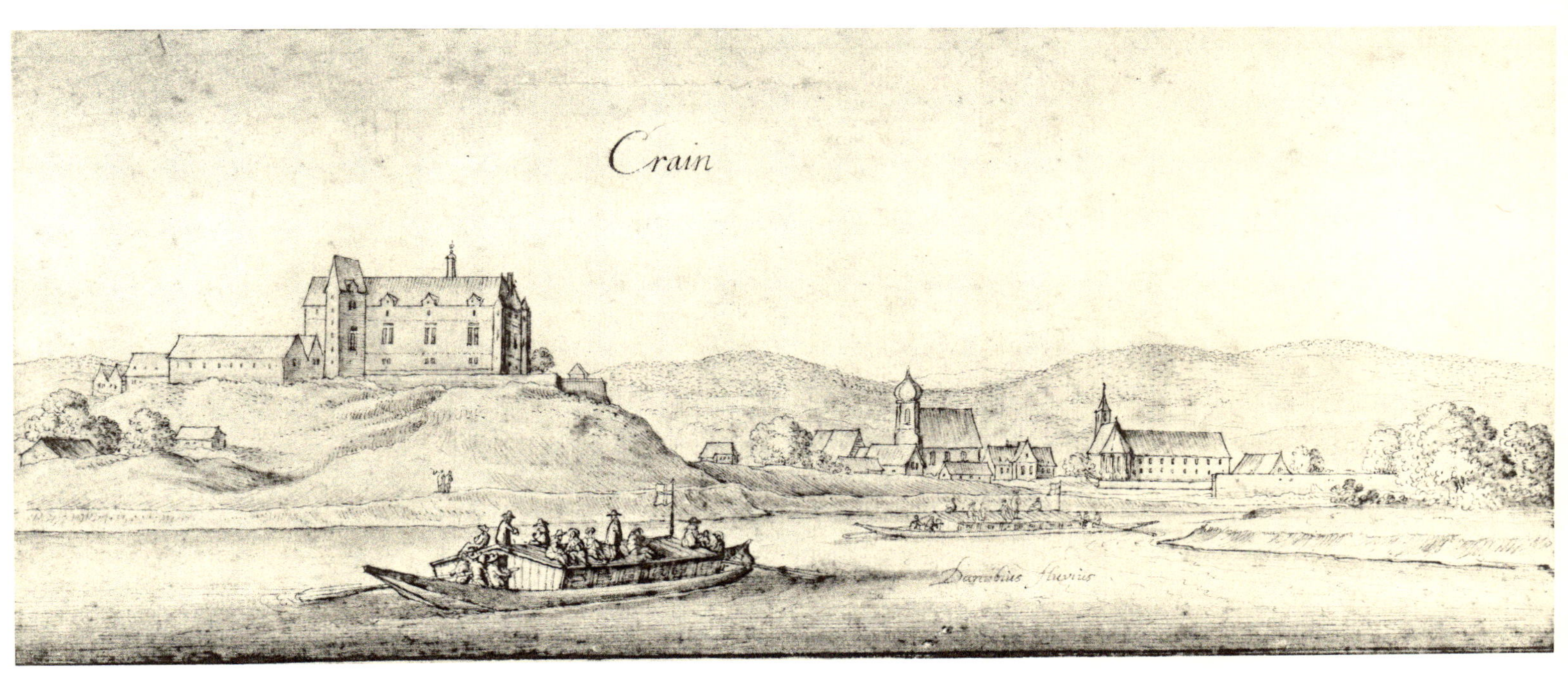
Crain
Danubius fluvius

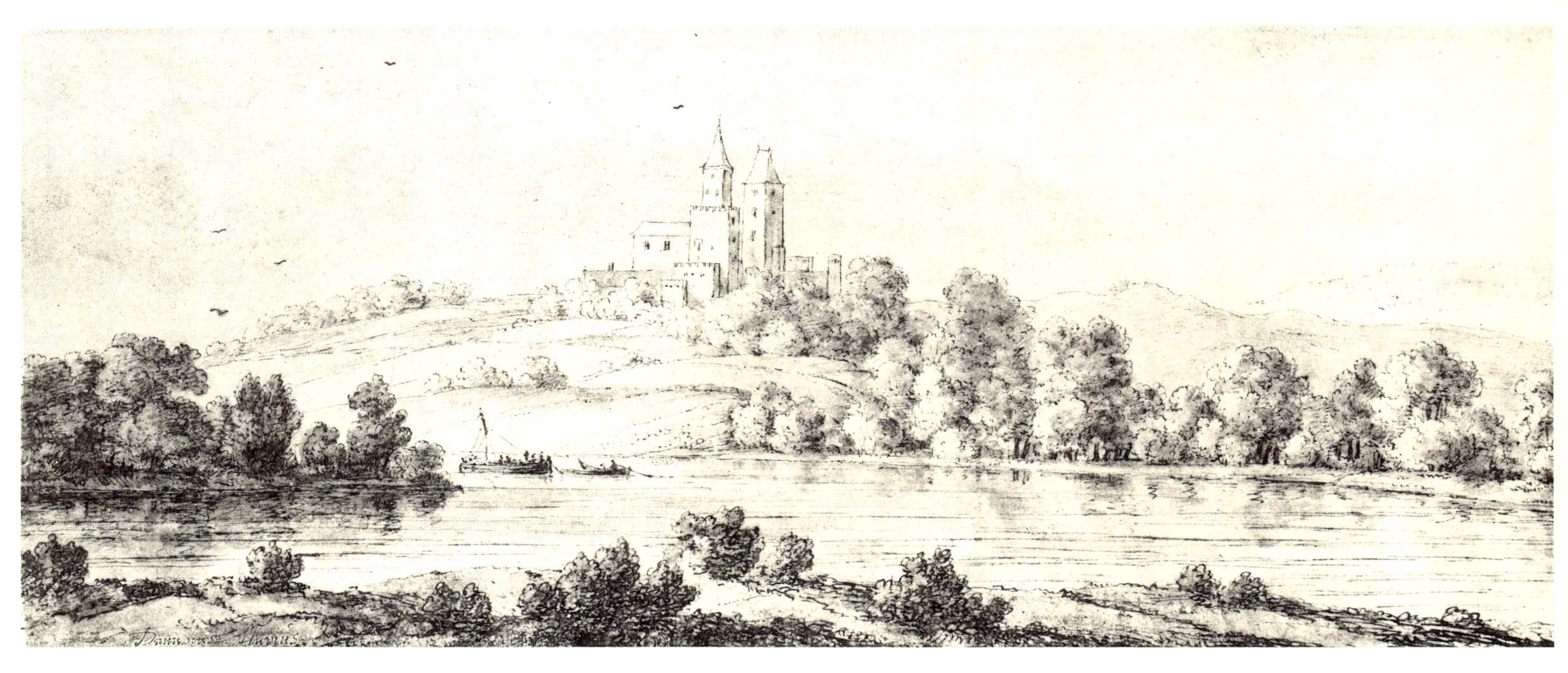

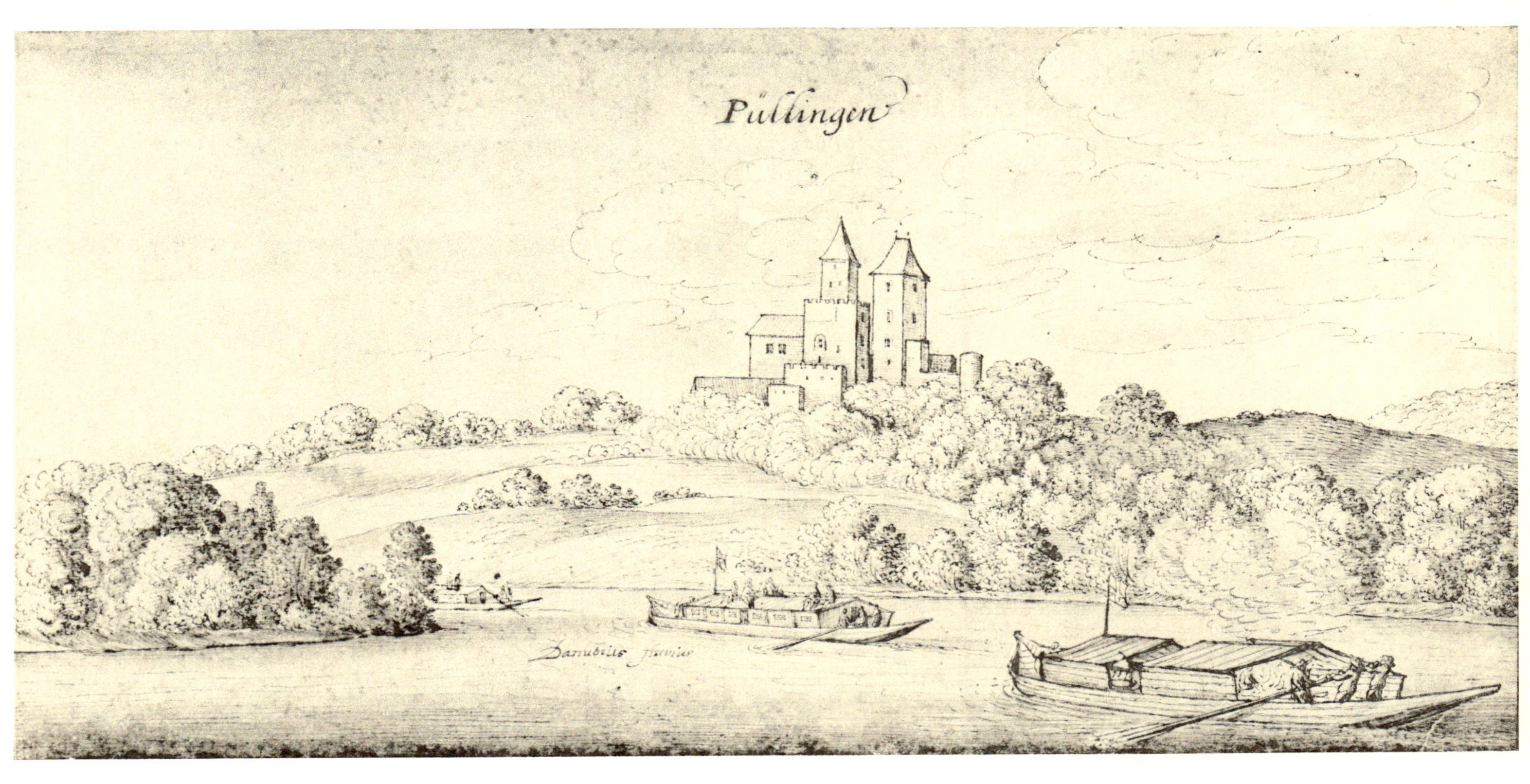
Püllingen
Danubius fluvius

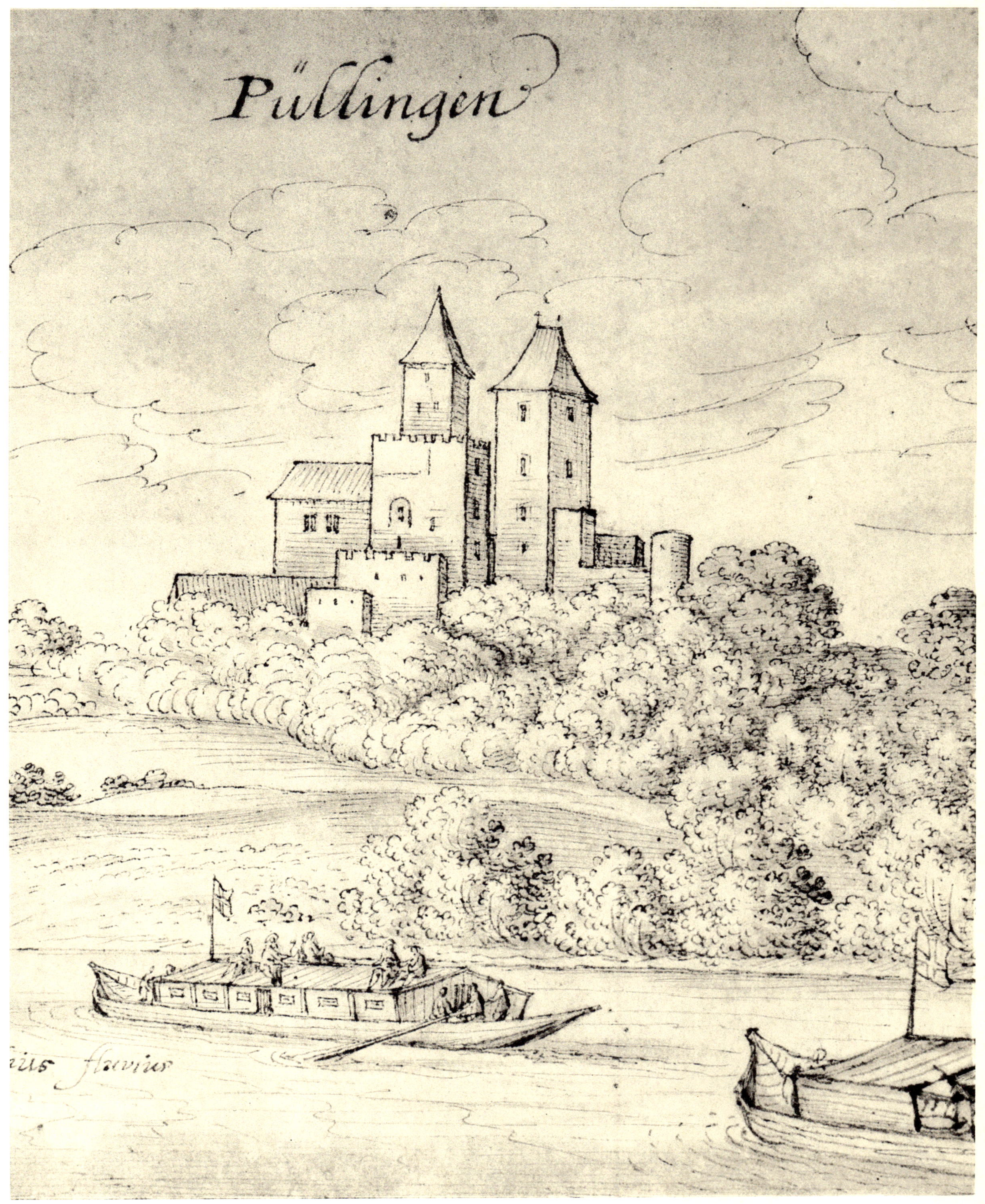
Püllingen
ius fluvius

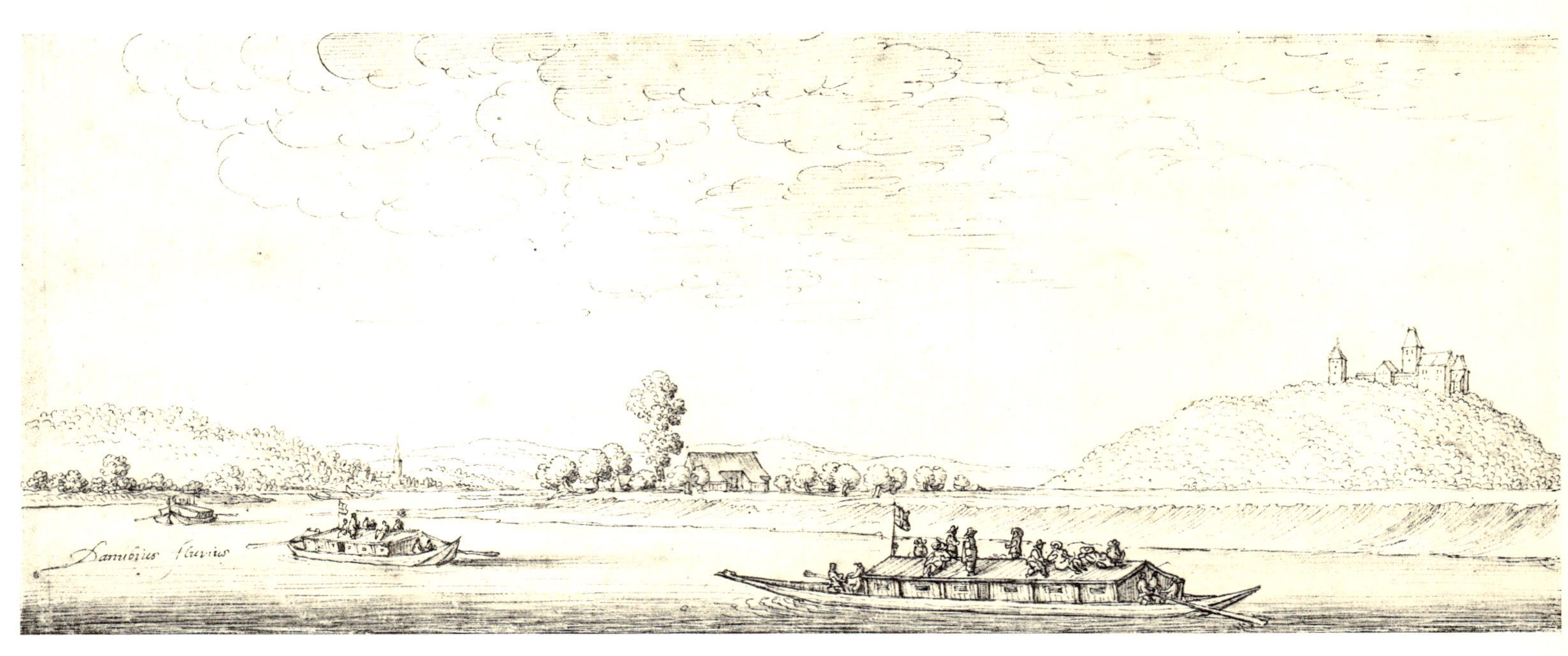
Danubius fluvius

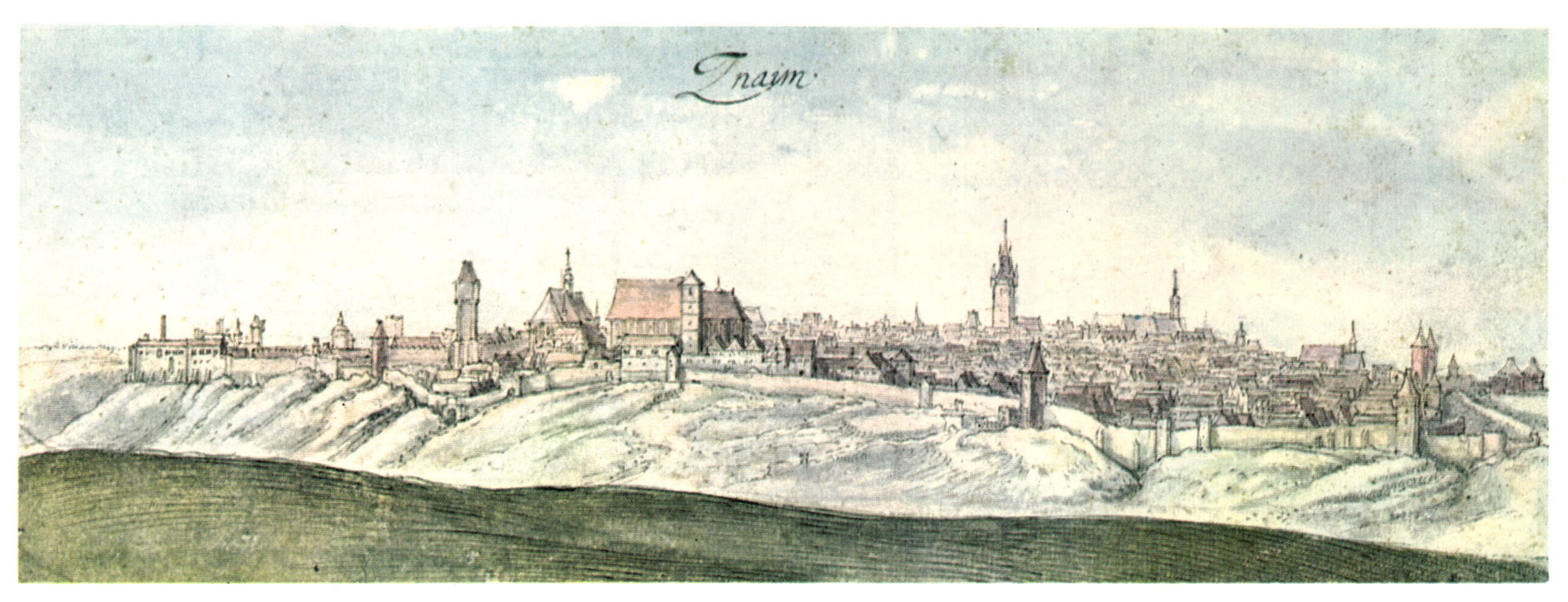
Znaim

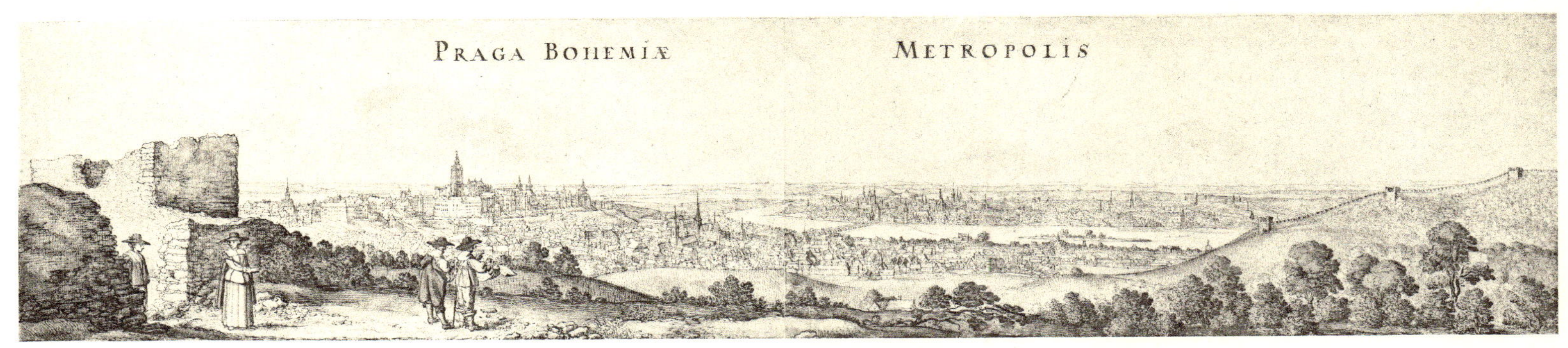

54/55

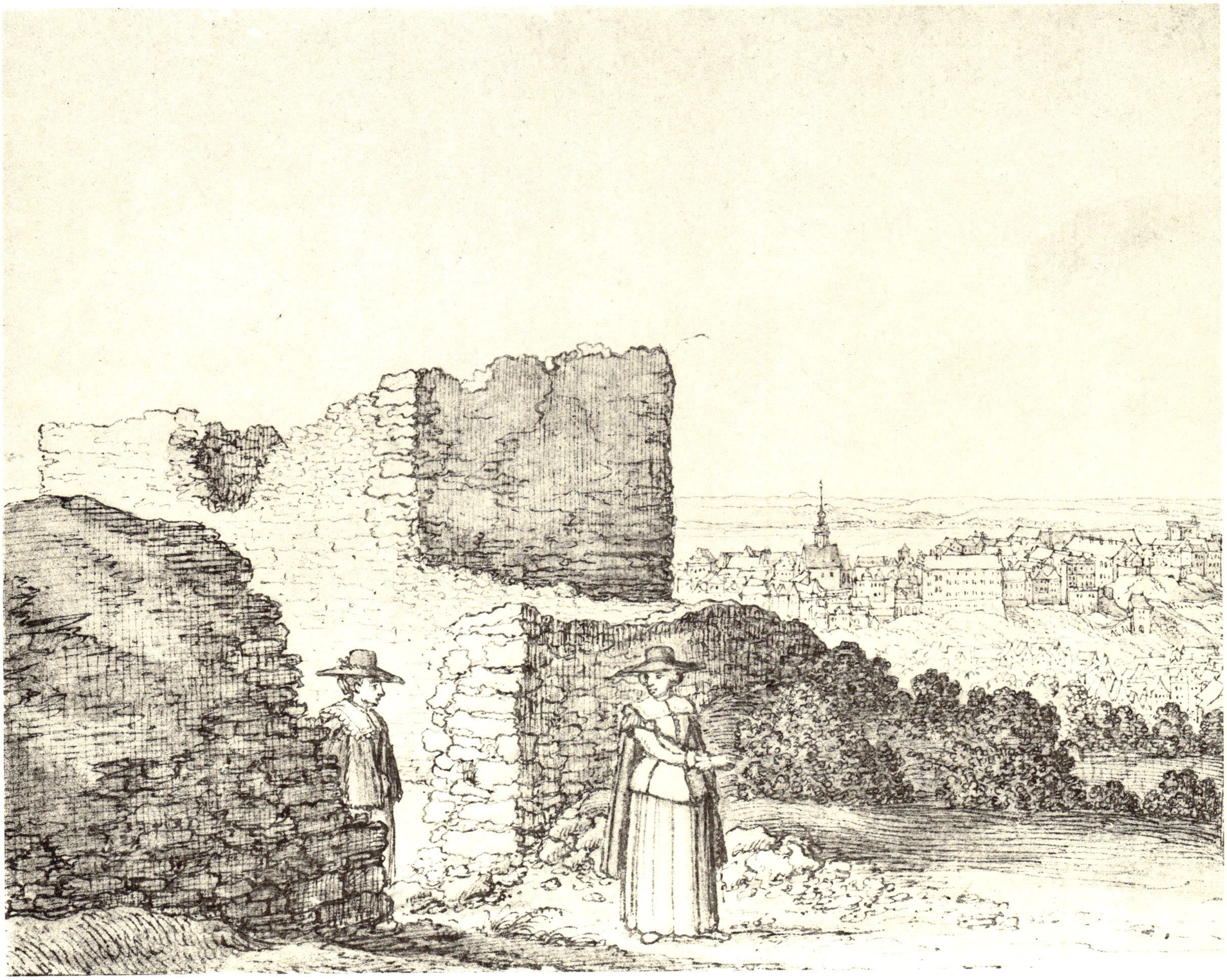

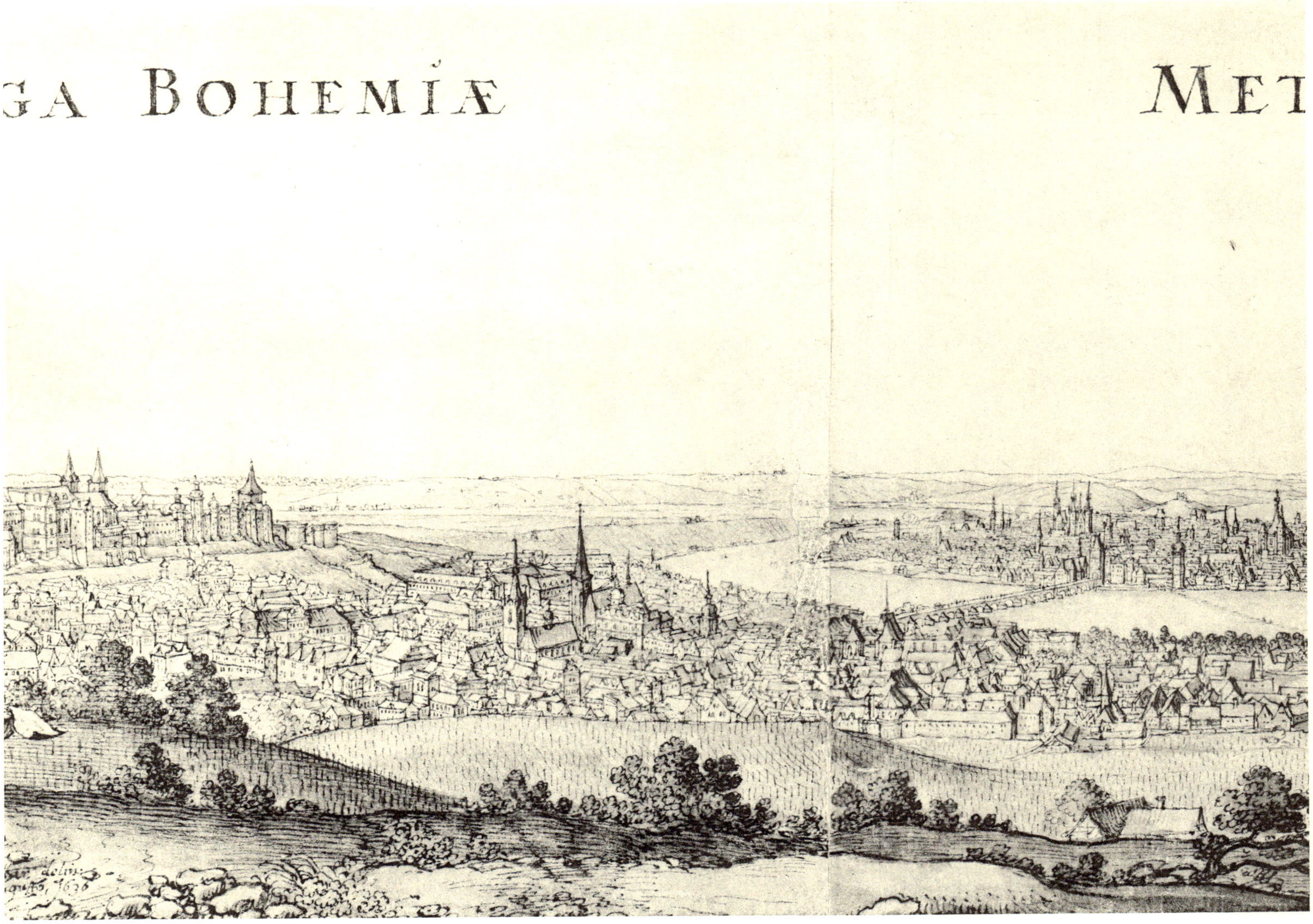

GA BOHEMIÆ MET

TROPOLIS

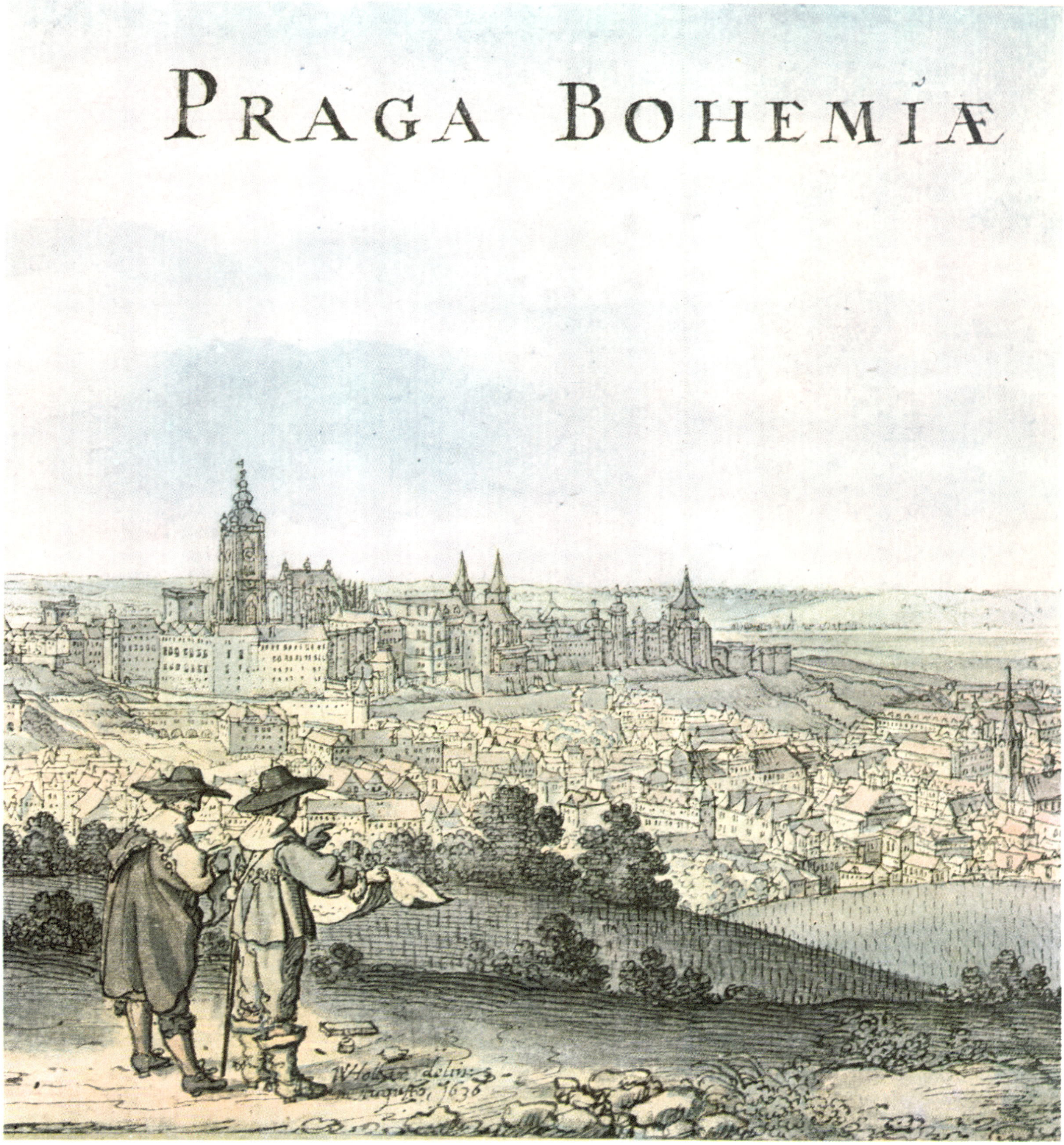

PRAGA BOHEMIÆ

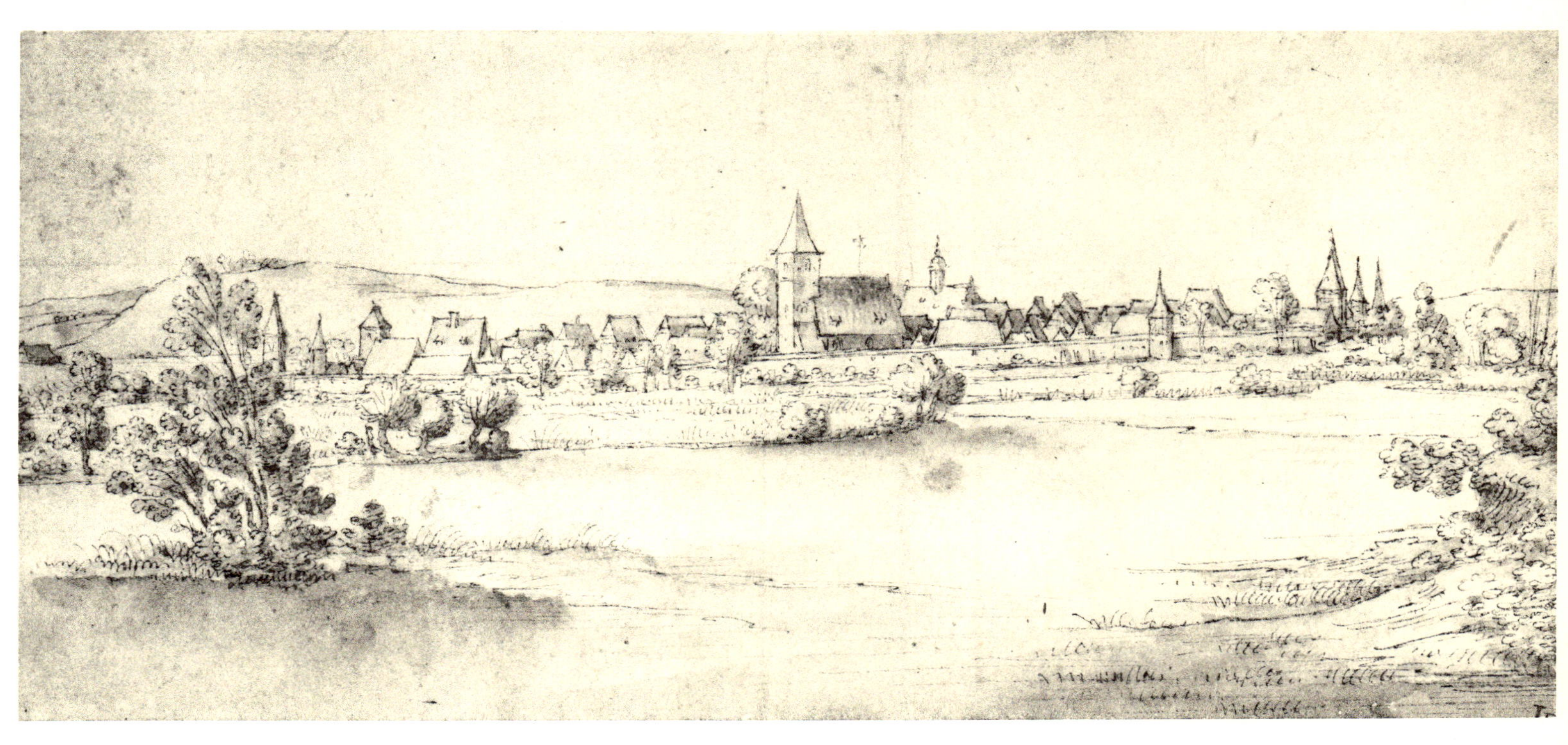

58

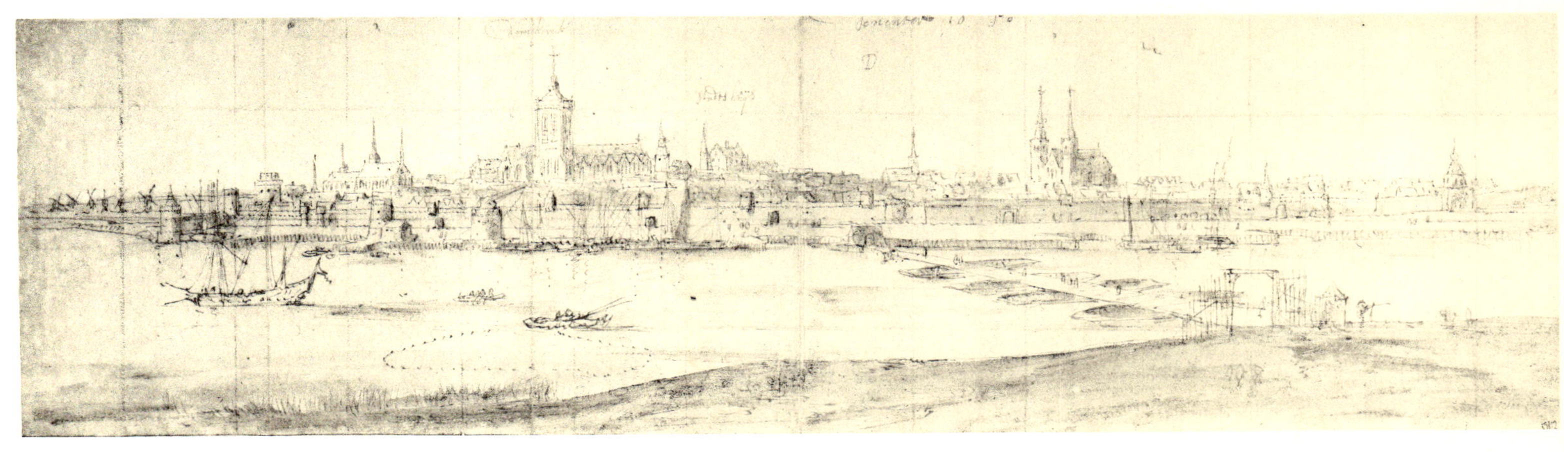

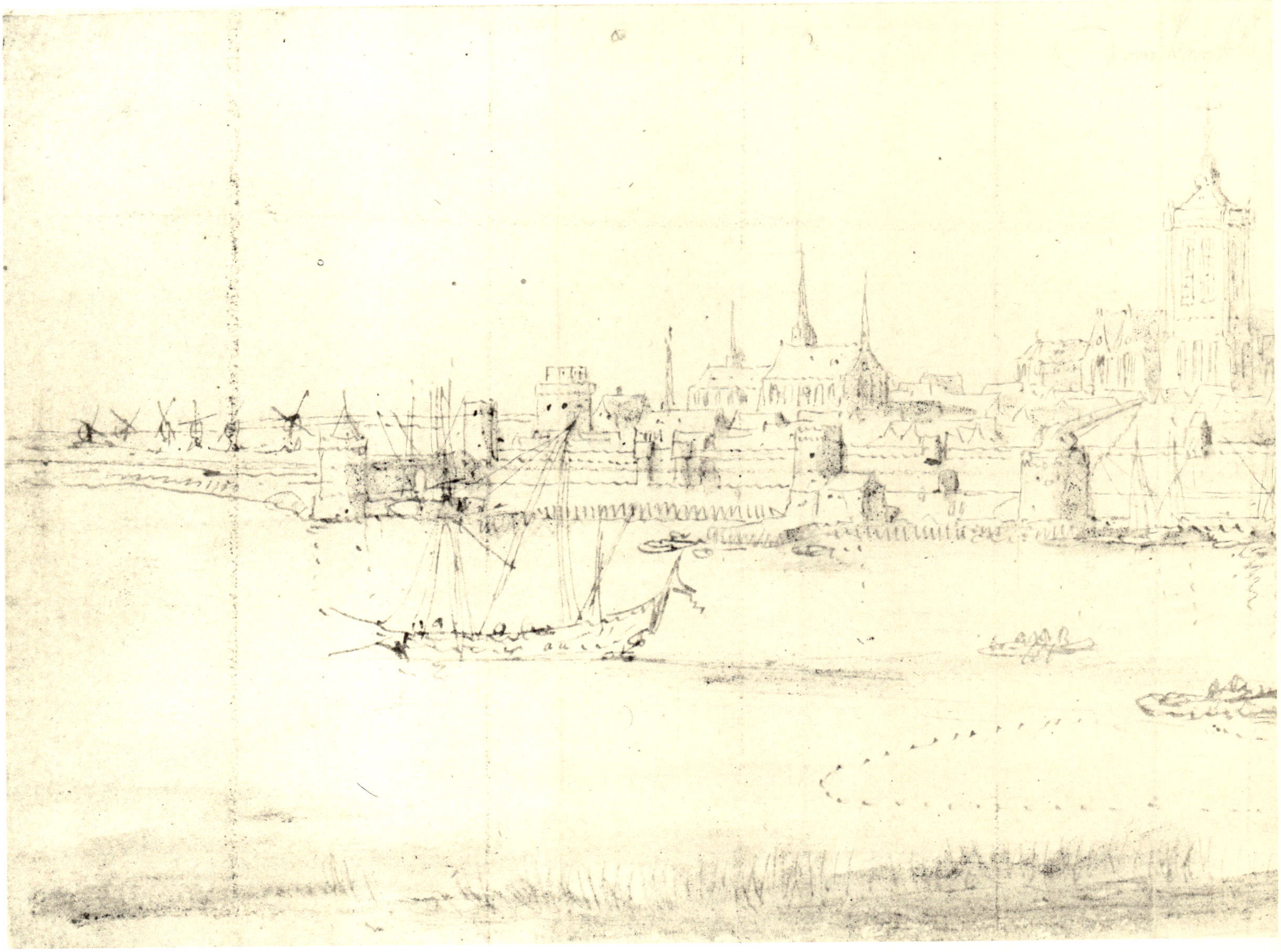

59/60

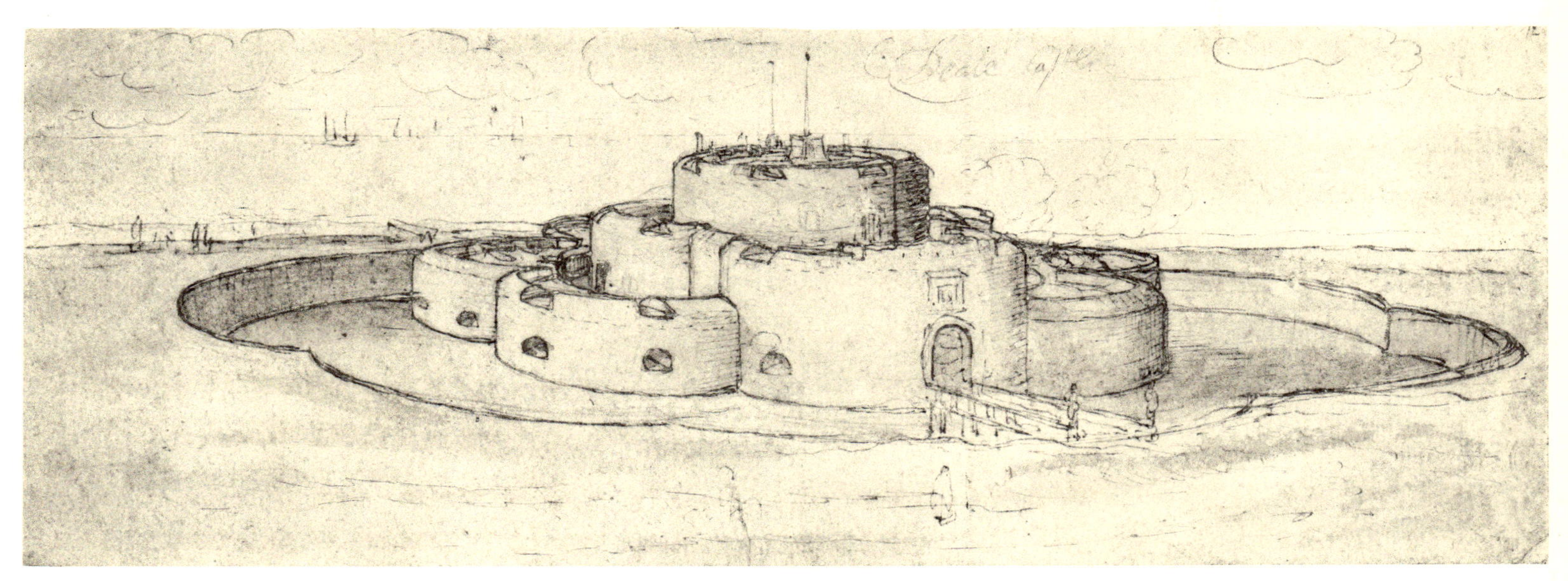

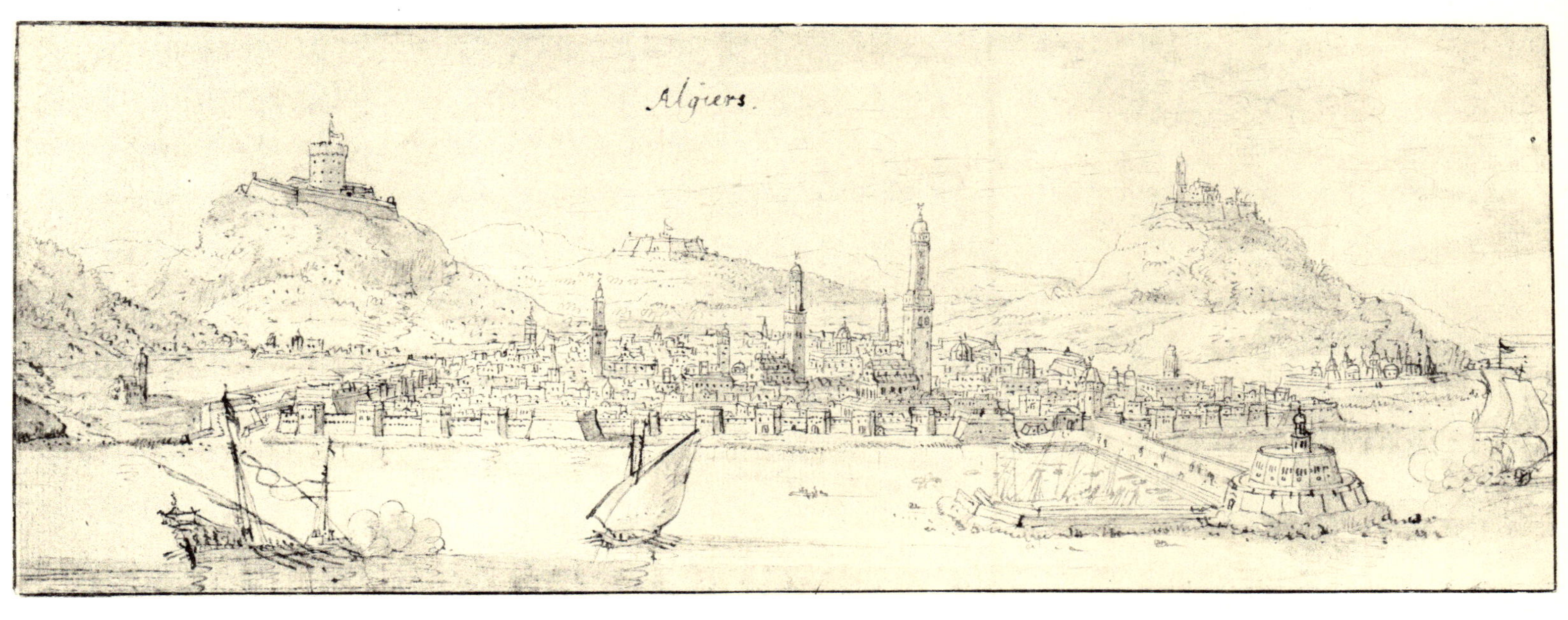
Algiers.

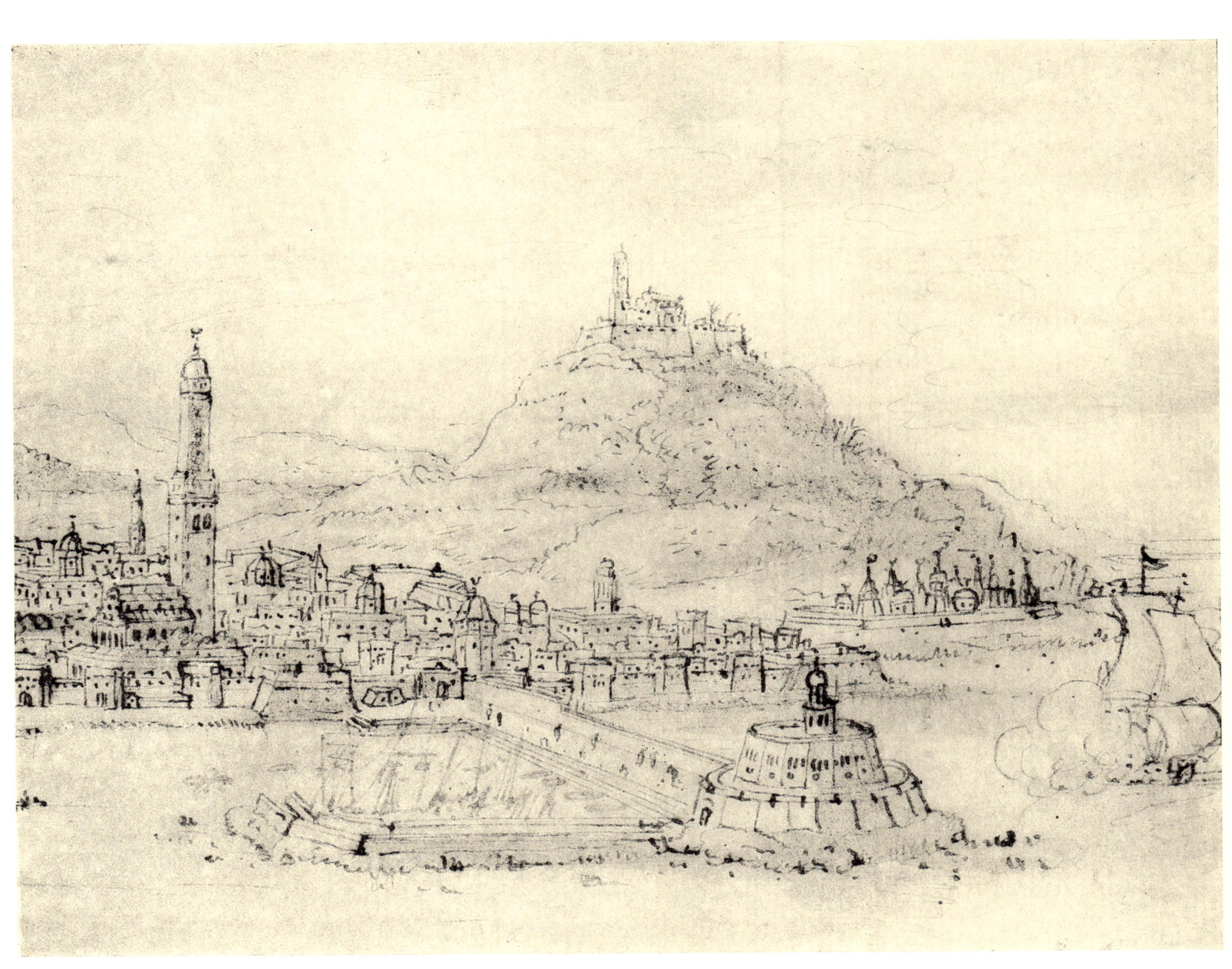

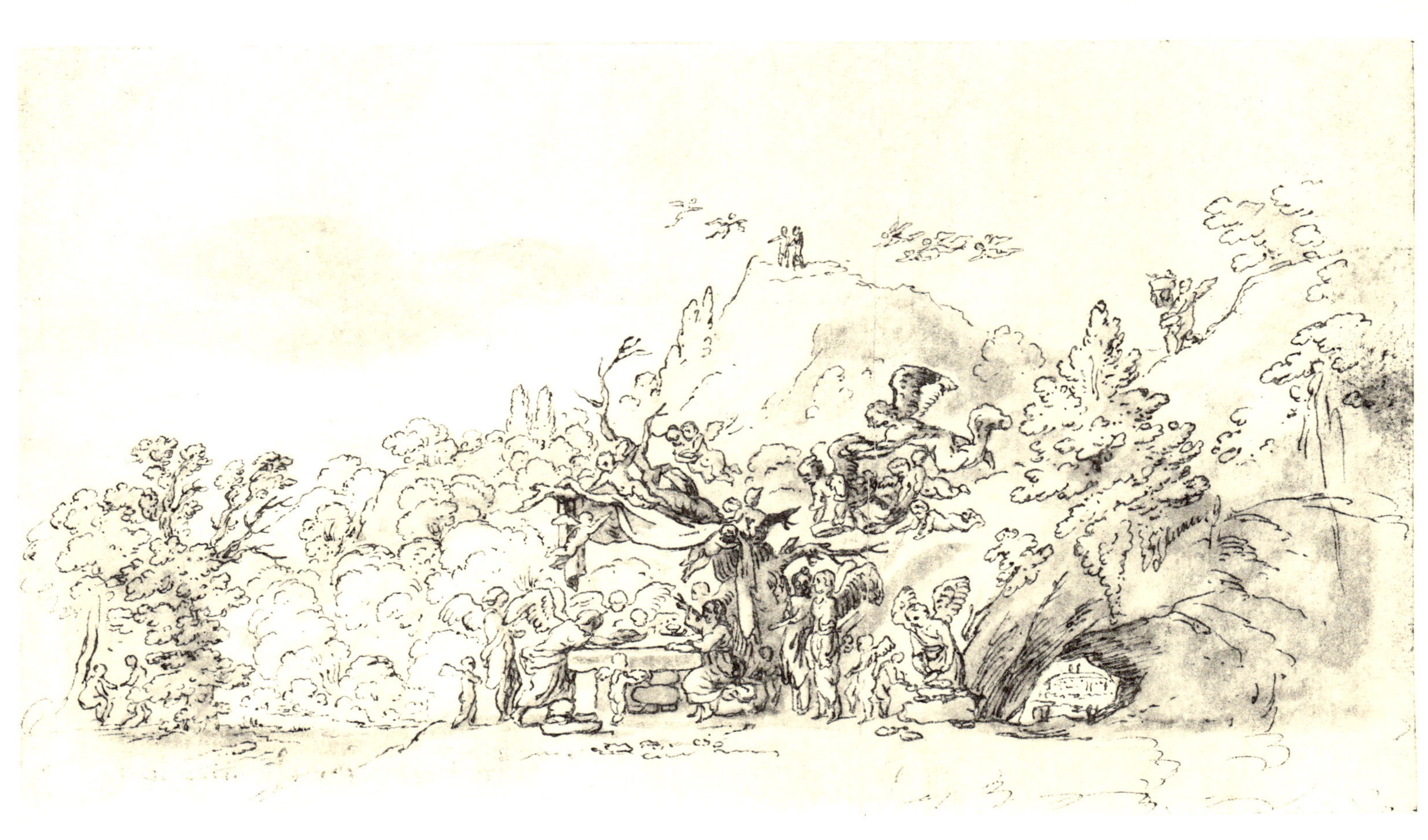

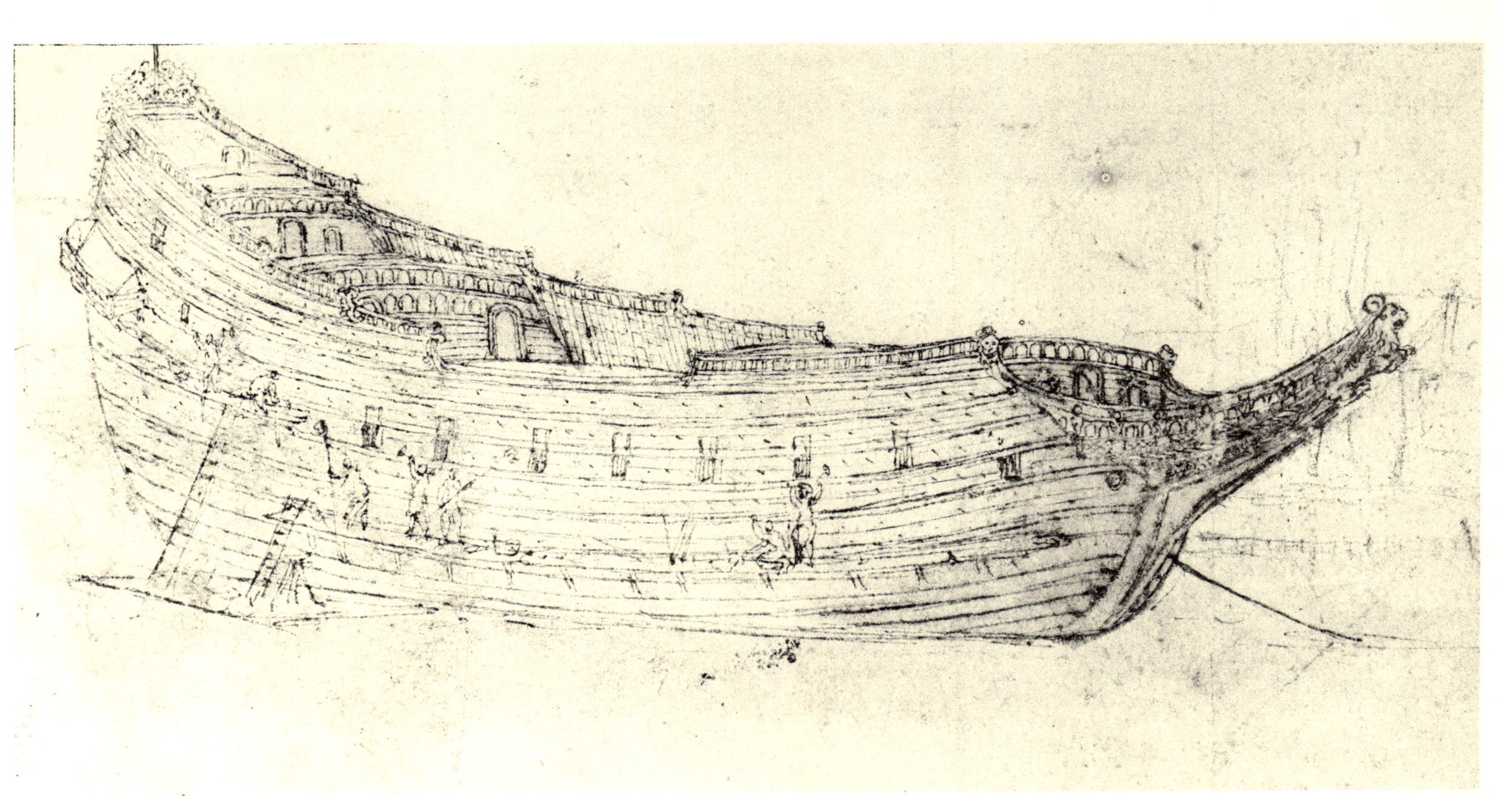

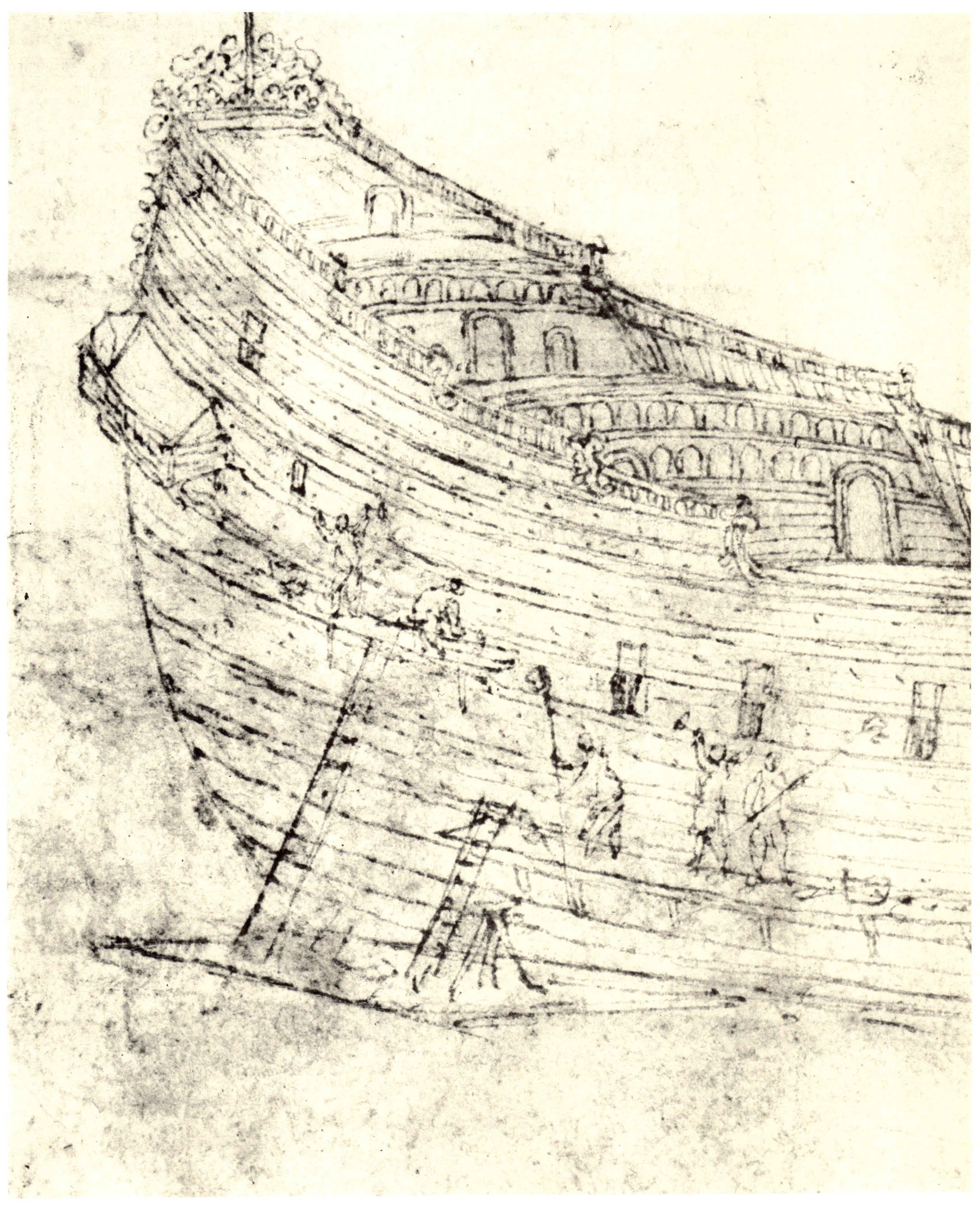

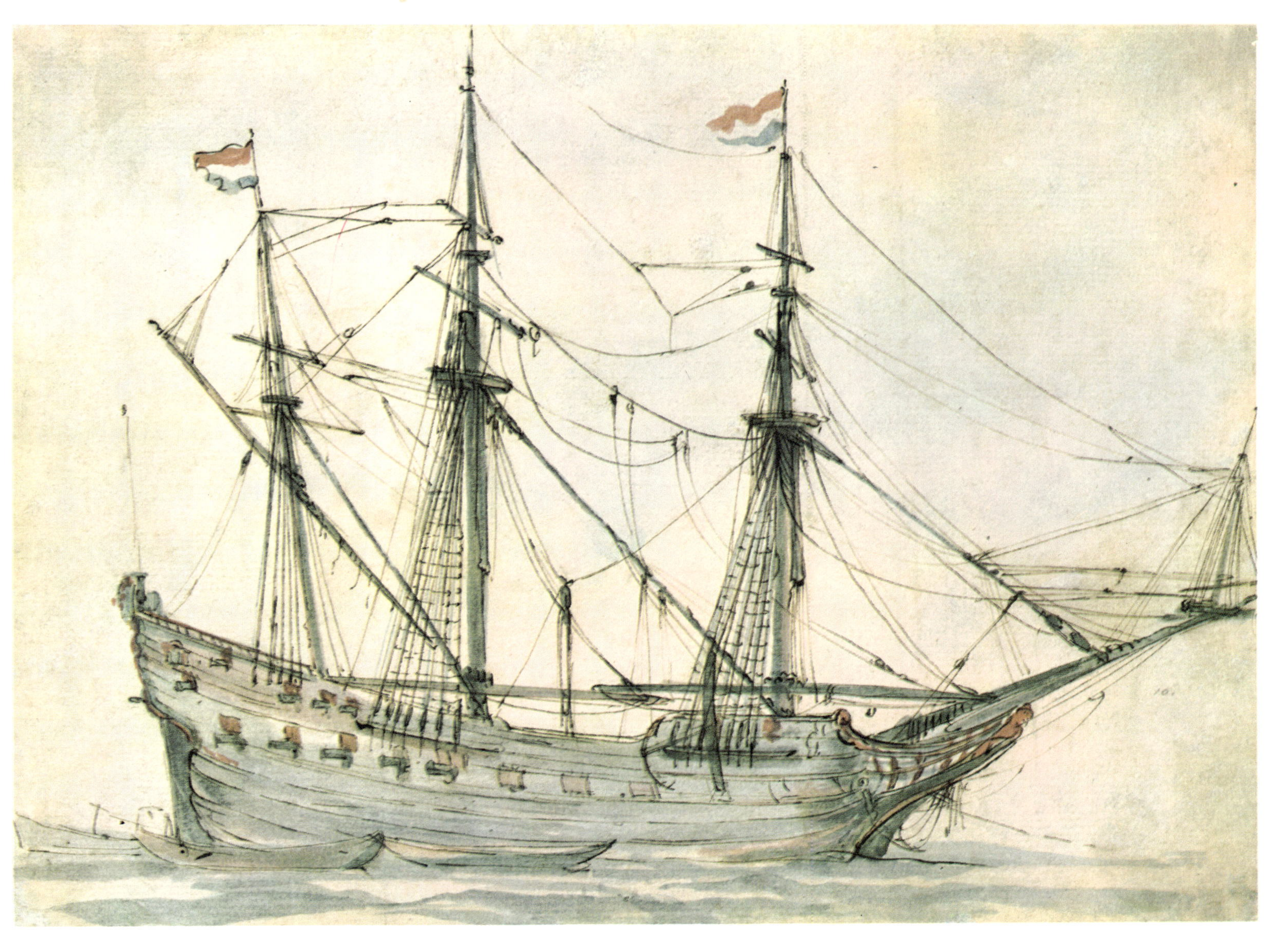

VIII

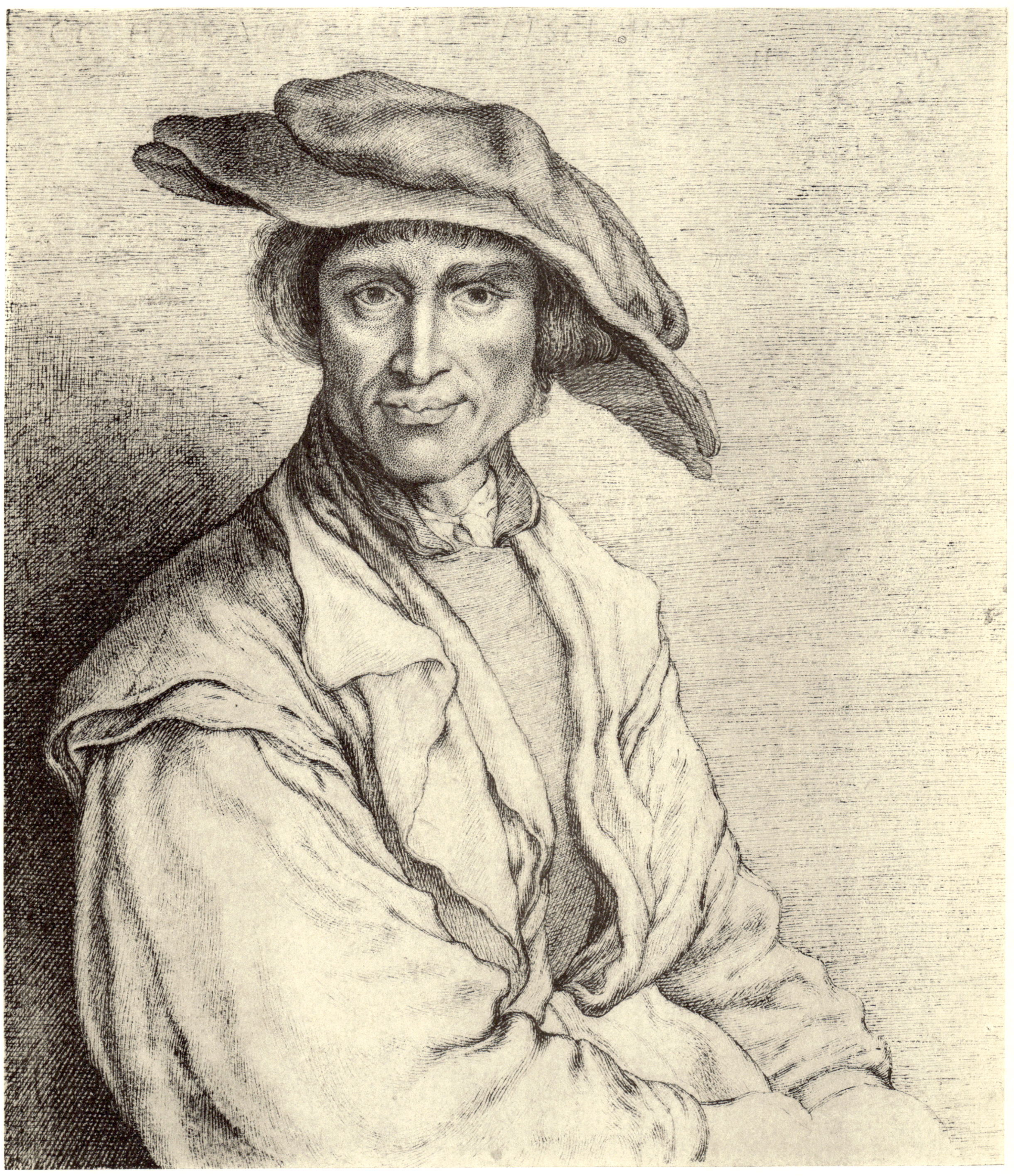

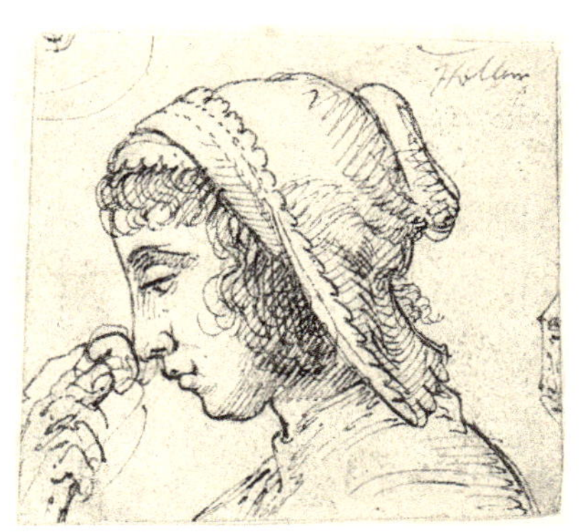

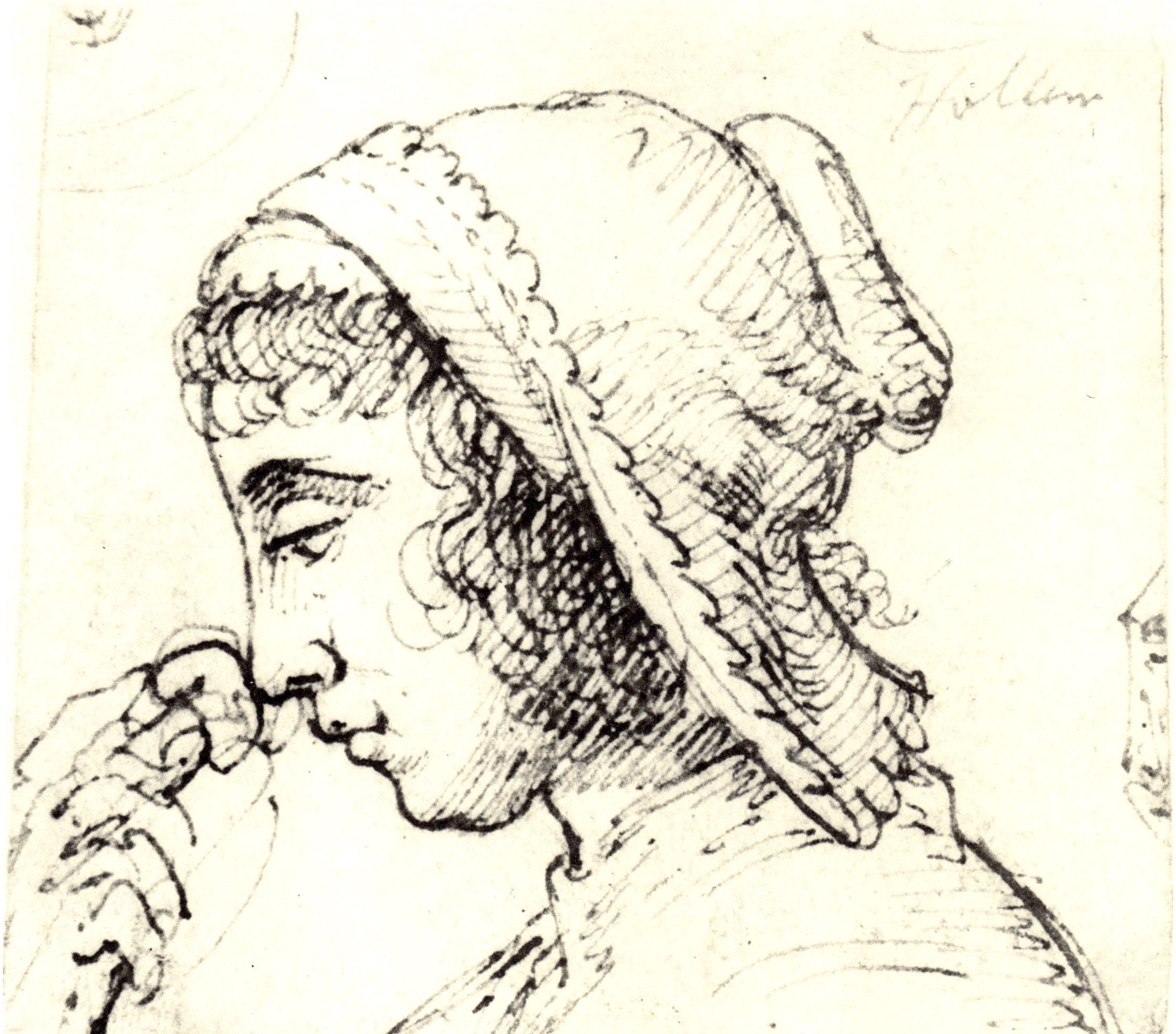

68/69

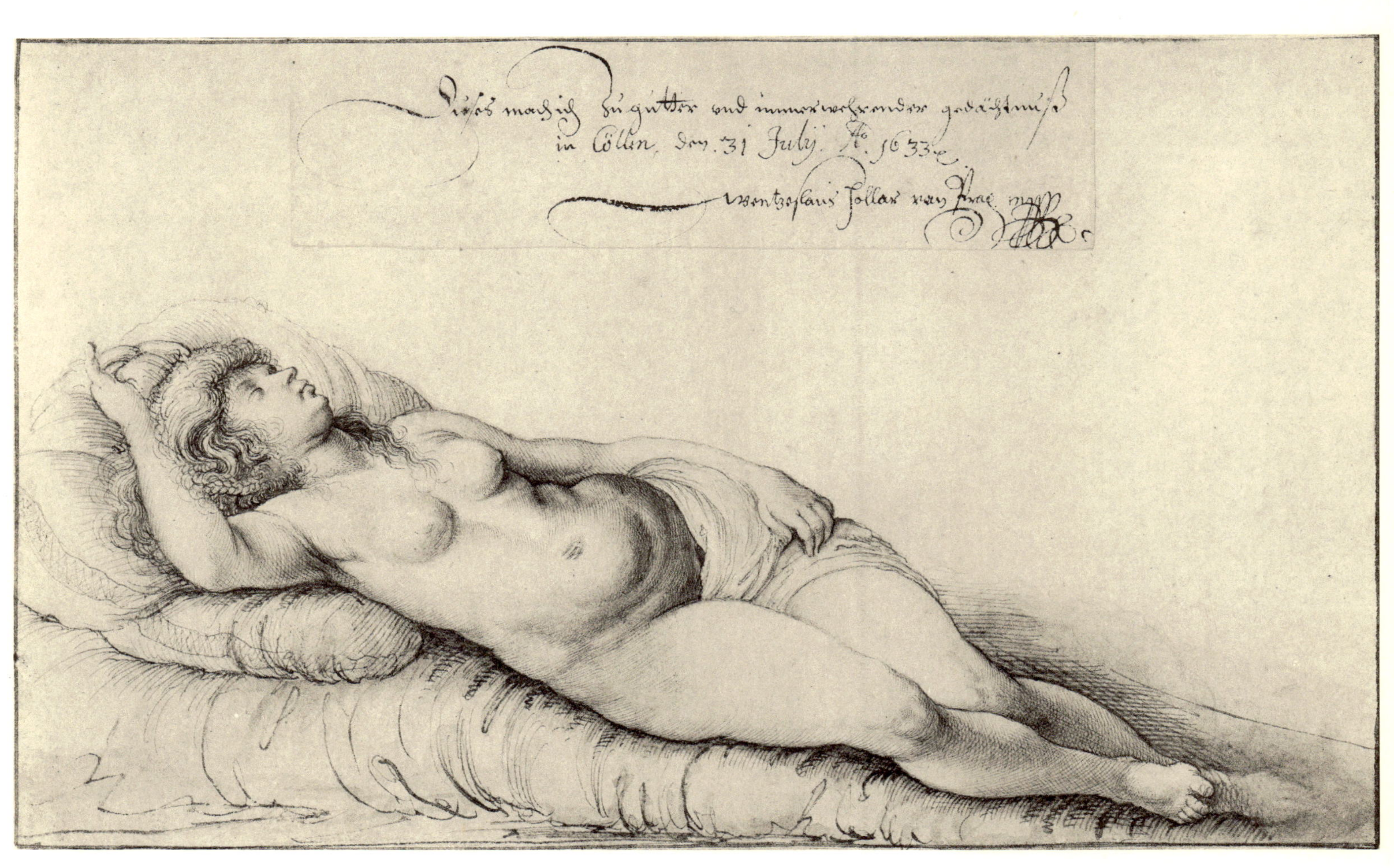
Dises mach ich zu gutter und immerwehrender gedächtnüss
in Cöllen, den 31 July. A° 1633
Wentzeslaus Hollar von Prag

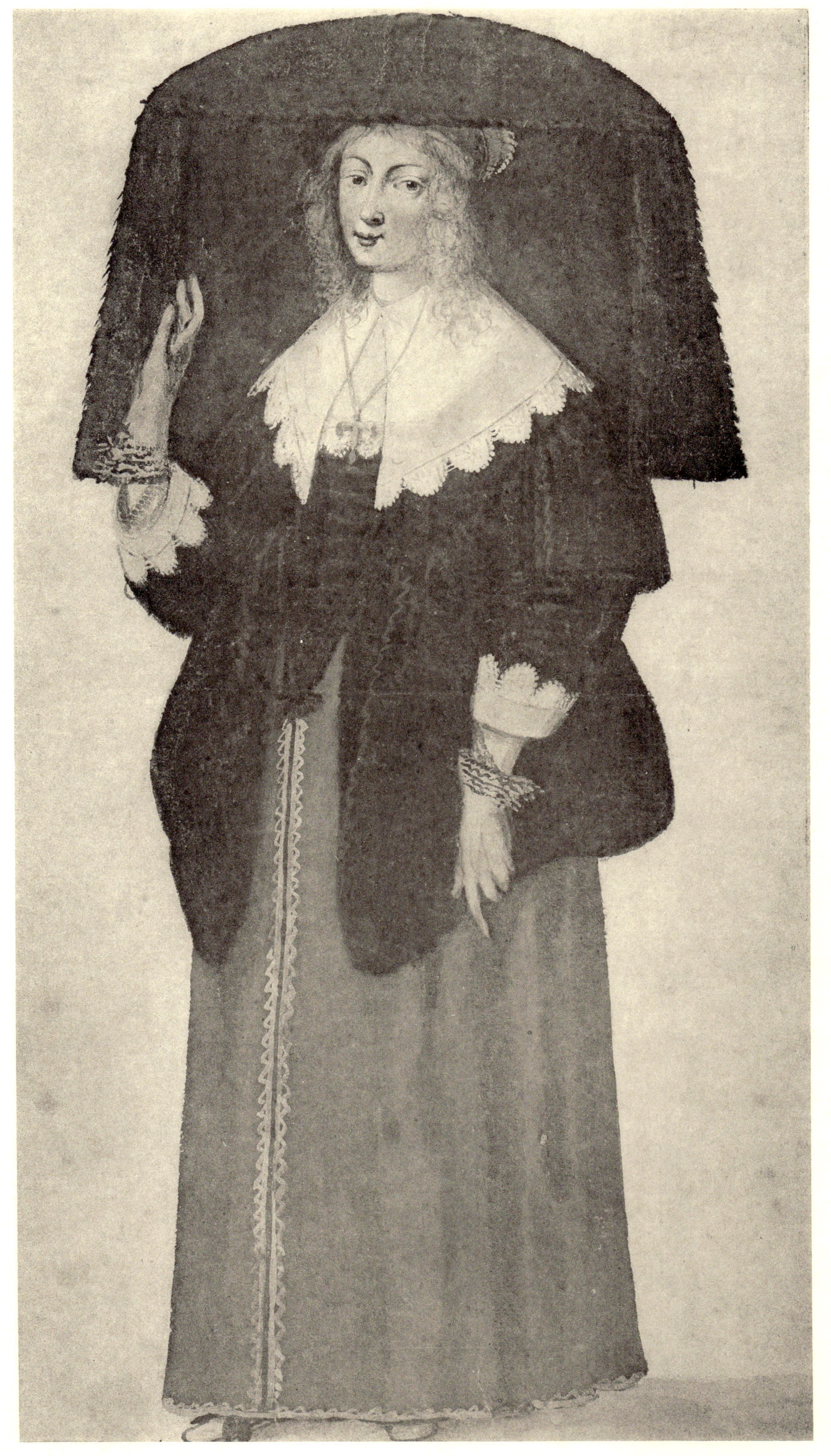

1607
13 July, Wenceslaus Hollar is born in Soukenická street, postal number 1195, in Prague's New Town, the son of Jan Hollar of Prácheň, a *Land* Records official. His mother Marketa, née Löwe von Löwengrün und Bareyt, died in 1613.

1627
Hollar leaves Prague for Germany, probably in the latter half of the year.

1627–28 (1629)
From November 1627, at least until March of the next year and probably until the spring of 1629, he works in Stuttgart.

1629–30
Works in Strasbourg for the printseller Jacob van der Heyden. In the same period he sails down the Rhine to Cologne and back.

1631
Hollar is probably employed in Frankfurt-on-Main by the printseller and etcher Mattaeus Merian the Elder.

1632–6
Freelances in Cologne for printsellers, among them Abraham Hogenburg and Gerhardt Altzenbach. Travels locally and makes some long journeys.

1634
Travels to Holland and has his first sight of the sea.

1635
Publishes a series of etchings in Cologne based on his own drawings of 1627–34, entitled *Velmi pekne obrazy nekolika mist – Amoenissimae aliquot locorum effigies.*

1636
Publishes in Cologne his *Reisbüchlein* including portrait studies partly based on his own drawings, as models for young artists. In May he meets the Earl of Arundel in Cologne, then in charge of a diplomatic mission to the Emperor Ferdinand II. He enters the earl's service as designer to the expedition, which brings him to Prague for a week in July.

1637–44
Hollar's first stay in England. He lives in the earl's palace on the Thames, making copies of items in his art and natural history collections and working for himself as well.

1641
He marries Mistress Tracy, a lady-in-waiting to the countess.

1642
The Earl of Arundel moves to Antwerp in the diplomatic service, taking part of his collections with him. Hollar works on in London in the service of the Duke of York, the future King James II.

1644–52
Hollar lives in the Netherlands. He revisits the Earl of Arundel in Antwerp, then an important engraving centre, and resumes work on copying his collections,

continuing to do so for some time after the earl's death in 1646. He comes into contact with Dutch artists and publishers and produces numerous graphic masterpieces.

1652–77

Hollar's second English period.

1655

Hollar's son, a gifted draughtsman, succumbs to the plague in London, Hollar's wife having died earlier. In the same year he marries Honora, a young girl he had adopted during the plague.

1666

In this year of the Great Fire Hollar is appointed Scenographer Royal.

1668–9

In this capacity he is attached to an expedition bound for Tangier to draw views of the Rock and Straits of Gibraltar. On his eventful return journey to Cadiz his ship is attacked by African pirates and narrowly escapes after a strenuous engagement.

1672

Hollar travels around the north of England drawing buildings.

1677

He dies in poverty on 25 March.

HISTORICAL LANDMARKS OF HOLLAR'S LIFETIME

1618

Revolt of the Bohemian Estates, start of the Thirty Years' War

1620

Defeat of the uprising at the Battle of the White Mountain

1627

New constitution outlaws all non-Catholic confessions in the country

1648

Peace of Westphalia ends the Thirty Years' War

1640–60

Civil War in England

1653–58

Oliver Cromwell rules as Lord Protector

1660

Restoration of the English monarchy, coronation of Charles II

NOTES

1 For a summary of their observations see F. C. Springell, *Connoisseur and Diplomat*, London 1963, p.142
2 Teréz Gerszi, *Die humanistischen Allegorien der rudolfinischen Meister*, Actes du XXIIe Congrès international d'histoire de l'art, Budapest 1969, tome I, texte, pp.755–62
3 F. A. Borovský, P. Toman and others. For an opposite view see L. J. Živný in *Naše doba* xviii, 1911, p.168
4 Katherine S. van Eerde, *Wenceslaus Hollar – Delineator of His Time*, The Folger Shakespeare Library 1970, p.7
5 Communicated by the District Archive of Klatovy. Attention was drawn to these sources as long ago as 1906 by the Horažd'ovice teacher Š. K. Vydra in *Památky archeologické* xxii, p.488. However, his article on the Hollars of Prácheň remained unnoticed. Likewise overlooked was the important finding about Jakub Hollar's will, quoted in full in that article with the signatures of Jan Hollar and Jakub's brother-in-law Pavel Aretin.
6 The unpublished *Album amicorum* is to be found in the Archive of National Literature in Prague, listed as D G IV 27.
7 J. Siebmacher's *Grosses und allgemeines Wappenbuch*, iii. Theil, Nuremberg 1656, plate 135 – on the Palatinate
8 L. Hlaváček, 'Kosmografie Vaclava Hollara', in *Umění* xv, 1967, pp.547 and 576–80
9 John Evelyn, *Sculptura*. Quoted in K. S. van Eerde, *Wenceslaus Hollar*, pp.79 and 89, note 13
10 K. S. van Eerde, *Wenceslaus Hollar*, p.48
11 K. B. Mádl, 'Hollarovy krajiny', in *Hollar I*, 1923–24, p.40 E. Dostál, *Vaclav Hollar*, Prague 1924, p.13
12 The drawing was published by F. Thöne in *Old Master Drawings* xiii, no.50, 1938, p.30, plate 32. For P. Jenisch and his valuable album see W. Wegner, 'Untersuchungen zu Friedrich Brentel' in *Jahrbuch der Staatlichen Kunstsammlungen in Bäden-Wurttemberg III*, 1966, p.175, note 91. I must thank Dr Heinrich Geissler of the Graphics section of the Stuttgart Staatsgalerie for pointing this article out to me.
13 For information about this drawing I am obliged to Dr Geissler, who is preparing it for publication.
14 For an analysis see Theodor Musper, 'Hollar in Stuttgart', in *Schwäbisches Heimatbuch 23*, 1937, pp.73–80
15 Musper, *op. cit.*, pp.76, 78
16 J. I. Pav, 'Wenceslaus Hollar in Germany 1627–36', in the *Art Bulletin* lv, March 1973, New York, pp.86–105
17 F. G. Grossmann in the catalogue of the exhibition 'Wenceslaus Hollar 1607–1677, Drawings, Paintings and Etchings', City of Manchester Art Gallery 1963, under exhibit D4
18 *Ibid.*, under D1
Hlaváček, *op. cit.*, p.561
Pav, *op. cit.*, p.98
19 F. G. Grossmann, who is preparing this drawing for publication, mentions it under D4 in his catalogue to the Manchester exhibition.
20 Springell, *op. cit.*, p.138 and p.155, note 12
21 Grossmann, *op. cit.*, commenting on another Prague drawing exhibited as D72
22 F. Roubík, *Soupis map českých zemí*, vol.1, Prague 1951, pp.35–9 and 56. F. Roubík, 'Zemští měřiči v Cechách v 16.–18. století', *Sborník archívních prací* xv, 2, 1965, pp.269 and 275
K. Kuchař, *Našě mapy odedávna do dneška*, in Prague 1968, pp.33–6. K. Kuchař, *Mapy českých zemí do poloviny 18. století (Vývoj mapového zobrazeni uzemí Československého republiky, I)*, Prague 1959, pp.16–20
23 The drawing S 283 with a view of Augsburg different from that of the etching P 699 is assigned by Sprinzels to the period of the 1636 Arundel mission; this is certainly older but can hardly be an *in situ* drawing of Hollar's. It is close to etching P 758, marked by Hollar as based on a drawing by M. Merian. See Grossmann's catalogue under D3
24 H. Geissler, 'Zeichner am Württembergischen Hof um 1600', in *Jahrbuch der Staatlichen Kunstsammlungen in Baden-Württemberg vi*, 1969. Much new information on architectural and artistic activity at the Stuttgart court has been collated by W. Fleischhauer in *Renaissance im Herzogtum Württemberg*, Stuttgart 1971.

25 J. Neumann, *Karel Škréta 1610–1674* (catalogue of the Prague National Gallery exhibition of 1974), pp.16, 17, 195
H. Geissler, *Zeichner am Württemburgischen Hof um 1600*, p.118

26 Geissler in *op. cit.*, pp.108–19 published a series of drawings from contemporary Stuttgart albums in which the allegorical subjects are almost all drawn from classical mythology.

27 This is certainly also true of the second, unpublished view of Cannstadt, see note 14. The real countryside around Stuttgart and the Neckar is also depicted in Hollar's etchings P 700, 759, 761, 762 and 784. Musper, *op. cit.*, notes a few topographical inaccuracies, but these probably arose when the sketches were revised for engraving.

28 Connections between Baur and Schönfeld were noted by Herbert Pée in his *Johann Heinrich Schönfeld – Die Gemälde*, Berlin 1971. Škréta's contacts with Baur and Schönfeld in Italy during the early 1630s were discussed by Neumann in the catalogue to the 1974 Karel Škréta exhibition in Prague, p.17

29 They were reissued in Augsburg, 1670–1, in several series of model compositions under the title *Iconographia.* See Pée, *op. cit.*, pp.62, 96 and especially 191. Under no.128 he argues that the sea-storm motif in Schönfeld's picture was taken from Baur's *Iconographia.*

30 Mádl, *op. cit.*, p.42; Dostál, *op. cit.*, pp.37–8 Pav, *op. cit.*, p.99

31 The final draft for etching P 625 was drawn from a different point and angle, taking in a row of half-timbered houses on the right side of the square and giving scope for rendering fine details in roofs and gables.

32 E. Croft-Murray and P. Hulton, *The British Museum: Catalogue of British Drawings I*, London 1960, p.358, no.25. Quoted by Grossmann, *op. cit.*, under D9

33 This drawing, dated 1629 and held in a private collection in Strasbourg before the war, was mentioned by S. Hackenschmidt and A. Reh in *Archives Alsaciennes* VI, 1927, pp.51–5. Its present whereabouts is unknown. It is mentioned on p.86 of Grossmann's catalogue.

34 'Domino Mattheo Meriano Basiliensi, artis chalcographiae peritissimo, Domino et patrono suo dilectissimo hanc tabellam dedicat Henricus van der Borcht minor.'

35 L. H. Wüthrich, *Die Handzeichnungen von Matthaeus Merian d.Ä.*, Basel 1963

36 In Wüttrich's list no.13, ill.16 (view of Basel) and no.14, ill.17 (Church of St Clare in Little Basel)

37 *Ibid.*, no.48, ill.47

38 Evidence of similar studies from Frankfurt and Hanau lies in etchings P 1846, 1847 and 1848 in the 1644 series showing women's costumes.

39 Wüthrich, *op. cit.*, p.22. In the case of several doubtful drawings in his list he raises the possibility of Hollar's authorship, but chronology and style speak against it.

40 The superscription to the *Smaller View of Cologne*, an etching of around 1635, states that Deutz was fortified in 1633. See on this also, J. J. Merlo, *Kölnische Künstler*, Düsseldorf 1895, p.396. The Swedish army occupied Deutz in 1632, see Pav, *op. cit.*, p.96

41 This can be seen by comparison with the etching P 864 of 1634–6, for which the drawing mentioned was the final draft.
See Jiřina Volková's note on no.11 in the catalogue of the Prague National Gallery exhibition of 1969.

42 Grossmann, *op. cit.*, under D31

43 Franz Winzinger, 'Eine unbeachtete Zeichnung Wenzel Hollars', in *Pantheon – Internationale Zeitschrift für Kunst*, Munich, 1964, pp.367–9

44 D80 in the Manchester exhibition catalogue

45 F. C. Springell, in his 'Unpublished Drawings of Tangier by Wenceslaus Hollar', *The Burlington Magazine CVI*, 1964, no.731, added another seven to Sprinzels's list of seventeen Tangier drawings, nos.373–89

46 Grossmann, *op. cit.*, under D27

47 Sprinzels, and also Springell whose collection includes this drawing.

48 Grossmann, *op. cit.*, under D41

49 Thus for example Wüthrich, *op. cit.*, under no.323 attributes a sketch of Augsburg to Hollar. But the painterly presentation, using wash and rapid brushstrokes with no prior drawing to express landscape details, particularly the foreground scrub, is completely at odds with the consistently linear character of Hollar's work.

50 Springell, *op. cit.*, pp.147–8

51 F. Sprinzels, *Hollar – Handzeichnungen*, introduction, pp.37 and 38

52 H. Weizsäcker, *Adam Elsheimer der Maler von Frankfurt*, Berlin 1936, I, p.167. The writer reproduces Hollar's etching in pl.101 and elsewhere mentions ten other Hollar etchings based on Elsheimer

53 K. Guth, 'V. Hollar a P. Pontius' in *Umění* v, Prague, 1932, p.148
Sprinzels, *op. cit.*, p.12

54 Grossmann, *op. cit.*, commentary to D107 and D108
Sprinzels, *op. cit.*, no.10

55 K. S. van Eerde, *op. cit.*, p.41

56 Dostál, *op. cit.*, p.121

57 Grossmann, *op. cit.*, commentary to D109

58 *Ibid.*, D111

59 A. M. Hind, *Wenceslaus Hollar and his views of London and Windsor in the seventeenth Century*, London 1922, pp.8 and 9

60 The author himself calls the picture a genuine portrait in his subscription to the large version: 'Le vray portrait du Chat du grand Duc de Moscouie'.

SELECTED BIBLIOGRAPHY

Appel, Heinrich, *Wenzel Hollar in Düren*, Düren 1957

Bock, E. *Die deutschen Meister*, Berlin 1921

Borovský, F. A., *Ergänzungen zu G. Parthey's beschreibendem Verzeichniss seiner Kupferstiche*, Prague 1898

Hollar a České Hollareum, pt.v, 1907–8, pp.97–146

'Hollar, Wenzel', in Thieme-Becker, *Allgemeines Lexikon der bildenden Künstler*, XVII, 1924

Denkstein, Vladimír, 'Hollarovy rané kresby z let 1625–1630', in *Umění xxv*, Prague 1977, pp.193-223; with English resumé

Dostál, Eugen, *Václav Hollar*, Prague 1924 with French resumé

Eerde, Katherine S. van, *Wenceslaus Hollar, Delineator of his Time*, in The Folger Shakespeare Library, Virginia University Press, 1970

Grossmann, F. G., catalogue of the 1963 exhibition 'Wenceslaus Hollar 1607–1677, Drawings, Paintings and Etchings', in the Manchester City Art Gallery

Guth, Karel, 'V. Hollar and P. Pontius', in *Umění v*, Prague, 1932, pp.145–250

Hind, Arthur M., *Wenceslaus Hollar and his views of London and Windsor in the seventeenth century*, London 1922

Hirschhoff, Alexander, *Wenzel Hollar, Strassburger Ansichten und Trachtenbilder aus der Zeit des Dreissigjahrigen Krieges*, Frankfurt-am-Main 1931

Hlaváček, Luboš, 'Kosmografie Václava Hollara', in *Umění* xv, Prague 1967, pp.545–85

Mádl, Karel B., 'Hollarovy krajiny', *in Hollar* I, Prague 1923–4, pp.34, 82, 133 and 196

'Nová kresba V. Hollara', in *Hollar VI*, Prague 1929–30, pp.93–101

Metzger, Paul, 'Wenzel Hollar in Bonn und Umgebung', in *Bonner Geschichtsblätter*, vol. 27, Bonn 1975, pp.51–76

Musper, Theodor, 'Hollar in Stuttgart', in *Schwäbisches Heimatbuch* 23, Stuttgart 1937, pp.73–80

Neumann, Jaromír, 'Václav Hollar', in *Hollar XXIII*, Prague 1951, pp.14–35

Pantheon – Internationale Zeitschrift für Kunst, 1964

Parthey, Gustav, *Wenzel Hollar, Beschreibendes Verzeichniss seiner Kupferstiche*, Berlin 1853, 2nd ed. with additional material 1858

Pav, John I., 'Wenceslaus Hollar in Germany, 1627–1636', in *The Art Bulletin LV*, March 1973, New York, pp.86–105

Springell, Francis C., *Connoisseur and Diplomat, The Earl of Arundel's Embassy to Germany in 1636 . . . with a catalogue of the topographical drawings made on the journey by Wenceslaus Hollar*, London 1963

'Unpublished Drawings of Tangier by Wenceslaus Hollar', in the *Burlington Magazine, vol.CVI*, no.731, London 1964, pp. 69–74

Sprinzel, *Hollar–Handzeichnungen*, Vienna 1938

Urzidil, Johannes, *Wenceslaus Hollar, der Kupferstecher des Barock*, in collaboration with Franz Sprinzels, Vienna and Leipzig 1936

Vertue, George, *A description of the works of the ingenious delineator and engraver Wenceslaus Hollar disposed into Classes of different sorts with some account of his life*, London 1945

Zivný, Ladislav J., 'Václav Hollar, nové příspěvky k jeho životopisu' in *Naše doba*, vol.XVIII, Prague 1911, pp.165, 259, 352, 426 and 525

Older sources are listed in Thieme-Becker, *Allgemeines Lexik on der bildenden Künstler*, vol.XVII, 1924 and Prokop Toman, *Nový slovník československých výtvarných umělců*, vol.I, Prague 1947.

INDEX

The page numbers which appear in italics refer to plates.

THE TRUE MANER OF THE EXECUTION
Lieutenant of Ireland, vpon Tower-hill, the

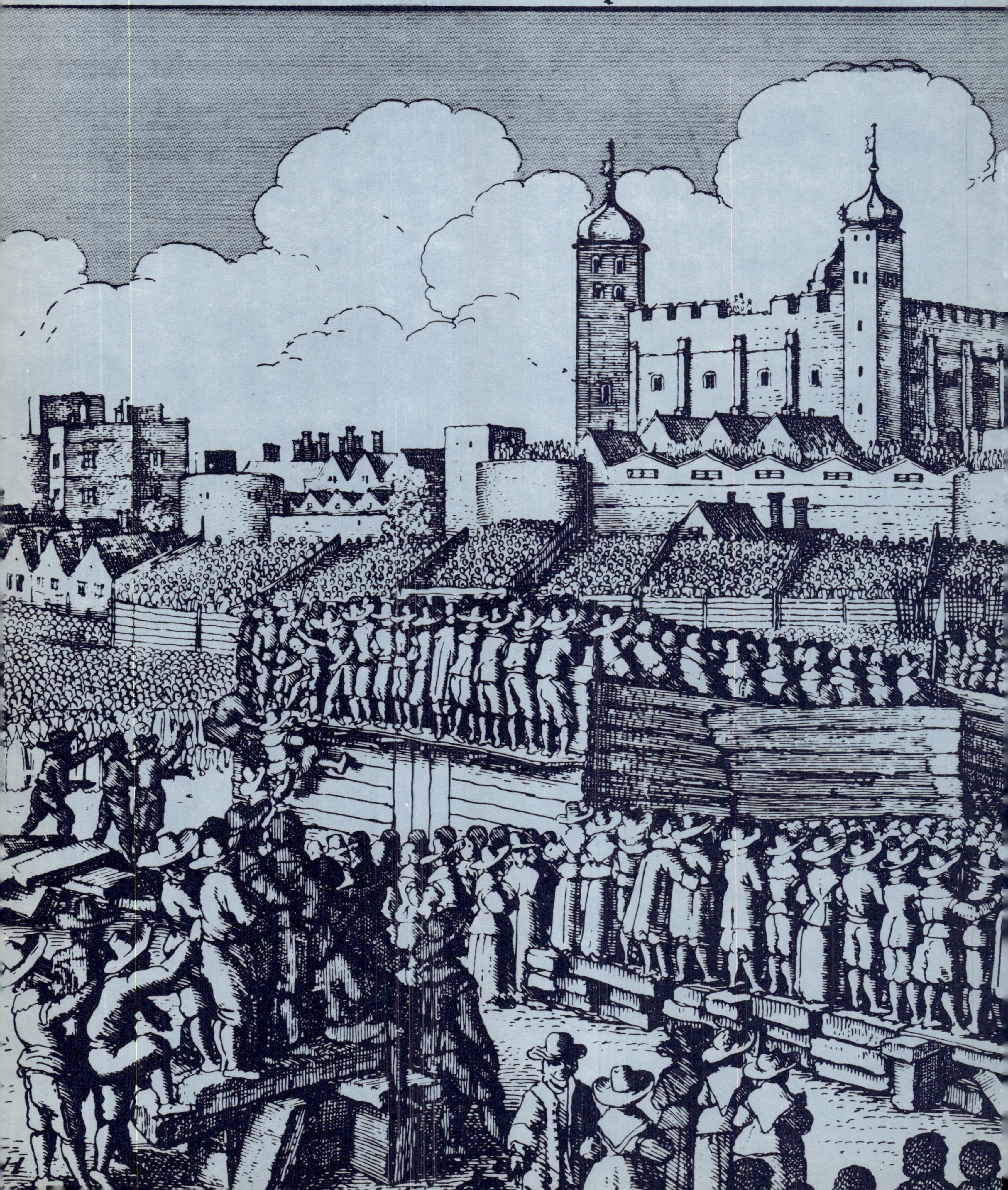